MASS MURDER IN CALIFORNIA'S EMPTY QUARTER

A TALE OF TRIBAL TREACHERY AT THE CEDARVILLE RANCHERIA

RAY A. MARCH

University of Nebraska Press | Lincoln

Library of Congress Cataloging-in-Publication Data
Names: March, Ray A., 1934– author.
Title: Mass murder in California's empty quarter: a tale
of tribal treachery at the Cedarville Rancheria / Ray A.
March.
Description: Lincoln: University of Nebraska Press, [2020] |
Includes bibliographical references.
Identifiers: LCCN 2020010780
ISBN 9781496217561 (hardback)
ISBN 9781496224842 (epub)
ISBN 9781496224859 (mobi)
ISBN 9781496224866 (pdf)
Subjects: LCSH: Rhoades, Cherie. | Murder—Cedarville
Rancheria, California—Case studies. | Northern Paiute
Indians—Cedarville Rancheria, California—Case studies. |
Northern Paiute Indians—Cedarville Rancheria,
California—Politics and government—Case studies. |
Cedarville Rancheria, California—History.
Classification: LCC HV6533.C2 M185 2020 | DDC
364.152/34089974577079423—dc23
LC record available at https://lccn.loc.gov/2020010780

Set in Minion Pro by Laura Buis.

While tribal sovereignty is limited today by the United States under treaties, acts of Congress, Executive Orders, federal administrative agreements and court decisions, what remains is nevertheless protected and maintained by the federally recognized tribes against further encroachment by other sovereigns, such as states.

—AN EXCERPT FROM THE BUREAU OF INDIAN AFFAIRS WEBSITE

The politics in the land is still volatile—a Molotov cocktail. I stand far from tribal politics because I see the 1934 Indian Reorganization Act as a most sinister piece of legislation. The contract tribes sign with the government is an "an act of surrender," a surrender in terms written by the government. The contracts come with built-in diseases that infect only the tribal members.

—DARRYL BABE WILSON

CONTENTS

Author's Note | ix
Prologue | xiii

Mass Murder in California's Empty Quarter | 1

Epilogue | 193
Acknowledgments | 197
Appendix | 201
Notes | 207
Bibliography | 219

AUTHOR'S NOTE

WHEN I TOLD A few journalist friends I was writing a book about a mass murder that occurred in rural Northern California—a murder carried out by a Native American woman killing her own relatives—I drew blanks. We're all so numbed by the stream of mass murders in this country that we brush off the flash headlines that don't set death toll records. One mass murder gets pushed off the front page by the next. The less spectacular are quickly forgotten or ignored. We know little of the story behind the story.

Mass Murder in California's Empty Quarter is an exposé of a family of urban Native Americans who took the Bureau of Indian Affairs up on its offer of free housing and federal funding and moved from the city to the reservation. Their displacement was a trial for which they were unprepared. They met lineal ancestry requirements for membership but they knew nothing of the Northern California Paiutes' cultural heritage, traditions, spirituality, customs, or language—and predictably, they did not know the tribal laws that governed them. That created the story's outline but not its boundaries.

To research and write the story of the Cedarville Rancheria mass murder, I posed a theory: If conditions for Natives are to improve there must be a broad cross-cultural understanding of the challenges they face as they govern themselves under the rules of sovereignty. Following this line of this thinking, I delved into the systematic events that led to Cherie Rhoades killing half of her immediate family. I compared the U.S. laws Native Americans must follow as citizens of this country and the laws they must follow under their own—and contrasting—tribal constitutions. One glaring difference I examined is the tribal use of sovereignty authority to purge its membership rolls. As the Cedarville Rancheria prepared to evict Cherie from the tribe there was an epidemic on the West Coast of what are known as "disenrollments." Blood quantum was the measuring ruler for disenrolling families from their tribes. There is nothing comparable in the U.S. Constitution to this tribal stripping of citizenship. Discussion of blood quantum and who gets to be a Native American and who doesn't is in chapter 5.

As I prepared to write this book I sought opinions from the contacts I had in Indian Country. What did they think of a white guy writing a book about a mass murder and questions he had about their tribal laws and justice? Was there confidence among them that I could write a truthful and informative book? The reactions were lukewarm. The warmest, which I took as inspiration, went like this: "I do not believe any research by a 'white guy' would be accepted by Native people. That said, with years of listening to many opinions and tales, it would be effective for you to align with respected individuals to carry the face of the book."

Those respected individuals turned out to be Kandi Maxwell and her husband, Lloyd Powell. They gave me the reliable source support I needed in researching *Mass Murder in California's Empty Quarter*. Kandi is Arkansas Cherokee and Lloyd is an enrolled Chickasaw. Not only did they willingly offer the credibility necessary to the work, they mentored me in the complexities of tribal law and provided intimate insights into Cedarville Rancheria life that were otherwise unobtainable. Under sovereignty status tribes are not obligated to conduct their business in public. I relied heavily on firsthand, for-the-record accounts, such as interviews and supporting documents of public record. Some interviews were conducted under the journalist's ground rule of "deep background," meaning the information could be used but the sources would not be revealed.

But Kandi and Lloyd knew the inner workings of the Cedarville Rancheria community. They knew Cherie Rhoades better than I did. My contact with Cherie was limited to the tribe's Rabbit Traxx gas station. I've recounted the Cherie and Rabbit Traxx episodes in chapter 3. Kandi and Lloyd knew the dysfunctions of the Rancheria. They knew the young Native students enrolled in Resources for Indian Student Education (RISE). On June 7, 2014, four and a half months after the killings, I met with them at their home west of Alturas and began a series of tape-recorded interviews. We quickly moved into the Native American world they called the "haves and the have nots," tribes living in third-world poverty while others basked in wealth, the disenrollment wave that was hitting casino tribes, Cherie's personality, her rivalry with her half-brother Rurik Davis, and the characteristics of her family—the Lashes.

The interviews covered the link between spirituality and culture, Native American politics, and the need for open and honest communication in Indian Country. Four years after the murders I had compiled a book-length collection of reporter's notes. All that remained was the final narrative. But two years after the murders a half dozen people, within the Native American community and outside, refused to be interviewed. They declined to provide any information about Cherie, the Cedarville Rancheria, or its voting members. The reasons varied but there was a common ring of intimidation. Too much violence, too many legal questions. They asked me to wait until the trial was over. They didn't want to comment. They asked not to be contacted again. I was threatened with a restraining order. Finally, there was a letter from a law firm representing the Cedarville Rancheria, strongly suggesting that it was inappropriate for me to contact any member or staff of the Rancheria before the Rhoades trial was resolved. In my reply I said I would be grateful to the tribal government for assistance with this book when they felt the time was right. I never heard back from the tribe's lawyers. I was not aware at the time that some surviving tribal leaders were deeply involved in an undercurrent effort to dictate the course of the trial—and ironically—its outcome after Cherie was found guilty.

PROLOGUE

THE EMPTY QUARTER IS windshield time, eye on the weather, shoulder-to-the-wheel, burning daylight. The Empty Quarter is an undercurrent of dying auction yards, rotting barns, cast-iron skillets, praying for rain to a white Christian God, a victim mentality of righteous farmers and ranchers over-regulated, under-appreciated, feeding the world, on the dole, ranting over coffee at the diner. The Empty Quarter is a diesel Ford 250 flatbed with three frenzied Border collies in the back, drivers who go-along to get-along waving hello as they pass each other through town. It's rock jacks, H-braces, disking fields, fertilizing, haying, grazing, irrigating, swabbing gun barrels clean. The Empty Quarter is one post office on an excessively wide street called Main, silent prejudices, daily gossip, a branch library open one half-day a week. The Empty Quarter is the contrail from an airliner on automatic precisely overhead at 9:13 a.m. local time on its way to Los Angeles. The Empty Quarter is an occupied window seat in that airliner seeing nothing below. No thing. The Empty Quarter is fatalism dominated by emptiness.

MASS MURDER
IN CALIFORNIA'S
EMPTY QUARTER

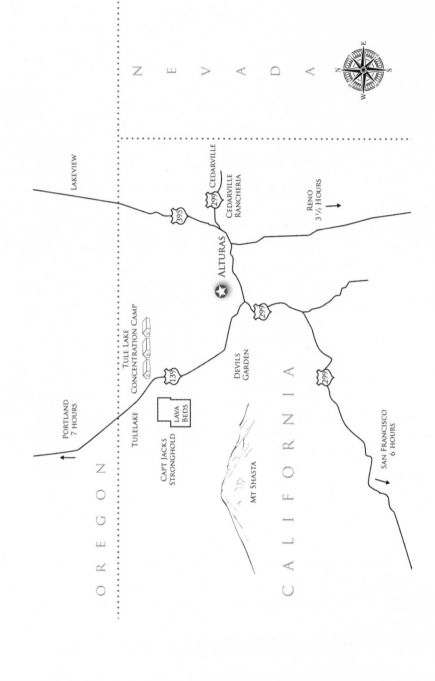

1

SHE WAITED IN THE empty lot for forty minutes before entering
the Cedarville Rancheria's offices. Her nephew Richard Lash told her
to stay outside. The tribe's executive committee wasn't ready for her.
Cherie rarely did what someone else told her to do. At her best she
was a rule-breaker. At her worst a tribal tyrant. She was suspected
by her little Northern Paiute tribe of embezzling federal funds. She
and her son Jack Stockton had been deposed three months earlier
as its leader and vice chair when a majority of the tribe voted them
off its executive committee. It was a family coup and her relatives—
nephews, nieces, and a half-brother—voted against her. Cherie and
Jack didn't have the votes. The tribe's newly formed executive committee, now led by her half-brother Rurik Davis, was poised to evict
them from their free federally funded Rancheria housing. If evicted
they would lose not only their two homes, but $80,000 each in gam-
ing money. The tribe received funds every year from profits earned
by Native-owned casinos under a California program titled Revenue Sharing Trust Fund.

She waited. It was a late February afternoon, close to three and
nearly fifty degrees. She wore polarized aviator sunglasses, summer
shorts, and a tank top that exposed her broad tattooed shoulders.
Earlier that day Cherie, her son Jack, and his family stopped for a
sandwich at the Alturas Subway. Jack told her he wasn't going to
their eviction hearing. His attorney told him not to. Cherie said she
saw no need for an attorney. Why spend the money? Her nephew
Richard Lash called her at Subway and told her the tribe had hired a
judge. Jack said he had an appointment at the Paiutes' Strong Family
Health Center. He gave her a hug and told her he'd see her after the

meeting. "Let me know how it goes," he said as he left Subway. Cherie went to her eviction hearing alone.

The day before, she asked Richard and another nephew, Jacob Penn, to clean two semi-automatic 9mm handguns. One was a Lorcin and the other a double-stacked Taurus. One of the guns was a Mother's Day gift from her husband, but she never test-fired either gun. There was idle talk of going target shooting on the hillside above the Rancheria. Talk of maybe selling the guns to a friend.

Now Cherie stood next to her car in the empty lot across the street from the tribe's offices. In each deep pocket of her shorts was a 9mm pistol loaded with full metal jacket bullets. She smoked a cigarette, drank some coffee, smoked another cigarette. Richard returned with an envelope.

"This is your appeal from yesterday. It's been denied. Wait here."

She heard voices and laughter coming from the conference room, a final wind down from a day of celebrating. For the first time the tribe was exercising a critical component of its sovereign authority—hiring a judge. Patricia Lenzi was an enrolled member of the St. Regis Mohawk Tribe of New York, a California licensed attorney, and a tribal judge in Arizona and New York. Lenzi was to oversee the eviction of Cherie and Jack. Rurik declared the day, February 20, a historic one.

"It was something very new for our tribe and we were excited yet nervous at how a court setting would take place and hopefully improve our tribe in the future," recalled Melissa Davis, one of Rurik's three daughters. The tribe was now going to conduct its business through an impartial court. This would eliminate having to deal directly with Cherie's dominating personality.

That morning they held a belated baby shower in the conference room for nineteen-year-old Angel Penn and her five-day-old son. The conference table was cluttered with colorful paper cups, plates of cookies, soda bottles, and a pair of bright pink sunglasses. On a side table was a child's stuffed brown and green toy monkey. Pinned to a wall were the brightly colored letters B-A-B-Y. Melissa tried to convince Angel to come to the baby shower but skip the hearing. It was too soon for a newborn to be out meeting people. But Angel insisted. She knew it was an important day and she didn't want to miss it.

Angel Penn walked into the conference room screaming with excitement to show Hedi Bogda little Nico. Hedi, an enrolled member of the Leech Lake Band of Ojibwe, was the tribe's attorney. All "the girls" planned to go out that evening. The night before Hedi and Sheila Russo, Hedi's best friend and the tribe's recently hired administrator, joked with a bartender about introducing him to Melissa.

Before the hearing started someone wondered if Cherie had been given enough time to prepare her defense. Hedi took Rurik and Glenn Calonico, the tribe's housing chair, into the open kitchen area. She suggested they should give Cherie more time. They said no. Judge Lenzi, after she was sworn in during a telephone conference call, suggested putting the hearing off to the next day so she could be there in person. "Make it ceremonial," she said. They said no again. Glenn was nervous. Just before the hearing began he showed Hedi a letter alleging Cherie had abused one of his children.

Lash returned to his aunt in the parking lot.

"They're ready," he said.

She walked up the handicap ramp and entered the building. The day before, Cherie and her son had appeared at their first eviction hearing. Then Hedi had asked Rurik to search them for weapons at the door; everyone knew Jack had a concealed weapon permit. But this time there was no weapon check. Carrying a black backpack, Cherie walked to the staff bathroom at the opposite end of the small building. There were no cameras in the bathroom. Until then Spencer Bobrow, the tribe's environmental resource coordinator, watched her on video surveillance live feed. There were nine cameras recording both inside the offices and outside in the backyard where children were playing. Leaving the bathroom, Cherie headed for the conference room fifteen feet away. Once inside, she paused and looked around. The laughing stopped and the atmosphere instantly changed. Her arrival in the tribe's crowded conference room was not only documented by live feed security but also captured by a live digital recorder sitting on the conference table. Because of her delay in the parking lot and a detour to the bathroom she was late in arriving. The already crowded room held one space-hogging focal point—the conference table. It left little room for people to move about, yet small children wandered in and out. Kids were playing in the backyard on a large plastic slide. People were talking over one another. As an enticement to attend board meetings, tribal members were typically paid a hundred dollars for each meeting. There was free pizza. An estimated eighteen people were in the building. They were all waiting for Cherie. The new tribal judge, Lenzi, was on the speaker phone from a tribal court in Arizona asking if Cherie was on her way.

"She's in the bathroom," said Glenn.

"She's in the bathroom," said Rurik.

"Okay, she's on her way in right now," said Hedi.

"Miss Rhoades is on her way in?" asked Lenzi.

"Yeah, she's just coming down the hall, I believe," Hedi answered. "Okay."

"Yes, okay, she's walking in the door right now," Hedi said. "Cherie, do you want to state your name?"

"Cherie Rhoades."

Cherie braced one knee on a chair called the "defense chair." She said she was cold. Told someone to close the windows that opened to the street. She tried to get everyone to look her in the eye. Getting attention came naturally to her. She was well known as a bully. She had a sneak-attack temper that could quickly turn violent. At five feet, six inches and 185 pounds she looked like a middle guard. Her graying hair was streaked in reddish-orange dye and braided in a single strand down the back of her neck.

Except for her nephew Richard Lash who was sitting in a chair in a far corner of the room, the entire tribe was at the conference table. Everyone—Rurik's three daughters, Monique, Melissa, and Monica, a fourth niece, Angel, with her new born baby on her lap, were sitting with their backs against a wall. Next to them were Hedi and Sheila. Filling out the lineup was Cherie's nephew Glenn. Only the conference table separated them from Cherie. Normally, as chair of the executive committee, Rurik sat at the far left end of the conference table. Today he was at the opposite end. On his right was Jenica McGarva, the tribe's non-Native head of housing. Also in the room, but not at the table, was Nikki Munholand, the tribe's non-Native assistant finance officer-administrator.

"I'm just calling the case CED-ED-2014-0001, which is Cedarville Rancheria Housing Authority, plaintiff, versus Cherie Rhoades, defendant," Judge Lenzi said in her opening statement. "And it's a complaint of unlawful detainer . . . And Mr. Calonico is there as housing chair . . . do you have counsel or anyone representing you, or are you representing yourself?"

"No," Cherie said.

". . . so you're there on your own. Correct?"

"I'm here on my own because they want to make sure that we have time for counsel."

It was puzzling who Cherie referred to when she said "they." In 2011 as chair of the executive committee she oversaw the formal adoption of the Bureau of Indian Affairs boilerplate sovereignty constitution that governed the internal workings of the tribe. Fatefully, the document was the final authority for evicting Cherie and her son. She knew the basic workings of the constitution. This exchange with the judge quickly set the contentious tone for their remaining dialogue. Cherie was composed as the judge led her through the preliminary stages of the hearing.

"Well, this is a complaint in unlawful detainer, so this is just a first hearing. If you need more time then we can talk about that," Lenzi told her.

Cherie began a counter diversion. She wanted to disrupt Lenzi's introductory judicial routine. She tried to correct the judge or sidetrack matters using the confusion of dates as to when the actual eviction notices were served. The judge systematically kept her course. For Cherie, it was an exercise in bantering, a warm-up drill for the right opening. That moment arrived in just a few minutes.

"Okay, so the administrative process of the eviction has happened, has been through the appeal and has been finalized on appeal," Lenzi said. "From my reading of the tribal law there is no avenue of appeal beyond what has already happened as of yesterday."

"Yes, there is," Cherie answered.

"You would agree that there's no other method to appeal," the judge asked her.

"No, I don't agree," Cherie told her.

"Where in tribal law is there authority to do something different?" Lenzi asked.

"It says you're supposed to be able to appeal to the community counsel 'cause three people shouldn't have the right to tell people they need to move."

"Well, where is that in tribal law though?" Lenzi asked again.

The judge was correct. Cherie was close to the wording of the tribe's constitution but not close enough. There is no provision in the tribe's constitution governing eviction. However, there is a clause covering disenrollment. If a member is being disenrolled by the executive committee she can appeal to the community council—the tribe at-large. But Cherie was being evicted, not disenrolled. She stood up, nodded to Rurik. He leaned over as if to speak with her confidentially. She took a gun from her pocket and shot him between the eyes.

Blood streamed from Rurik's forehead. Everyone in the room scrambled for safety.

"Holy sh . . . hold on, aw no Cherie, aw fuck, Cherie, Cherie . . ." Glenn screamed. "Oh my god," one of the Davis sisters cried.

Nikki saw what she called an "interaction" between Cherie and Rurik, thinking they were going to have words. Then she saw Cherie put the gun to his temple and shoot him. When Cherie swept around to her left, Nikki ran down the hallway leading to the backyard where children were playing. She yelled for everyone to get away from the building, Cherie was shooting people.

Monica looked up from her laptop screen. Cherie and Rurik's eyes were locked when Cherie pulled the trigger. Monica thought it was some kind of joke. Then she saw blood pour out of her father's head. Instinctively she ducked under the table and tried to hide.

"She . . . I honestly thought that maybe she was . . . going to run off because she killed somebody," Monica said. "So I was hoping that maybe, you know, the rest of us are safe. But then she just started opening fire. And I was ducked underneath the table. I couldn't see what was going on. And I kept weaving in and out between the pillars because it was a really nice, thick pillar. So she would be on one side, so I whipped over to the other side hoping that would protect me. I remember actually locking eyes with her before she shot me. And I ducked underneath the table and I tried going back over, and that's when I felt something hit me, but I lost all feeling, so I just laid down and tried to pretend I was dead." She was shot through the leg and the bullet exited underneath her tailbone.

Melissa couldn't remember if she was teasing Angel about being a mom or if she was looking at Monica's laptop. She thought Rurik, whom she called Papa, and Sheila were talking to Cherie. It was hard to hear with the background noise and people getting up and moving around. She heard a pop. The room went quiet. She looked in the direction of the noise and saw her father very still. A trail of blood ran down the center of his forehead and then he fell forward on the table. Pulling the rapid fire trigger as fast as she could Cherie turned on the others at the conference table. The "pops" didn't sound like typical gunshots to Melissa. She ducked down and tried to hide behind a thick wooden table leg. She ended up next to Angel and her baby. Cherie was now on her hands and knees, eye level.

"She looked right at me and shot," Melissa said. She didn't realize she was hit until she saw a bullet shell next to her right arm. "That's when it clicked that it was really happening. This wasn't a BB gun. At that moment, I felt something go through my right calf and I instantly knew I was shot again. That's when I screamed. Not from the pain, but from the realization that I was going to die."

Cherie kept yelling that she wasn't going to let anybody leave the room alive. She was going to kill them all.

"And I believed her," Melissa said.

Melissa lost all sense of time. She guessed maybe less than a minute. She pretended she was dead so Cherie wouldn't go for her again. The room went quiet and she wondered if this was how she would die. She wondered if she should wait for help as she played dead. What if Cherie went to her car to reload and came back and shot everyone in the head to be sure they really were dead? The Lorcin jammed. Melissa crawled out from under the table as Cherie came back into the room with a knife from the nearby kitchen.

"I ducked back under the table with her in pursuit, her eyes locked on to me. She got under the table and tried to get on top of me with the knife. I don't know how I managed, but I used all my strength to keep that knife away from my body, even if it meant grasping the blade with my bare hands. I screamed again."

Melissa didn't know if there were others near her during the shooting. Her hearing was narrow and selective, picking up certain sounds and leaving others out. She heard Glenn crying out to Cherie to stop, please stop. It was then, Melissa thinks, that Glenn distracted Cherie. She was able to kick Cherie off and get out from under the conference table.

"I know she went after Glenn, and it still haunts me knowing he saved my life, but at the price of his own," Melissa said. She tried to run out of the building, but her legs weren't working. She had just one shoe on and her glasses were missing. As she passed the office front desk she heard a phone ringing. Desperately hoping someone was on the other end she cried for help. "Someone help, send help!" she screamed into the receiver but no one was there. She dropped the phone and ran out of the office. Cherie, kitchen knife in her hand, ran down the handicap ramp after her, yelling she was going to cut the head off the snake.

"Cherie kept repeating she was going to cut the head off the snake and my thoughts immediately were that she cut off everyone's head inside the building. I didn't know who all were still in the building, but I knew Papa and Glenn were gone. Did she use the knife to do it?"

Melissa collapsed in Spencer Bobrow's arms. He turned and tackled Cherie, knocking the knife from her grip. He yelled, "That's enough." He asked her why, Cherie, why did you do this—all for a house? She told him no, it wasn't over a house; it was a matter of principle.

Hedi thought: why would Cherie bring a toy gun to this hearing? Was she trying to scare her brother, Rurik? She watched Cherie put the gun to Rurik's head and pull the trigger. He fell to the floor. Shocked, Hedi stood up thinking this isn't happening.

"Cherie walked over in front of me and shot Glenn, who was sitting right next to me on my right side. She looked at me and said, 'You're next, bitch.' Sheila grabbed me and threw me on the floor." She remembered they were crawling around, screaming as they tried to figure out how to get out of the room. They were trapped under the table and Cherie was standing between them and the door.

Cherie shot Sheila in the back of the head and Sheila landed partially on Hedi, pinning her to the floor. Unable to move, Hedi covered her head. She could hear the screams as Cherie kept shooting people. With every shot Hedi was certain the next one was going to be for her. Partially pinned under Sheila, she found there was nothing she could do but lie there and wait to die.

"I thought about my children and how they were going to get a phone call telling me I was murdered."

Hedi sensed that Cherie had left the room but didn't know where she'd gone. Hedi's breathing was out of control. She knew she had to quit breathing and play dead. She heard Glenn's pleading, his moans as he died.

"Aw, Cherie, no. Cherie, no. No, Cherie, no, no. Cherie, Cherie stop. Cherie stop," Glenn pleaded as Cherie shot him again and again.

"No. I'm not . . . not till you're dead."

She heard Melissa's cries. She heard baby Nico crying. She didn't know he was under Angel. His cries were muffled. Maybe someone put him in a closet. She was going into shock, her body shutting down. She grabbed her St. Christopher's medal and said a prayer. When she heard Cherie come back into the room she moved as close as she could to her best friend. They were now cheek-to-cheek. She heard victims' blood spilling onto the floor.

"Sheila's face was directly next to mine; she had been shot in the back of her head. The blood was pouring all over my face. I swallowed it and breathed it in and it kept dripping on me." Hedi heard Sheila gasping for air as she took her last breath.

Judge Lenzi, hearing by telephone the announcement of Cherie's arrival in the conference room, pictured Michael Corleone from *The Godfather*. She shook off the image as crazy. When Cherie became agitated, Lenzi spoke calmly. There was a crash followed by a silence. Then crashing sounds, again and again, over and over.

"Finally, I heard a woman cry out and the line went dead," she said. "I expected a call back in minutes, explaining Cherie had a tantrum and tossed furniture or something and that they would have to convene on a different day."

She called back but reached the tribe's voice mail. She texted Hedi and called her cell. No answer. She asked advice from her colleagues at the Arizona tribal court. One jokingly said, "I hope no one came in and killed your whole staff." Distraught and calling continuously, she boarded a flight to California and drove to Alturas. On the plane she poured out the story to a complete stranger. She was crying uncontrollably. In Alturas she picked up Hedi. "We were in a restaurant sobbing, crying, trying to get the horror out of our souls," she said. "This was in public. There was no private place to be in a town where neither of us lived." Her phone record timed the entire killing scene. It took nine minutes.

Jenica, hysterical and covered in blood, frantically pushed her way past Cherie and ran two blocks to the Alturas police station. The rookie desk officer's first reaction was to radio "11–99." Extreme emergency. An officer needs help and is in immediate peril. Whether this was the most accurate alert to transmit may be debatable, but under the circumstances the use of "11–99" resulted in the quickest possible

9

response. Among those first on the scene were five on-duty sheriff's deputies plus an off-duty deputy and a court bailiff who was also the only E M T in the sheriff's office—the sum total of Sheriff Mike Poindexter's administrative staff. At the time he did not have the staffing for a day patrol shift. He emptied out his entire department.

Within minutes of the killings Cherie, held down by Spencer, was handcuffed and taken to the Modoc County jail three blocks away. She was booked and secretly transferred to Susanville, one hundred miles to the south, because Sheila's husband, Phil Russo, was a part-time jailer at the Modoc County jail.

Melissa knew it was over when deputies arrived. Her adrenaline was dropping and she was losing her strength. She braced herself against a car. She told someone there was a baby in the conference room. An ambulance arrived. She was placed on a stretcher. Her clothing was cut and completely removed. Her stomach hurt and was beginning to bloat. At the hospital she asked a nurse about Angel. The nurse, who had helped with the delivery of Nico five days before, told her, "You have to be strong for the baby."

As Hedi waited to die, she heard police sirens coming closer. She prayed they would hurry. She heard voices when police knocked down the front door and entered the room. She listened as they found body after body. The metallic scent of gun powder was still in the room.

"Hey, she . . . quiet."

"That's a baby."

". . . come on. Is there a pulse?"

"Any . . . anybody else hear a baby?"

"I hear a baby."

"I just heard a baby."

"Right over here somewhere."

"He's got it, right here. Let's get that . . . let me get that out of here."

"Holy fu-ay-ay-ay."

"Injury to the baby?"

"It doesn't appear so."

"Baby appears fine."

"Holy fuck."

"We've got a baby alive."

"She, this victim here, actually saved a life of a baby. The baby was under her body."

During her trial Cherie saw the video of her killings for the first time and was shocked. She was shocked by what she described as her "weird ass crazy grin" as she killed one person after another. She was shocked to see two toddlers coming and going in the murderous chaos. It was "crazy" that children were present at the hearing. "Who brings children?" she asked, as if children were never a part of the Native social fabric.

When Hedi thought it was safe she lifted her head. She saw terror on the officer's face as he stared into her eyes. She scared the hell out of him when she popped up like a jack in the box. He asked if she was injured and she said she didn't know. Her ribs and side hurt but she didn't know if she was wounded. He told her to stay still while they checked on the others. She wrapped her arms around Sheila and tried to wake her up. She felt one of the bullet holes in the back of Sheila's head and knew she was dead. Hedi began to cry as she held Sheila to her.

She couldn't move when the officers came back for her. They shifted Sheila just enough to lift Hedi up. She was terrified Cherie was still there and was going to kill her. They covered her with a blanket to prevent shock. They had trouble getting her out of the room. Everywhere they turned there was a body. Hedi was hysterical. Outside she saw Brandi Penn and Nikki. Penn, Angel's sister, had left the meeting earlier to run to the bank to get money for a truck she was buying from Rurik. They thought Hedi was dead. When they saw her they screamed and cried. Sobbing, they wrapped her in their arms, asking if she was hurt. The officer who helped her out of the building cleaned the blood off her. She started vomiting.

"I had brain splatter on me and blood all over my face, arms and hands."

Richard Lash and Monique Davis, Rurik's third daughter, left the room seconds before the shooting started. They went to the backyard, but Monique, who was pregnant, stopped in the staff bathroom.

Phil Russo held a credential from the California Department of Corrections. He had voluntarily taken a core course to prepare him for entry-level work in local jails or probation departments. His name had been on Sheriff Mike Poindexter's extra help roster for the last four months when his wife was killed. Sheila and Phil Russo were recent arrivals to Alturas, having moved there from Bakersfield eight months earlier. About noon Russo went home after a twelve-hour night shift. He was scheduled to go back to work at midnight.

Sheila worked regular day hours at the Cedarville Rancheria's Alturas office. At about two o'clock she went home to change her shoes. She told her husband she had finished one meeting and it had gone better than she expected. She was getting ready for a second meeting in an hour. This was the hearing to enforce the tribe's eviction order against Cherie and her son Jack. On the strength of an outside auditor's findings the previous December, Sheila had taken to local authorities—presumably Sheriff Poindexter—her suspicions that money had been misused. She was told the county didn't have jurisdiction.

Sheriff Poindexter said he didn't recall meeting Sheila Russo but conceded that his undersheriff may have been contacted without Poindexter's knowing it. With four federally recognized tribes in the county, the sheriff was familiar with PL 280—the congressional law passed in 1953 that transferred criminal and civil jurisdiction over tribal lands from the federal government to six states. California was one of those initial states.

Cherie retaliated to the allegations of embezzling federal money. She bullied, she threatened violence, and she attempted to fire Sheila, but she lacked the authority. Sheila told her mother she was worried about what Cherie might do. Sheila had good reason to worry. She had executive committee voting power to break a tie vote. This was not reflected in the tribe's constitution or by-laws and remains unwritten. Past administrator Duanna Knighton used it frequently. Sheila would vote against Rhoades. Russo's door bell was ringing. It was Sheriff Poindexter and Russo's sergeant-in-charge.

At the police station Hedi's clothes were stripped off and photographs were taken of the blood on her body. She was given fresh clothes while she gave her account of the murders. She called her parents to tell them what had happened and that she was alive. It was the one call she made. Their number was the only one she knew, and her cell phone was still at the murder scene. Philip Russo walked into the police station. He looked at Hedi. She shook her head. He broke down and they held each other. At that moment she believed he still had hope Sheila was alive.

After giving police her statement Hedi went back to her hotel room, picked up her clothes and went to Sheila and Philip's house to shower off her blood-stained body. When Philip returned they didn't know what to do, so they went back to the parking lot across from the Cedarville Rancheria's offices. All that night they watched crime scene investigators from the Department of Justice take photographs as they moved through the building. At sunrise, after the bodies were taken away, she and Phil left. The day was starting for Hedi. With Rurik dead, some form of tribal government was needed and that meant Hedi had to return to the murder scene, the chairs and tables flipped over, papers strewn all over the room, the blood on the carpet, and the smell.

All Phil desperately wanted that night was to be by his wife's side, but he wasn't allowed in the tribal office building. He stood in front of the building until the last person cleared the scene. He watched as Sheila was taken out in a body bag.

In those nine minutes of havoc four people were killed and two injured. There were sixteen spent rounds scattered on the conference room floor and eight live rounds remaining in the jammed Lorcin. Rurik Two Bears Davis, fifty, was shot once in the head. Glenn Calonico, thirty, was shot eight times, including two shots to the chest that killed him. Sheila Russo, forty-seven, was shot twice in the head. Angel Morningstar Penn, nineteen, was shot once in the chest. The wounded were Melissa Davis, twenty-eight, shot four times, and Monica Davis, twenty-five, shot once. All were shot at close range—two to three feet.

The media descended on Alturas and Cedarville the day after the murders. People on the street were interviewed. Neighbors were interviewed. The Alturas city clerk was interviewed. A woman directing a theatre rehearsal for children a few blocks away was interviewed. Even the town bullies who knew Cherie were interviewed. "She bullied her way through life," said one. "She kept pushing and plowing to get her way, but I would never think she would start blowing people away in a meeting." Telephones at city hall didn't stop ringing. One exuberant news story began: "The people of Modoc County are stunned. Their small community is getting national attention after a mass shooting Thursday in Alturas." A mass murder had never occurred here. Police called the murders "isolated." A mug shot of Cherie taken at her booking went viral. Photos of the victims were lifted from Facebook. Associated Press took exterior shots of the Rancheria's offices, wrote a matter-of-fact story, and sent it out with photographs to its nationwide subscribers. Embezzlement and eviction were the tantalizing headlines. One metro newspaper investigated the tribe's source of finances tied to the state's Revenue Sharing Trust Fund. Cherie was profiled as unpleasant, a tangle of sheer meanness, forceful, and a loudmouth, threatening all the time. Five days later AP followed with more details and for the moment the story stayed alive. Gleaning what they could on short deadlines, the reporters left. Story over.

Sheila was the only non-Native victim. The coverage of her killing was an automatic aside, a statistic in the aftermath reporting by the major press—"also killed was . . ."

Phil immediately set in motion a crusade to give his late wife the recognition she deserved. He did this by systematically using major media outlets—television, print, and social media. He invited a regional television crew into his Alturas home about a week after the shootings. His message was clear and consistent. Shelia was caring, loving, and non-judgmental. She had a passion for helping others. "The one thing I want to make sure of going forward is that we don't just tell the story of a killer or this tragedy." He pursued this message over a five-month period, making a half-dozen internet postings and giving at least five television interviews.

Phil worked to give his wife the credit he felt she deserved. He used the internet to draw attention to National Crime Victims' Rights Week. A month later he posted an opinion piece titled "Please Stop Turning Killers into Celebrities." This was followed by "Mixed Emotions over the Evidence" and then a question and answer interview with a crime victim advocate, titled "Where's the Heart in Journalism for the Plight of Victims of Violent Crimes?" He was using his wife's death as a platform for changing how victims were publicly perceived—and the media was the culprit.

"It is our responsibility to let them know they've gone too far," he wrote in a nationally read blog. He said there was a need to shame the media publicly—that the media were "traumatizing" the surviving victims. He said it was offensive to the public's intelligence. He asked the public join him in his effort to hold the media accountable for their coverage of something as horrific as a mass murder.

2

IT WAS A SLOW week at the Bureau of Indian Affairs office in Redding. Until Thursday evening, when a local newscast reported four people, including three Natives, killed in a mass shooting in Alturas. The murders were less than two hundred miles to the northeast.

On Friday Dr. Virgil Akins, Redding BIA superintendent, sent his first dispatch to BIA officials in Washington. The murders were in his territory. He repeated information he'd picked up the night before. It was a routine report. He didn't say if the BIA was sending a team of emergency counselors to Alturas. The BIA's only crisis help plan is for fires and other natural disasters. Unprepared, the BIA's only choice was to improvise and look for outside help.

Also on Friday, the morning after the murders, Joshua Simmons, an acting fire management officer in Akins's region, sent an email to Steve "Sid" Caesar, chief of emergency management in the BIA's Office of Justice Services in Washington DC. He said, "We are in the process of getting a CISM team ordered to assist the Cedarville Rancheria regarding the shooting that has occurred there." Critical incident stress management teams, known as CISM, are trained to respond to catastrophes such as multiple murders. He told Caesar, "We are using this team because they have BIA employees who are also tribal members . . . this team would have more cultural sensitivity for working with tribal members." Simmons was trying to get the team to Alturas the next day. His message went out at 10:26 a.m.

At 1:23 on Friday afternoon a message from Jay Hinshaw, the BIA's regional emergency management coordinator, went to the Department of Interior's Watch Office (DOI). After September 11, 2001, the Watch Office was responsible for coordinating law enforcement, emergency management, and security. "A critical stress management team is being deployed to assist the surviving tribal government officials and Indian community members in the aftermath of a shooting incident at the Cedarville Rancheria tribal office involving multiple fatalities," Hinshaw confirmed. The team was an interagency team. It was not BIA. But, he added, "BIA employees will be directly involved in helping the community recover from this devastating event." Hinshaw copied Caesar and nine other BIA officials. In four minutes Hinshaw got a reply from the Watch Office. "Thanks for the update, Jay . . . that must be horrific for such a small community." Eight minutes later, at 1:35 p.m., the DOI's Office of Environmental Policy and Compliance responded, "So very, very sad," and added an FYI informing Hinshaw that he was using an old email address for Caesar. A new address was added to the FYI.

At 4:39 Friday afternoon Lynda Zambrano, executive director of the nonprofit Northwest Tribal Emergency Management Council in Snohomish, Washington, received an email detailing the murders in California. The email was from an unidentified BIA source.

Sensitive to false or inaccurate information regularly circulated on the internet, Zambrano was cautious. She immediately went online and found the Associated Press coverage of the mass murders. Once she was confident her information was valid she sent out an "email blast." At the bottom of her email she copied and pasted the AP story. She was the only one in the email thread who did this. She knew everyone on her email list needed to know her source of information. If it was not in writing, Zambrano knew there was too much room for interpretation and misquoting. She also knew it didn't always work, but it made for fewer mistakes.

Following the Northwest Tribal Emergency Management Council's prepared call out plan, Zambrano sent out an appeal for help. "We are looking for any assistance that we can in finding counseling services or a CISM team," she wrote. First, she notified Washington state officials and first responders. Then she notified neighboring tribes, knowing they came to the aid of other tribes. She used social media: Instagram, Facebook, Twitter, Snapchat, LinkedIn and the Northwest Tribal Emergency Management's website. Also on call was the National Tribal Amateur Radio Association. Its six hundred emergency amateur radio specialists are under the umbrella of the Northwest Tribal

Emergency Management. Most of her resources, like the radio operators, are aligned with the Emergency Support Functions (ESFs) of the National Response Framework (NRF). Zambrano knew that by quickly identifying and deploying the right people and resources to a crisis, damage to people's health and well-being could be reduced. Her call for crisis counseling aid for the Cedarville Rancheria took just twenty-four minutes.

She didn't worry that the reach of her emails might fail because on the list was a personal hero of Zambrano's, Sue Bush, director of the Office of Emergency Management in Washington State's Department of Social and Health Services Administration. Zambrano knew the minute Bush received the email alert she would respond to the call for crisis counseling help. Bush was back to Zambrano in three minutes. She asked for telephone numbers so that they could coordinate through the weekend. She told Zambrano, "I am trying to drum up culturally competent resources here. I will try to get an after-hours POC in SAMHSA ASAP." POC was point of contact. SAMHSA was the federal Substance Abuse and Mental Health Services Administration. Zambrano introduced Bush via email to Hinshaw. This was the first link between state, federal, and non-government agencies in the search to fill the Cedarville Rancheria's emergency needs.

Zambrano widened her net. She continued to contact additional sources. The Cedarville Rancheria tribe needed help quickly. She knew that crisis counseling is about addressing a person's immediate needs, including their safety. "Time is of the essence," she wrote in her emails. She had confidence her email alerts were reaching the right people. But she knew many federal agencies, the BIA being one of them, were ill prepared to respond to major catastrophes like mass murder. "That's where the Northwest Tribal Emergency Management Council comes in," Zambrano explained. "We exist to aid in filling the gaps where any shortfalls may occur. We identify and deploy alternate resources when the traditional federal system fails. One of our tribal elders says it best and it has become our organization's motto: 'The creator placed us on this earth to take care of one another.'"

She quickly dropped off the email thread. Zambrano said her job was to fill the gap only until federal officials responded. "We are not here to enable the Federal Government or any other responsible party from their trust or fiduciary responsibilities," she wrote in an email to me. "I knew that the BIA may not have the resources that the tribe was in need of, but they did have an obligation to assist in finding the appropriate resources. We provided information to assist all parties involved." She was comfortable knowing that the Washington state governor's office, SAMHSA, and the state's Medicaid program were notified and were following through with her urgent calls. "I had even greater confidence that fellow tribal nations were notified and would assure that the Cedarville Tribe received everything that it needed. I remained on standby if anyone needed further assistance but there were no requests."

In the meantime the BIA continued to improvise. On Friday afternoon, following up on Zambrano's introduction, Hinshaw sent Bush an email at 5:24. He told her the Department of Interior's Watch Office in Washington DC didn't have a 24-7 telephone number for her, so he was using the email address Zambrano provided. His news wasn't promising. "We had ordered an interagency wildland fire CISM team this morning. This afternoon the team cancelled and will not be coming." Hinshaw gave no explanation for the cancellation. "We were wondering if you are aware of a standing team or possible team members who can be brought in to provide assistance to surviving tribal government officials, tribal members." Included on his list were BIA, Bureau of Land Management, and U.S. Forest Service employees. He added: "We're working with Indian Health Service (IHS) in Sacramento, but IHS will not make any decisions about sending people until Monday. Josh Simmons and I . . . are traveling to Alturas early tomorrow morning to meet with . . . surviving tribal officials and employees. We will complete a needs assessment, but neither of us have any experience with mental health crisis counseling."

Cancellation of the interagency wildland fire CISM team left Hinshaw in limbo. He was the first to admit the BIA was unprepared to provide crisis counseling, not only for its own employees but for the surviving Native victims of the incident.

Over the weekend Bush compiled a list of possible sources for Hinshaw. On it were names and telephone numbers for the Federal Bureau of Investigation, the California Governor's Office of Emergency Management representative in Modoc County, the American Red Cross Sacramento chapter that covers Modoc County, and a mental health professional who works with Native children. She gave detailed information on how to contact other agencies specializing in disaster distress help. She sent the list to Hinshaw on Sunday at 6:42 p.m.

The next morning, Monday, at 7:53 Hinshaw got back to Bush. He didn't need her help. "Thanks so much, Sue. I was . . . able to confirm from Candace Deaton, director of Strong Family Health, that the needs assessment is ongoing. There appears to be no unmet needs at this time. . . . Candace is the tribally appointed point of contact for all emergency aid offers." The BIA's search was over. In Deaton the BIA conveniently found someone who filled the agency's gap in crisis mental health care. Strong Family Health is a nonprofit run by the Cedarville Rancheria. Its purpose is to provide healthcare for tribes in Modoc County, but it does not have a crisis counseling program. Ironically, the governing boards for Strong Family and Cedarville Rancheria are the same. Thus when Cherie killed Davis, Calonico, Penn, and Russo she also killed the key members of Deaton's Strong Family board of directors. Deaton had the support of the tribe's survivors, presumably Bogda, Munholand, and Brandi Penn. No one asked Deaton for her qualifications. There was an implied assumption that as director of Strong Family Health she had experience in putting together a crisis management team. No one asked if Deaton, too, might be a victim.

To keep legally within its BIA-written constitution and by-laws the tribe asked for the BIA's help in forming a new tribal executive committee. But Tina Penn, the surviving vice chair of the executive committee, was missing. She lost three of her family in the shootings. Tina wasn't at the eviction hearing when Cherie went on her killing spree. Now she was critical to re-establishing the tribe's government. No one seemed concerned that Tina might also be a victim and that she hadn't been found. Alturas police considered putting out a missing person notice, but there's no indication they did so. On Monday, with Akins and the BIA's Southern California superintendent Robert Eben monitoring, the tribe selected an interim government. Brandi Penn, Tina's surviving daughter, was named temporary chair. Tina's name dropped from the BIA's email exchanges.

The BIA didn't escape severe criticism for its failure to respond with its own crisis counseling team. The week before the shootings William Wiley retired as the BIA's national emergency manager. He was now working with a Zambrano subcommittee. Wiley didn't wait for an outcome to the BIA's scramble for help. It was apparent the BIA was floundering. By 2:11 on Sunday morning he could not contain his irritation any longer. In an email to Sue Bush, and copied to Lynda Zambrano, he pointed at the National Interagency Fire Center in Boise, Idaho, the National Interagency Coordination Center, and the National Multi-Agency Coordination group. Wiley said he thought those agencies had been directed two years before to include "all hazards" in a website database that managed state and federal wildland fire-fighting resources. All hazards, Wiley thought, meant threats other than just fires. He said he was frustrated that these agencies "have not enthusiastically . . . effectively embraced this assignment." This was something they claimed they'd been doing for the last two years.

Wiley wrote, "There is much foot dragging from old 'fire dogs' to fully embrace the functioning in the real world of all hazard management. I am shocked. I hope that we can use this incident to encourage management in all agencies that have such risks . . . to establish, train and use such teams, dedicated to active shooter, officer shooting and disaster response. This type of counseling is needed immediately and not after the weekend or days of fumbling later . . . and putting such needs and deficiencies in our after action reports over and over literally for decades without any corrective actions, is most frustrating."

Wiley went directly to the Cedarville Rancheria tragedy.

"I can imagine how the children in the building and those in the local schools who knew or were related to the victims, or their children and grandchildren are feeling now," he wrote in his email. "These people and the first responders need immediate debriefing and counseling quickly and potentially for a substantial time." He said crisis counseling is lacking in almost all planning, not just at the tribal level, but throughout the BIA. Hinshaw was on Wiley's copy line.

On February 26, 2014, a week after the murders, at 1:34 p.m. Hinshaw sent an email to Darren Cruzan, director of the BIA's Office of Justice Services (OJS) in Washington DC. Cruzan is a career BIA employee and a member of the Miami Tribe of Oklahoma. He is responsible for the overall management of the BIA's law enforcement program. Its main goal is to uphold the constitutional sovereignty of the federally recognized tribes and preserve peace within Indian country. Hinshaw didn't defend Wiley's criticism of the BIA. Instead, he gave Cruzan a candid assessment. Disenrollments in California and school shootings nationwide were two examples that could trigger future attacks on tribal offices. The Cedarville Rancheria murders could lead to copycat shootings. He suggested the BIA examine the shootings and create a crisis counseling plan tribal governments could use.

He told Cruzan: "In speaking with the victims and law enforcement officers who were involved, it's clear to me that there were some prior warning signs. This was the most significant attack on a tribal government in my memory." Hinshaw continued, "In the Pacific Region and elsewhere there have been many tribal disenrollments as competing groups and families exert their power. Groups of disenrolled Indians are reportedly now having heated discussions through social media. With this in mind I'm concerned that attacks at tribal offices may now begin to increase similar to the increase in school shootings in the aftermath of Columbine copycats." At the time of the murders Hinshaw, also a career BIA employee, had been with the BIA for thirteen years.   It took Cruzan two weeks to get back to Hinshaw.

On March 13, 2014, Cruzan wrote: "I agree we need to coordinate and develop a strategy. From my experience these things are impossible to predict, but in hindsight there are always clues that could have at least provided some warning. Can I ask you to assemble an after action report from the regional perspective. After we have a chance to review all of the AARs that you receive we can make a better decision on the proper direction this effort would take. . . . As you know any efforts (by) the BIA . . . will need to be coordinated with all of the partners, including state, county and local police jurisdictions, especially in the PL 280 state of California."

Cruzan made no mention of the BIA's failures in reacting to the Cedarville Rancheria. Instead, he fell back on Wiley's criticism of the BIA's bureaucratic procedures. Cruzan asked Hinshaw for an after action report. He stressed the hurdle of working with multiple federal and state jurisdictions.

Nearly a month after the four were killed at the Cedarville Rancheria, an after action report was completed. Hinshaw was one of three BIA officials making the report. There were twelve suggestions for improvement. The last was Hinshaw's warning that the BIA had to prepare for attacks on tribal governments and copycat school shootings. The report's summation had a familiar ring to it: "Local, state and federal law enforcement and security personnel would need to be consulted during any such study and prevention tool development efforts. It seems this would need to be a national level effort where the BIA-Pacific Region would provide some support."

October 24, 2014, Lynda Zambrano was in a meeting with employees from the Federal Emergency Management Agency's Region 10. The meeting was at the Snohomish Public Library. It was eight months after the Cedarville Rancheria mass shootings. Region 10 covers Alaska, Idaho, Oregon, and Washington. Within those states FEMA is responsible for 271 tribes. There was a telephone call for her. It was a reporter from a Seattle newspaper. A fifteen-year-old Native boy at Marysville Pilchuck High School, up the road from the library, had shot five students. Only one survived. He then put a 40-caliber Beretta PX4 Storm semi-automatic handgun to his head and killed himself. All the victims were of the neighboring Tulalip Tribe. It was the second deadliest high school shooting since Columbine.

The staff at the Marysville School District took the lead and formed their own CISM team. Later there was a bomb threat, followed two days after by another. Zambrano's son is a student at Marysville Pilchuck and also of the Tulalip Tribe. All the victims were his relatives. He asked her, "Mom, how can you guarantee when you send me to school, I'll be safe?"

In August 2016 Cruzan appeared before a U.S. Senate committee on "Addressing Trauma and Mental Health Challenges in Indian Country." It was two years after he received Hinshaw's email and nearly two years after the Marysville Pilchuck High School shootings. In a prepared statement Cruzan briefly acknowledged the need for crisis counseling as a way to prevent suicides among Natives. He did not address the BIA's failure to provide traumatic crisis counseling after the mass shootings at the Cedarville Rancheria and Marysville Pilchuck High School.

In late 2019 the BIA announced that the problem of providing aid to trauma victims like the Cedarville Rancheria killings was answered. An occupational safety and health manager (from OSHA) was hired for the BIA's Pacific region. But OSHA is under the U.S. Department of Labor. It only oversees working conditions in the private sector and some cases the public sector—not mass shootings. That duty falls to the Federal Emergency Management Agency (FEMA). FEMA is under of the U.S. Department of Homeland Security. The agencies have different responsibilities. There is no intersection.

Did the BIA have a crisis emergency plan in place for the Marysville Pilchuck High School shooting that killed students from the Tulalip Tribe? No one from the BIA contacted Zambrano.

3

CEDARVILLE IS A DOT in the far northeastern corner of California's Empty Quarter. With a population of five hundred and waning, it's the largest of four settlements in Surprise Valley. Twenty-five miles and a 6,000-foot mountain pass separate it from the murder scene in Alturas. It's the home of the Cedarville Rancheria and Cherie Rhoades and her family.

In the late nineteenth century settlers planted grasses and grains and put their cows to grazing in Surprise Valley. A three-block downtown was laid out with a park and churches. In a nostalgic moment Cedarville was named after a town in the Midwest. The town remains much the same today as it was in the late 1880s. Back then the townsfolk believed the Northern Paiutes would stay on their reservations. But 150 years later in 2005 the Cedarville Rancheria Northern Paiutes went public with their plan to build a gas station-convenience store off-reservation. Now the town's fourth and fifth generation merchants saw the Northern Paiutes' gas station plan as overstepping their boundaries. Time to bring out a petition.

Cedarville relies on bulletin board notices for news—or grocery store counter petitions, depending on the urgency of the issue. In this case a petition was soliciting objections to the Cedarville Rancheria Northern Paiutes' plan to build a gas station and convenience store at the main entrance to town. The petition asked the Bureau of Indian Affairs to deny the Cedarville Rancheria's request to put 1.3 acres adjacent to Indian-owned land into a trust. The trust was the Rancheria's first step toward construction of what is often referred to as a "travel center."

More than a hundred customers put their signatures on the anti–

travel center petition. It was easy to pick up the pencil. Not much thought was required for an uninformed citizen to have an effective grass roots voice. The store keeper was the first to sign. The petition stated that if the Paiutes were allowed to build on 1.3 acres that were off-reservation, Modoc County would remove the land from the tax rolls. Land purchased by a tribe is held in a trust by the Bureau of Indian Affairs. Under U.S. law governing tribal lands, it cannot be taxed. Backers of the petition argued that the loss of taxes on vacant land was more important than the addition of a new, customer-based income-generating business.

However, the petition wasn't really about tax loss or a truck stop, even though it said truck stops negatively impact a town's business community. This petition was a propaganda tool against the American Indians at the Rancheria: a tactic of fear and falsehoods designed to persuade a biased citizenry.

How exactly would the American Indian-owned gas station impact Cedarville's business district? The town had one grocery store, one motel, two cafes, a beauty shop, a Napa Auto parts store, and a seasonal used book store. The self-serve gas station was open infrequently. But some people believed that the Cedarville Rancheria Paiutes didn't buy local. There was an attitude of: "What have those Indians ever done for the community? They don't even shop here."

Yes, the tribe conceded, it would not pay $412 in property taxes on the 1.3 acres. However, the tribe voluntarily contributed money to local school programs, the district fair, and the two county hospitals, one in Cedarville, the other in Alturas. Through the Modoc Indian Health Project the two hospitals had recently split tribal grants from the Cedarville Rancheria of $200,000 and $245,000. The business community and petition pushers chose to ignore these donations. The petition organizer sent a letter of complaint to the BIA's Northern California office.

"I believe that a truck stop in this town would change our community permanently because of the nature of what a truck stop brings with it, drugs, prostitution, vagrants and overall unsafe conditions our community has not had to face. We are remote and blessed with low crime, wonderful people, peace and quiet and quality of life. This is not what we need in our community."

The truck stop and threat of prostitution on the outskirts of town were a diversion away from recessed racism and social silence. Social silence is a governing factor, often controlling the most important—and unsaid—issues of a small town because the fact that no one speaks openly about their racism or prejudice doesn't mean those attitudes don't exist.

The BIA had no obligation to consider the petition or deny the Cedarville Rancheria's request to put the vacant acres in a trust. The petition disappeared from the grocery counter, and eventually the new gas station was built. Cherie Rhoades was the project manager.

If the tribe wanted an intimidating woman to buffer them from the townsfolk, Cherie Rhoades was a good choice. She was an imposing front person. Her legacy of bullying matched that of the best of the petition manipulators. Everyone knew she picked up a table and threw it at someone who pissed her off. "You want to fight? Go ahead, fuck with me. I dare you," was in every stride she took. At that time she was the leader of the Cedarville Rancheria tribe.

In August 2011 Cherie gave my wife Barbara, also a journalist, and me a short tour of the Rabbit Traxx gas station construction site. We were there to take photographs and get information on the grand opening. Cherie said the station would open in November, and it did. There is no law in California that requires station attendants to pump gas for customers. But on opening day Cherie was out front asking customers, "Fill 'er up?"

Idle conversations while she pumped were short and to the point. One morning when I pulled in for diesel I said I'd heard her mother had died.

"Yeah. Down in Reno. She was cremated."

"Cremated?"

"Yeah. Only cost $500 in Nevada."

"Not bad."

"That was you who wrote that negative editorial about Strong Family and Belinda Brown the executive director." Cherie, head of the Rancheria's executive committee, was on Strong Family's board of directors.

"You got the wrong newspaper, Cherie. I never wrote a negative editorial about Strong Family Health."

"Yeah. You did."

"Sorry, but you got the wrong newspaper."

"Yeah. You did."

She was convinced she was right and I was wrong.

A congenial Cherie showed up the night the Burners came through Cedarville on their way home from Burning Man, the mega-gathering at the Black Rock desert, about 100 miles south of Cedarville. Rabbit Traxx is a last stop-and-gas-up for the Burning Man exodus heading north to Oregon, Washington, and British Columbia. There was a large dumpster behind the gas station where Burners dropped off their recyclables for free, courtesy of Cherie as the tribe's leader. The makeshift recycle center was run by volunteers as a fundraiser for Cedarville non-profits. Barbara and I were working the late afternoon shift. Cherie walked across the parking lot. When she walks it's as if nothing moves. She's a single gliding unit, no arms swinging from side to side.

"You guys like ice cream?" she asked us. Burners, many still in costume, were lined up at the dumpster.

"Sure thing," we said.

"ok, I'll be right back," and Cherie quickly returned with ice cream sandwiches.

"This one's my favorite. Strawberry." She passed them around. She had a name for the sandwiches, something that sounded like Bunny Rabbit.

"How about a picture with the Burners, Cherie?" Barbara asked.

And Cherie stood camera-connected but unsmiling between a man in a kilt and a woman from Portland.

4

CHERIE WAS BORN DECEMBER 13, 1969, to an impoverished Native American mother living off-reservation in the Sacramento metropolitan area. She is the youngest of five children. All of them have the same mother but three different fathers. Her mother, Virginia Lash, was an eighth grade dropout. She had her first child when she was sixteen. All the children grew up as whites with no cultural connection to their Northern Paiute ancestry. One of Cherie's half-sisters, Gina, a paranoid schizophrenic with antisocial behavior, is imprisoned at Patton State Hospital in San Bernardino, California.

When Cherie was eleven years old she was raped by a twenty-three-old man. The rape, never reported, evolved into a three-year consensual sexual relationship. She stopped going to her middle school classes on a regular basis. She was expelled from the ninth grade when she hit a male teacher who wouldn't let her play volleyball. She transferred to an alternative school, where she flunked five of her six classes. The only class she narrowly passed was reading. She dropped out. Cherie was twenty-one when she earned a general education diploma. By then she had a son, Jack Stockton Jr. The father was a married man thirty years her senior. He eventually divorced his wife, but instead of marrying Cherie he took up with another woman and left the state. She was briefly homeless and moved back to her parents. She met Marvin Rhoades, a bartender, and they lived together for nine years before marrying. He was forty-two years older than Cherie. After her mother moved to the Cedarville Rancheria, Cherie and Marvin Rhoades followed in 1993. Rurik and his family arrived the next year. Until then Cherie and Rurik's relationship was typical for teenaged brothers and sisters. "He took me to the roller skating rink because he used me to get girls to dance with him at their sock hops," she said. But after their move from an urban life to the reservation, the relationship changed.

Cherie and Rurik knew nothing of the Northern Paiutes' traditions, language, or spirituality. They were not raised as Natives and were unprepared for the substantial responsibilities of tribal self-government. Now the Lash family, Cherie, Rurik, their mother Virginia, and various cousins and children over age eighteen, held the controlling bloc of votes when seats on the executive committee came up for election. Facing them was the adoption of the Bureau of Indian Affairs' stock constitution. The constitution guaranteed the tribe sovereignty status and with it came supporting federal funding. Cherie and Rurik's enrollment in the tribe also qualified them for a share in California's lucrative Native gambling revenues. The Lash-controlled tribe had to agree on the final wording of the constitution and put it before the tribe for ratification. But Cherie and Rurik couldn't come to an agreement on one constitutional clause: should enrollment in the Cedarville Rancheria be based on blood quantum or ancestral lineage?

The BIA does not set blood quantum requirements for tribal enrollment. To be eligible for enrollment in a tribe, the BIA requires applicants to submit a request for a Certificate of Degree of Indian or Alaska Native Blood (CDIB). Anyone seeking enrollment in a specific federally recognized tribe has to show a blood-line relationship to an ancestor already enrolled in that tribe. This can be a parent, grandparent, or great-grandparent and so on. Dead or alive. Proof of this blood line or descent requires a certified copy of the birth or death certificate of the ancestor. Tribes obligated by their constitutions to use blood quantum—which has been called "statistical genocide"— are increasingly seeing a dilution of Native blood through outside or inter-marriages. As a result they are lowering the percentage of Native blood required for enrollment. The range is dramatic: the Yomba Shoshone tribe in Nevada, for example, requires one percent Native blood for enrollment, which is equivalent to one parent. The Utu Utu Gwaitu Paiute tribe, in California, requires one grandparent, and the Karuk of California one great-grand parent.

The other enrollment choice under Native constitutional sovereignty is ancestral lineage, or lineal descent. Tribes using ancestral lineage do not have a minimum blood quantum or minimum degree of Native blood requirement. However, members must be direct descendants of original enrollees. If there is a loophole in lineal descent it's required that enrollees be "direct descendants." In theory at least, the descendants are full-blooded Natives and their descendants can be from outside or inter-marriages. An example is the Oklahoma Modocs, widely known in Indian Country as the whitest tribe in America. The tribe is originally from the California-Oregon region that includes Modoc County. Weak on blood quantum, the Oklahoma Modocs are strong on lineal descent. As a result, the tribe will always have a viable membership. Most Modoc tribal members, living in twenty states, have never been to their homeland and do not know its history.

Rurik's daughters weren't certain on which side of the blood line he stood, but they thought he was against the blood quantum criteria. This made sense. The Lash blood line was running thin as a result of non-Native marriages. The Cedarville Paiutes, like many tribes nationwide, were faced with a monumental decision that could determine their future: should the tribe require lineage or blood quantum as proof of Northern Paiute heritage? The question was answered when the tribe adopted the BIA-written constitution with the proviso clause that "all lineal descendants of persons eligible for membership" can be members of the tribe on the condition that they live on the Rancheria. No blood quantum required.

After Rurik gained the chair of the executive committee he tried to get Cherie, their mother, and another half-brother disenrolled. He failed to realize that he would have disenrolled himself along with his entire blood-related family. Cherie pointed out that Rurik was about to cut off this limb of the family tree. Rurik's disenrollment attempt was never made public under the tribe's sovereignty protection, leaving Cherie with intense bitterness toward her half-brother. She did not like anyone threatening Virginia. Cherie saw her as a loving and caring mother, even if the threat came from Rurik, one of Virginia's own children. "When my mother's feelings get hurt, it doesn't make me very happy," Cherie said.

The family quickly dissolved into a deep state of dysfunction because of vagueness, disagreement, and ignorance of sovereignty rights. Rurik still was not prepared when he struck on the idea of using the embezzlement allegation to evict his half-sister—instead of disenrolling her. He didn't know the tribe's legal process on how to carry out the eviction. Nor, apparently, did Hedi Bogda, the tribe's recently hired attorney. It was Modoc County's Sheriff Poindexter who told them he couldn't carry out an eviction without a court order. The tribe had to form its own court. Hiring Hedi was the first step. Contracting with Judge Patricia Lenzi was the next. Now, with an attorney and a judge in place, the tribe could hold an eviction hearing and then go to Poindexter with a legal court order to enforce. What Rurik didn't wait for was an official Department of Justice determination on the embezzlement allegation.

Blood line has always been a part of the BIA's plan to add Natives to the great American melting pot. Native Americans were forbidden to wear Native clothes, speak a Native language, or even wear their hair long. But there's a glitch in this BIA vision of assimilation. Native Americans who are officially enrolled in federally recognized tribes like the Cedarville Rancheria are distinguished from other ethnic groups in the United States by their enrollment cards. It's the enrollment card identifying them as "Indians" that sets them apart. The Cedarville Rancheria's decision to define who is an American Indian by adopting ancestral lineage as its criteria guaranteed a future for Cherie and Rurik's descendants—regardless of their blood quantum.

5

CHERIE AND HER FAMILY didn't look like American Indians. They didn't know the Paiute language, its traditions, customs, songs, and spirituality. Did this make them less American Indian? Or did it matter? They were officially documented by the U.S. government as members of a recognized tribe—regardless of their level of ancestral lineage or percentage of blood quantum.

"Here's a story about two brothers," said Kandi Maxwell, an Arkansas Cherokee and English teacher at Modoc High School in Alturas. Kandi knew Cherie and her victims.

There were two brothers who were enrolled in the Chickasaw Nation, which uses the same criteria—ancestral lineage—as the Cedarville Rancheria. Both brothers had their DNA tested. One brother's test showed Native heritage. The other brother's did not—even though the brothers had the same family tree and their grandparents were enrolled members and listed on the Dawes Rolls. The Dawes Rolls, also known as the "Final Rolls," are the lists of individuals who were accepted at the close of the nineteenth century as eligible for tribal membership in the "Five Civilized Tribes": Cherokees, Creeks, Choctaws, Chickasaws, and Seminoles. These five tribes continue to use the Dawes Rolls for determining tribal membership.

"So, who gets to keep their story?" she asked.

Kandi contends that the question who is an Indian goes back to the two brothers. Should the brother without Native DNA in his test results be denied his Native heritage? Or is enrollment in a federally recognized tribe, like the Cedarville Rancheria, the deciding factor proving Native linage? The government recognizes that tribes are distinct entities unto themselves. As sovereign nations, tribes decide who is eligible for enrollment. The BIA sets no minimum blood quantum requirement. So does tribal enrollment or blood quantum make a person more Indian?

"Look at Cherie and the Cedarville Rancheria. How 'Indian' are they?" Kandi asked. "It feels like these late-comers to Native heritage are putting on something that doesn't belong to them. I admit I have a problem with this because I believe you need to be a part of a Native community to be Native." Her belief was borne out in 2004 when she was given the Distinguished Service award by Resources for Indian Student Education (RISE) for her culture and academics work with Native youth. In 2016 California's American Indian Education Centers recognized her work with its annual Honored Elder award.

Kandi knows that much of Native culture has been misappropriated. However, she believes identity is more than paper. She thinks it's inappropriate to deny Elizabeth Warren her heritage and her family stories based on a DNA test. "Warren didn't claim tribal membership, she always stated heritage. She understands that heritage is different from tribal enrollment."

Kandi continued that she believes Warren grew up listening to her family stories and thought of herself as Native. "Some people never identify as Native, but through DNA tests find out they are. They have the blood but they have no cultural heritage."

Trump's problem with Warren's identity may be that she didn't look Native. In 1993 he appeared before the House Subcommittee on Native American Affairs of the Committee on Natural Resources. He was trying to block Indian casinos in Connecticut and New York because they would compete with his Atlantic City casino operations. In his argument the future president quipped, "They don't look like Indians to me."

Who gets to keep their story?

"You can't please every tribe because they each have their own beliefs, and many are contradictory," Kandi pointed out. "As for Trump, he just repeats his Pocahontas garbage. More of the same from his small-minded brain."

6

THIS ADVISORY IS ON the Cedarville Rancheria's website:

"Be cautious when visiting reservations. These areas are not designed for visitors and are inhabited by real people. These peoples will not look the way Hollywood portrays . . . they will look like all other peoples of the area."

The tribe states it clearly: we look like our white neighbors.

Cedarville Paiute oral history says the Bureau of Indian Affairs, promising free land, free houses, and free money, enticed Cherie's family to move from the Sacramento area to the Cedarville Rancheria.

The Rancheria is tucked into a hillside that climbs away from Cedarville. Near the back entrance to the county fairgrounds a wooden sign, "Cedarville Rancheria," marks the entrance at the corner of Patterson Street and Rancheria Way. The Rancheria has one block-long paved street that ends in a cul-de-sac. There are less than a dozen structures in all, distinguished from each other by their colors: gold, blue, brown, red, turquoise and beige. Cherie's house is off-white with turquoise window trim. The lot sizes are larger than those in town, and there are fewer trees. There is a small community park and a kids' play area, and assorted vehicles are parked at random.

The twenty-acre tract was purchased for the tribe in 1914 under the authority of President Theodore Roosevelt's Antiquities Act of 1906. By the 1970s this BIA free housing amounted to a few shacks. All eight residents were on welfare. On average their formal education ended with the eighth grade. They spoke Paiute and practiced Native arts and crafts. Indian religion was the dominant religion, according to the demographic data published by the Government Printing Office. Today the shacks have been replaced by a program administered by the U.S. Department of Housing and Urban Development. Federal housing grants and gambling revenues known as "casino allotments"—profits from Native-owned casinos—have replaced the welfare checks. All federally recognized tribal members in California share casino allotments on a per capita basis.

This is the reservation community to which Cherie and Rurik moved when they left their urban life in the Sacramento area to live at the Rancheria. New houses were being built. The offer of a free home and a casino allotment each quarter was an opportunity they couldn't refuse. The entire family cashed in. To make the move to the Rancheria official, Cherie and Rurik enrolled themselves and their children as members of the tribe. When they arrived at the Rancheria their mother, Virginia, was the tribe's leader.

Of the nearly six hundred federally recognized tribes in the United States, about two hundred have their own court systems. Typically, larger tribes maintain their own civil courts. Smaller tribes like the Cedarville Rancheria contract with outside attorneys and judges to conduct legal proceedings. This is what the Cedarville Rancheria did the day of the murders. Hedi Bogda was already on board as tribal attorney. Judge Patricia Lenzi was hired that afternoon and was waiting by the telephone to conduct her first hearing.

Requirements for practicing law in a specific tribal court vary widely. Tribes do not necessarily require that attorneys be members of a given state bar association. However, some tribes require attorneys to pass a tribal bar exam and hold membership in their tribal court bar. Other tribes require attorneys to complete a cultural awareness training program in addition to passing a tribal bar exam. The American Bar Association recognizes the sovereignty of Native nations and tribal courts by allowing tribal court practitioners to be full members of the ABA. The courts, large or small, are as varied as the tribes themselves. They range from Native American tradition-based systems with few or no written rules or codes to sophisticated procedures that reflect the formal, rule-based, adversary system of the federal and state courts. This general principle applies to civil cases only. It does not include criminal matters. In 1953 the U.S. Congress passed Public Law 280. This statute, with some exceptions, transferred federal criminal jurisdiction over Natives on tribal lands to six states, California among them.

The types of cases heard in tribal courts can change over time and are as wide-ranging as the tribes themselves. Currently tribal courts in California deal with matters such as child welfare, guardianship, civil disputes, tribal ordinance violations, restraining orders, and eviction notices and appeals. For small tribes like the Cedarville Rancheria tribal judges usually conduct court sessions via conference calls known as remote telephonic hearings. And instead of the juried trials common in state courts, complaints are heard by the tribe's executive committee. In the case of the Cedarville Rancheria this is an elected three-member board. If the defendant appeals the executive committee's decision, the appeal is made to the same body that made the decision in the first place. This was exactly what happened in Cherie's case.

Judge Lenzi: "Where in tribal law is there authority to do something different?"

Cherie: "It says you're supposed to be able to appeal to the community counsel 'cause three people shouldn't have the right to tell people they need to move."

Judge Lenzi: "Well, where is that in tribal law though?"

The tribe's effort to evict Cherie came at a time when disenrollment was widespread among tribes on the West Coast. The complaint of detainer filed by her nephew Glenn as the tribe's housing authority was a legal counter reaction to her refusal to obey the eviction order.

7

CHERIE WAS TWENTY-FOUR WHEN she and her older brother became reservation Paiutes.

That was when the bitterness started. Rurik was on a personal vendetta. He deliberately humiliated her, made fun of her. Is it possible Rurik's bitterness caused what psychiatrists call a "reality-based pathological component" in Cherie?

They interpreted rules and regulations differently. In every instance they disagreed. They fought over everything tribal, wording of the constitution, use of grant monies, who got the larger house, which applicants were qualified for a house, environmental violations, even upkeep of her yard.

The fights turned violent. Alturas police were frequently called to keep the peace at routine meetings of the tribe. In 2009 Cherie unseated Rurik as tribal chair because he wanted to be paid for his chairmanship out of grant money. It wasn't ethical. Dethroned, Rurik was angry. Cherie said, "When we were in meetings he would kick his daughters under the table to make them vote the way he wanted. If they didn't, he took them out in back of the office and yelled at them." Rurik physically threatened her. Power plays like this divide Native families. Natives like the Lashes who act on emotions, have adversarial personalities, and don't know their tribal traditions often exploit sovereign authority. It was the wording in the constitution, not the future accusation of embezzlement, that first divided them. Once Rurik stretched as far as he could across the conference table to get as close to Cherie's face as possible. She thought he was crawling up on the table to attack her and she pushed her chair back to escape. Rurik was anxious, in a hurry, as if he was running out of time. He devised a plan to banish her from the tribe.

"This all happened because of the stupid court thing," Cherie said. "Rurik was a piece of shit."

8

AT THE SAME TIME as Cherie faced her half-brother's eviction order a disenrollment epidemic was raging through California's tribes. Disenrollment of a member of a federally recognized tribe carried severe penalties. The harshest was loss of identity.

In the decade leading up to the Cedarville Rancheria mass murders—and peaking in 2016—at least two dozen California tribes removed an estimated 2,500 Natives from their membership rolls. Nearly all the disenrollments argued that the targeted person failed the ancestry or blood quantum test. Disenrollments resulted in decline of nearly 10 percent in total tribal membership statewide. Tribes that disenrolled their own people lost from 10 to 50 percent of their total membership.

Those targeted for disenrollment suspected that greed and political corruption were the motives behind the reduction in numbers. They said tribal leadership groups—typically a one-family majority like the Cedarville Rancheria's Lash family—were corrupt and were exploiting Native sovereignty. They manipulated their constitutions to justify cultural genocide legally. Tribal executive committees and tribal members who survived the purge denied that greed or power motivated them. They argued that they were upholding membership rules established in their constitutions. Disenrollment was simply the removal of unqualified members who falsely joined their tribes for the benefits: scholarships, housing, and the regularly arriving "casino" checks. Those who were disenrolled countered that disenrollment was antithetical to the self-determination principle of tribal sovereignty. They said disenrollment is not tribal and is not an inherent right of Native peoples. Disenrollment was unique to "per cap" tribes; it was not happening among tribes that didn't receive casino money. And finally, as they pointed out: disenrollment doesn't exist in any traditional American Indian language.

The origins of the disenrollment outbreak can be traced to two U.S. Supreme Court decisions.

The first, *Santa Clara Pueblo v. Martinez* in 1978, made it virtually impossible for a Native woman to contest her disenrollment outside the tribal court system.

Julia Martinez, a full-blooded member and resident of the Santa Clara Pueblo in northern New Mexico, married a Navajo and they had several children. A daughter, Audrey Martinez, joined her mother in a federal court lawsuit against the Santa Clara Pueblo. Martinez went to court because two years before her marriage the Pueblo had passed a membership ordinance barring her children's membership in the tribe. The reason? Their father was not a Santa Claran. The new tribal law denied membership to children of female members who married outside the tribe. Children of male members who married outside the tribe were exempt. Martinez sued for discrimination. She said the tribe was violating Title 1 of the Indian Civil Rights Act of 1968. The tribe countered and the suit went to the U.S. Supreme Court. Martinez lost. The court ruled that Title 1 of the Indian Civil Rights Act did not authorize federal courts to hear civil actions against a tribe or its officers—in this case the validity of a tribe's ordinance, regardless of its timing. The ruling opened the floodgates of disenrollment without recourse.

The second U.S. Supreme Court decision came in 1987, when California sued the Cabazon and Morongo bands, which operated a card room and two bingo parlors on Cahuilla Mission Indians' land near Palm Springs in Riverside County. Both bands were federally recognized. A year earlier the State of California said the bingo parlors and card room were in violation of state law. The state cited criminal provisions of Public Law 280. This 1953 law granted six states—Alaska, California, Minnesota, Nebraska, Oregon, and Wisconsin—criminal jurisdiction over Native American tribal lands within the states' borders. Riverside County joined the California suit, saying that bingo, poker, and other card games violated a local ordinance prohibiting gambling. The two tribes countered, protesting that the games came under civil regulatory law, not criminal law, and the state had no authority over them. The California-sanctioned lottery was given as an example. The U.S. Supreme Court agreed. In 1987 the court ruled 6–3 that California and Riverside County did not have Public Law 280 authority to regulate bingo or card games held on Native-owned land. The case, which became known as the Cabazon decision, effectively turned a modest reservation poker parlor and bingo enterprise into a nationwide gaming phenomenon that spurred Congress into passing the Indian Gaming Regulatory Act the next year.

In California there are sixty-nine tribal-owned casinos and ninety tribal card rooms, all highly profitable. Total revenue from Native-owned casinos in the state averages an estimated $7 billion a year. This places Native-owned casinos in California second only to Nevada's gambling industry. California ranks first nationwide with nearly twice as much gambling revenue as second place Oklahoma. The majority of the eighty-nine tribes in California—regardless of size and their rural isolation, like that of the Cedarville Rancheria—receive approximately $275,000 each quarter based on annual statewide gaming revenues for the period. Tribes including the Cedarville Rancheria have received a total of over $17 million since the trust fund was established in 1999.

The $275,000 per tribe every three months is not necessarily paid out equally among its members. Distribution within each tribe is governed by tribal executive committee policy. For example, when Duanna Knighton was the Cedarville Rancheria's administrator she set up two financial plans. One called for a portion of the casino money to be deposited into an investment plan. Other funds went into an account for education. Annual donations were also made to the perennially cash-strapped Surprise Valley Health Care District. Some of the Rancheria's casino money was supposed to go to economic development, such as the Rabbit Traxx gas station and convenience store. Instead at about the time of the Rabbit Traxx opening, tribal members voted to increase the amount each member received quarterly. Each member of the Cedarville Rancheria receives $80,000 annually. A recent cost of living analysis by the California Budget and Policy Center found that the annual budget for a family of four with two working parents ranges from a high of $110,984 in San Francisco County to a low of $55,032 in Modoc County.

On the afternoon she walked into the Cedarville Rancheria tribal offices with two pistols, was Cherie aware of the epidemic of disenrollments, accusations of corrupt tribal governments, charges of greed, alleged manipulation of tribal constitutions, and fear of Native sovereignty being exploited? Rurik could have delayed the hearing. He and Calonico saw no alternative solution or temporary detour, no turning back. They were at an end point. Disenrollment fever was sweeping through Indian Country. Now was the time to use this momentum against Cherie. Even if her eviction fell short of disenrollment, she would be soon be off the Rancheria.

The only punishment in the social structure of tribes comparable to disenrollment is eviction. Rurik discovered he couldn't disenroll Cherie, as that meant disenrolling the entire Lash family because they were blood relatives. Disenrollment meant Cherie would lose her home. It also meant losing $80,000 yearly in casino money and her job at Rabbit Traxx. She would forfeit her tribal citizenship, educational stipends, and access to tribal schools, grants, and tribal-funded healthcare, and all cultural ties to the tribe. Severing her cultural bond to the tribe was debatable because as an urban Native American she had no connection to its historical traditions. Penalties such as eviction or disenrollment are prevalent today in Indian Country. The two are interchangeable. However, there is a third form of punishment: banishment. If Rurik was aware of banishment, it's unlikely he considered it. The point of banishment was to hold the family together, unlike disenrollment or eviction. Banishment would not remove Cherie from the Rancheria.

Banishment is a milder form of punishment. Traditionally it was used before tribes began adopting the BIA constitution. Only in the 1990s did banishment begin to appear in tribal constitutions. Usually temporary, banishment decisions can carry heavy penalties similar to disenrollment. However, the use of banishment as an exercise of punishment under Native American sovereignty poses a legal question. Does it violate the Indian Civil Rights Act of 1968? The Indian Civil Rights Act is similar to the federal Bill of Rights and the Fourteenth Amendment. It addresses citizenship rights and equal protection under the laws. At issue is the severity of punishment imposed.

U.S. constitutional law has no provision for stripping naturally born U.S. citizens of their rightful citizenship. Native Americans can be federally recognized enrolled members of their tribe, but they do not have the same protection as naturally born U.S. citizens. The Cedarville Rancheria's enrollment ordinance, for example, has a clause that allows for the disenrollment of a citizen-member on the grounds of falsehoods concerning lineage and blood quantum. This includes descendants of someone who has been disenrolled on grounds of falsehood or anyone holding dual or simultaneous membership in another tribe. The Cedarville Rancheria's executive committee was also the tribe's enrollment committee. Anyone disenrolled from the Rancheria could appeal that decision to the tribe's general membership, also known as the community council. However, the tribe as a sovereign nation has the final word. There is no due process, no avenue of appeal to state or federal courts available to non-Native U.S. citizens. Many tribes in California—tribes receiving sizeable quarterly subsidies from Native-owned casinos under California's gaming laws—have disenrollment beyond blood quantum falsehoods or dual tribal citizenship.

There is nothing in the Rancheria's eight-page constitution explicitly dealing with eviction. The tribe had no reference or guiding criteria in its constitution for enforcing eviction. Rurik, Bogda, and Lenzi therefore used a section in the tribe's constitution covering disenrollment. That section gave members facing expulsion the right to appeal to the entire membership of the tribe. Cherie may have been right when she said she could appeal the executive committee's decision to the tribe's membership-at-large. But there was a flaw in her thinking. In appealing to the tribe's members, she risked going before the same majority that kicked her off the executive committee. She was sandwiched.

9

KANDI GOT THE CALL at the hospital. She was having numerous cardiac diagnostic tests.

"I . . . I'm sorry to bother you like this," it was her Modoc High School principal, "but there was a shooting at the RISE building."

The RISE name had stuck even though the Cedarville Rancheria purchased the building two years before the murders.

"Cherie must have shot Rurik," Kandi thought. She knew he was holding an eviction hearing for Cherie and her son, Jack.

"Were there any casualties?"

"Four people were shot. All four are dead."

She reeled. She turned to her husband, Lloyd, who was sitting next to her, and told him there had been a shooting at the Rancheria office.

"Rurik?"

"Can you provide us with some names," the principal asked, "so we can be prepared to help the affected students tomorrow at school?" He had no names, and a police officer was listening on the line. All they had time for were names, no questions.

Of course. She knew several students who were friends with the kids on the Rancheria, including the sons of Rurik's girlfriend, Holly Cox.

One of Holly's boys was a student of hers. Rurik and Holly were planning a family trip to Hawaii in a couple of days. And there was the boy's best friend, Jack Stockton's stepson, and Angel's friends from the continuation school for at-risk students.

She gave the principal names of possible victims.

Kandi was released from the hospital the next day with a clean bill of cardiac health. Back home she read about the killings: Rurik, Calonico, Angel, and the new tribal administrator, Sheila Russo, had been shot and killed. Two of Rurik's daughters had been wounded. Kandi had spent years as a volunteer with Resources for Indian Student Education (RISE), where the murders took place. She knew everyone personally. She knew the layout of the room. The chrome and gray padded chairs, the conference table where the tribal members sat during their meetings. She saw their faces and she knew intimate details of their lives. But it was Angel's death that affected her the most. She imagined her holding her five-day-old son on her lap as she was shot.

Kandi admitted to herself she had no real affection for Angel. Angel was hard to like, too manipulative, too loud, too defiant. Kandi knew Angel struggled with depression and cutting. She knew Angel had been sexually abused as a young girl and had been abandoned by her drug-addicted mother.

"I knew Angel was lost, but she didn't deserve to die, not for this. She wasn't caught up in tribal politics. She simply had cast her vote against the more vengeful relative."

10

THE LAST TIME KANDI saw Angel Morningstar was at a grocery store in Alturas a few days before the shooting. Angel's hair was dark, almost black, streaked with red highlights. She wore square-framed glasses over her dark-chocolate eyes. Instead of one of her usual low-cut, spaghetti-strap tops with her breasts popping out, she wore a dull-colored, oversized sweat shirt and sweat pants. She giggled as she picked foods off the shelves. Held each item and posed like a model on television. She was trying to impress some guy. Kandi had noticed that Angel was getting bigger and thought to herself, "God, she just had her two-year-old son taken away because she neglected the boy. The two-year-old was with his father. Now she's having another baby, this time without any father figure in the picture." Angel flashed a smile.

"Hi, Angel."

She thought back to when Angel was eight and a chubby, awkward girl with thick glasses. Even then, her clothes were too tight and her voice was too loud. If there was something inappropriate or out-of-place to be said, Angel said it. She had no impulse control. When she was a volunteer for RISE, Kandi tutored Angel. She chaperoned cultural camps and activities that Angel attended. She remembered when Angel was about nine years old. Lloyd built a sweat lodge at the Cedarville Rancheria so that the kids could participate in a traditional ceremony.

"I went with him to the first sweat. Chaos was a mild way to describe the afternoon," she said. "Lloyd built the lodge on a vacant lot across the street from Cherie. Cherie's son, Jack Stockton, gathered wood for the lodge fire from a stack of trashy lumber next to his grandfather's house.

"Who said you could have my fucking wood?" his grandfather yelled at him. "What the fuck will you do this winter? You asshole. Who's fucking going to replace it?" That was his grandfather, Larry Lash. The old man kept swearing at Jack, but a fire was built and the sweat lodge began.

A sweat lodge is a place of prayer. Traditionally there are four rounds of prayer, and hot stones are brought in at the beginning of each round. Water is poured over the stones as a form of purification, and the door stays closed until the round of prayer inside the lodge is completed. With young ones it was typical to allow children to go out when they needed to, but the sweat lodge on the Rancheria was beyond typical. Kids ran in, kids ran out.

"Angel was the one I remember most," Kandi said. "She was wild. Her grandmother, Virginia Lash, had her hands full raising her and her brothers and sisters. Angel was dirty and unkempt and she flew inside the lodge, stayed briefly, and then crawled back outside. She was a whirlwind of energy throughout the ceremony."

Angel was a middle child. She had an older brother, Donnie; an older sister, Brandi; and two younger brothers, Brandon and Jacob. Her mother was Tina Penn. They all lived with their grandparents. Not long after that sweat another cousin, Richard Lash, came from out of state to live at the Rancheria. Because there were not enough rooms in the house, some of the boys lived in trailers in the back yard. Jacob moved in with his aunt Cherie. The children were frequently unsupervised. Sweat day was no different.

"Maybe it's understandable, but Angel's growing into a teenager didn't improve her attitude," Kandi said. "She wouldn't listen to authority of any type. She cut slashes up her arms as a way to cope with her anger and frustration. Angel ran away and was frequently in trouble with the law. Out of control at fourteen. Her grandmother and grandfather sent her off to an out-of-state boot camp, which is a long-term non-Native boarding school that is supposed to provide security and structure and offer programs to help troubled kids like Angel develop better coping and behavior skills. She attended the boot camp for more than a year, but her troubles continued. Not long after Angel returned home, she was put into foster care."

Once Kandi chaperoned a few students including Angel on an outing to a climbing gym and a bowling alley. Angel wore a short, black skirt, black tights, a low-cut, revealing shirt, and knee-high boots with laces up the front. Climbing or bowling in that outfit was impossible. She spent the entire time texting on her cell phone, wandering off, which was against the rules, or pissing off her roommate, Jenny, by trying to coax her into banter. "I hate you," Jenny snapped back.

Angel went to Warner Continuation High School on the Modoc High campus. When she got pregnant at seventeen she was transferred to adult education. After Angel's first son was born, Kandi sometimes saw her pushing her toddler downtown in a stroller or at a local powwow or RISE event.

"We weren't close, but I watched her grow up and we talked about school, her family, her baby."

11

A WEEK AFTER THE shooting at the tribal office, Kandi read news articles on the internet about the murders. Several women remarked how sad it was that "the good looking ones seem to be the ones to die."

It was easy to see the contrast between them. In Cherie's police mugshot, taken soon after her arrest, her eyebrows were arched, and her eyes and mouth scowled. Heavy double chin, spiky hair, and tattoos were menacing. Then there was Rurik, standing under a tree, tall, his long, dark hair streaked with gray, dark eyes set deep under thick eyebrows. He was wearing a buckskin shirt with a bone choker. Kandi remembered that he wore that outfit for his driver's license photo. He had the Hollywood Indian look, high cheek bones and thin lips. She said some people called Rurik the Indian Fabio after the Italian fashion model from the 1980s and 1990s.

"It was easy to picture Rurik on the cover of some sleazy Native romance novel," Kandi laughed.

In an article titled "A Call for Justice over a Mass Shooting in Indian Country" Rurik is pictured with his girlfriend. The photo caption reads: "As you can see, Rurik 'Two Bears' Davis has a kind smile. He was full of life. At the memorial site in mid-July, one of his daughters was making 'BBQ ribs that Papa always loved.'"

"Photos can capture only a piece of the story," said Kandi. "Rurik was more complex then he appeared in the photograph. He was angry with Cherie and determined to expose her embezzlement of tribal funds, even if it meant her eviction or disenrollment." Kandi didn't know how far back their feuding went, but she knew they fought.

"Sometimes, Rurik could be a real ass. I was in a school meeting with him and his girlfriend a few weeks before his death," Kandi said. "His girlfriend's son was failing his classes, and I was the boy's English teacher. Rurik wasn't living with his girlfriend but he played the father role at the meeting."

The meeting included the school's principal, counselor, all the boy's teachers, an advocate for the boy, and the county's school psychologist. Courtesy dictated turning off cell phones. However, Rurik left the room several times to talk on his cell phone and missed a great deal of the discussion.

"He was rude," Kandi continued. "Each teacher explained in detail all of the strategies they had used to help the boy complete his homework, how they met with him at lunch or after school to give extra help, how both the principal and the counselor met with him daily to help him organize his backpack, but Rurik roared, 'Well, what are you going to do about this? He's failing and it's your job to prevent that.' It was as if he had not heard the entire conversation, hadn't even heard how much time and effort each person was giving to help the boy. One teacher felt so insulted that he left the room."

The next day Kandi's principal came to her classroom and apologized for how he had handled the meeting. He said he should have stopped Rurik from talking; no one disrespects his hard-working teachers. Kandi told the principal who Rurik was, and described Rurik's relationship to the boy and his mother. She found herself defending Rurik because she understood him. Rurik was playing the tough guy, the protector. He had offended others in the process, but it was his way to prove how much he cared for his girlfriend and her son.

"If you look up Rurik's name on the internet, you'll find photos— Rurik laughing in the snow, Rurik snuggling with a puppy, Rurik riding his four-wheeler on the playa. But looking at the photos is like looking through a veil. Too much of Rurik is hidden. Rurik could be kind and he could be vengeful. His name Two Bears, was appropriate."

12

LLOYD POWELL REMEMBERED THAT Rurik tried several times to get Cherie disenrolled and kicked out. She violated the tribe's housing policies. Her junky yard was filled with propane tanks, old cars, and trash. She broke the tribe's drug policy by failing her drug test. "When Cherie failed the drug test, she said she was on antihistamines. She fought Rurik's accusations," he recalled. "She was retested and her second test came back clear."

Lloyd is an enrolled Chickasaw and 2010 recipient of California's American Indian Education Centers Honored Elder award. He worked with Cherie's mother, Virginia Lash, when Virginia was the Cedarville Rancheria's tribal chair. Virginia held the single most powerful position in the small tribe. Under Virginia's leadership an unwritten tribal policy was set in place: Lloyd said she was always trying to disenroll somebody.

"It was like that all the time, back and forth with each other, all of them. Virginia, Rurik and Cherie," Lloyd said. Cherie used tribal funds to add a large bedroom and another bathroom onto her home. She said an elder relative was coming to live with her. No elder moved in, nor was it clear who the elder may have been. "A lot of bitterness and anger was fueled. Duanna Knighton, the tribe's administrator, helped stir the pot, sometimes to the point that it scared me."

Lloyd knew about tribal adversity and conflict. Before joining RISE he worked as a drug and alcohol counselor at Wemble House, a group home in Klamath Falls, Oregon, for Native American teens with drug and alcohol addictions. There was friction with the Klamath tribe staff members because he was Chickasaw. Some of the Klamath workers did not want outsiders in the program—even though the Native drug offenders came from both Northern California and Oregon tribes. The harassment and the two-hundred-mile roundtrip commute were tiring. When Knighton asked if he would come to work for Cedarville Rancheria, he accepted.

In 2000 he volunteered to supervise the Medicine Wheel Project, the RISE after school cultural program. Some of the students were mixed-blood. Others came from the Alturas Rancheria or the Pit River XL Reservation. He also ran the RISE outreach program for Paiute students from the Cedarville Rancheria and the Fort Bidwell Rancheria. Lloyd's style in working with conflict and youth in cultural arts came from his belief in the value of Native American traditions and culture, but he wasn't taken seriously by some of the students, who were unruly and defiant. The younger students, however, captured his heart, and Lloyd stayed on as a volunteer for more than a decade.

"That's how I started with the tribe, first working with Cherie's mother. Later, after Virginia retired there was an interim tribal chair, and Duanna and I continued to work with her," he said. "I knew Duanna when I was a volunteer doing powwows and chaperoning kids on outings at RISE. When Duanna asked me to come to work for the Rancheria I accepted. She filled a dual role. She was also assistant director of RISE. She did the fiscal records for both the Rancheria and RISE. She also had the voting power to break a tie in executive committee deliberations."

The ordeal of performing under pressure was just beginning for Lloyd. Soon he took on additional Rancheria jobs under the department headings of economic development and environmental protection, or, as Lloyd put it, "Anything that fell under anybody else's job, I did." His main challenge was enforcing Environmental Protection Agency (EPA) regulations. There were plenty of environmental hazards on the Rancheria.

"I was hired to clean it up, diesel and other hazardous waste. I had a real runaround with Cherie and all of them over getting them to clean up their messes," he said. Getting Cherie and her mother up to the EPA standards put him constantly at odds with them. "I had to put up with Cherie and her nastiness and things she did daily, but I did get it cleaned up."

Getting Cherie to clean up her yard triggered her. For example, she'd barge into the tribe's offices and make physically threatening demands of the staff. "Everyone had to handle her bullying as best they could," Lloyd said. When there was an opening for tribal chair, Cherie and Rurik fought over who was going to be the tribe's new leader.

"Duanna didn't want Rurik in there and she had a lot of influence. Tribal chair was an elected position, elected by the tribe's members," Lloyd said. "So it wasn't a surprise to me that when Cherie was elected tribal chair a lot was going to happen. She was after Rurik all the time for any little infraction, anything. And it was payback when Rurik became chair; it was reversed and he became the bully."

Lloyd's desk was near Duanna's. "I heard Duanna go after Rurik all the time because he wanted to see the books, things like that. If somebody like Rurik wanted something from her she would sic her bulldog on them, which was Cherie. God, some of the stuff that went on."

When Cherie became the tribe's chair of the executive committee she retaliated against Rurik. She tried to disenroll him for asking to see the books. "She and Duanna said Rurik was interfering with tribal administration stuff," Lloyd explained. "They'd come up with stuff and they'd have these hearings and everybody would get off. But when Rurik got in as chair I didn't know much about his trying to kick Cherie out. I talked to him a couple of days before the shooting and he told me. By then I was retired. Rurik said he was cleaning it up. It could've been handled differently, of course."

Lloyd believed the anger between Cherie and Rurik could be traced back to generational trauma. Rurik didn't want to talk to Lloyd about generational trauma. "You could take it all the way back to see brother against sister, sister against brother, family members against each other. All that inability to be a family and their bringing that here to the Rancheria. It was revenge and anger. Over and over."

13

THE LAST TIME LLOYD saw Rurik was at Starbucks in the Niles Hotel in Alturas, when Lloyd stopped by for coffee in the Stronghold Room. Someone called him from the balcony overlooking the main floor. It was Rurik and his girlfriend, Holly.

"Rurik had many good qualities and I liked him. We worked together, traveled to conferences together, and kept a friendship for twelve years. He was playful, trustworthy, and there was never any bullshit. Rurik loved talking about cars, Indian politics, and women. He was a 'man's man.'"

Rurik and Lloyd traveled together to Native Youth Empowerment conferences. "On those trips everybody, the people at the conferences and the children, all loved Rurik," Lloyd said. "Rurik was gracious to everyone he met. He could disagree with someone and still be okay with that." The White Bison Conference in Colorado Springs taught culturally based healing methods and provided resources on sobriety, recovery, and addiction prevention. The conference Lloyd and Rurik attended was about mentoring youth. Lloyd recalled: "The speaker said, 'We should all be out there in the pool playing with the kids, like that man out there.' That was Rurik. He skipped the meeting to play in the pool with the kids."

In 2004 Lloyd attended an Indian Board Members Conference organized by the Falmouth Institute and held at Mandalay Bay Resort and Casino in Las Vegas. Most of the tribe, including Cherie, her mother Virginia, and Rurik, went to the conference. None of them went to the workshop sessions.

"Cherie went to one but she came in late and said the facilitator 'was from the Planet Apes,' and walked out," Lloyd said. Cherie and her family also skipped a workshop titled "The Role of the Board in Internal Disputes" and another called "Steering Your Board in Troubled Waters."

"Rurik was playful with the kids, but he was also the disciplinarian on the Rancheria," Lloyd said. When the kids had problems Virginia sent them to Rurik, and he decided on their punishment. "He usually assigned them a job, like mowing lawns or doing yard work for Grandma Virginia." On the Rancheria some of the yards were littered with old junk and cars. Lloyd said Rurik's yard was landscaped and he kept his cars immaculate. "He was also a sharp dresser." Rurik often wore his shiny NASCAR jacket with new jeans, or a sporty black hat. He loved to dress "Indian'd up" in his buckskin shirt and Native jewelry.

"I'm cleaning up the Rez," Rurik called down from the balcony. "Things are happening. You should come back and work for us." Rurik was always offering Lloyd a job.

"I'm retired now," said Lloyd. He took the stairs up to the balcony and they shook hands.   "We're having a hearing. We're going to do it," said Rurik.

"Good for you, Rurik, so what's up?"

"We're cleaning up."

"I heard about that." What Lloyd had heard were the allegations that Cherie had embezzled tribal funds.

"Well, in two days we're taking care of it."

"Good for you, Rurik, good for you. Keep in touch."

14

ON JANUARY 9, 2014, Rurik and Sheila Russo took their suspicions of embezzlement to the U.S. Department of Interior's Office of Inspector General in Sacramento. Modoc officials had told them the alleged embezzlement was a federal offense. Now, as Rurik and Sheila saw it, they were forced to take matters into their own hands.

An independent auditor's report of the tribe's financial records confirmed that an estimated $60,000 in federal grant funds was "potentially" misspent. The evidence was the misuse of a tribal credit card. The suspects were Cherie and her son Jack Stockton, who were members of the tribe's executive committee. Cherie's daughter-in-law Erin Stockton, the tribe's chief financial officer, was also suspected.

Sheila and the tribe's financial and administrative assistant Nikki Munholand were the first to discover the bookkeeping discrepancies. Munholand told U.S. Department of Interior investigators she "found it odd that Erin Stockton maintained possession of the tribal credit card at all times instead of keeping it in a locked drawer at the tribal offices." Erin, the report noted, "was pulling money from accounts wherever she could, with no actual thought of what she was doing to pay for extravagant things the office was buying."

According to the DOI investigation, three months before taking their embezzlement allegations to the DOI, Sheila confronted Erin Stockton over her failure to generate financial or payroll reports. Sheila and Nikki felt that they were "treading on really thin ice" because the Lash family had majority control of tribal politics. Nikki did not tell Jack Stockton or Cherie. "Munholand believed," according to the DOI report, "that based on the types of purchases she observed on the credit card statements, Jack Stockton would have been aware of Erin Stockton's use of the tribal credit card for personal purchases."

Nikki said a furniture purchase was made using both the tribal credit card and Stockton's personal debit card on the same date. She urged Stockton to review the credit card statements, but he never provided any documentation to support the questionable purchases as legitimate. The outside auditor also questioned an item tagged as "inmate packages." The inmate was Cherie's fifty-two-year-old half-sister Gina, who was under treatment at the forensic psychiatric hospital in Southern California. The auditor's report revealed Cherie and Erin Stockton's purchases using a tribal credit card as a potential misuse of federal funds. They did not have tribal authorization. The auditor believed Erin Stockton made these purchases using her tribal credit card on behalf of her mother-in-law, Cherie. Munholand told the DOI she did not believe Cherie used Erin Stockton's credit card but she felt Cherie benefitted from the unauthorized card use.

A follow-up investigation by the DOI found that Erin Stockton—not Cherie—used the tribe's Bank of America credit card to make $24,084.92 in "unallowable" personal purchases over a nine-month period prior to the mass murder—from March until December 2013. Using the credit card, according to the DOI, she bought furniture and made "other purchases unrelated to tribal business." She paid the bills by using the tribe's checking account but made no attempt to reimburse the tribe.

It was also found that Cherie used her tribal credit card in 2011 for less than $500 in unauthorized purchases. And the investigation found that she had made another $3,911.04 in "unallowable" purchases. These unauthorized purchases were the only evidence the DOI found that Cherie was an embezzler of federal funds. The report did not give any details on what those purchases were. Jack Stockton did not have an assigned tribal credit card, according to the investigation report. Both he and Erin refused to be interviewed during the investigation. Cherie, the Department of Interior report dutifully noted, was not available to be interviewed because she was in the county jail awaiting trial for multiple murders.

The audit also revealed that on January 19, 2016, the tribe's insurance company had reimbursed it for the unauthorized $24,084.92 in expenses run up by Erin Stockton after the tribe filed an employee dishonesty claim. "When tribal administrator (Duanna) Knighton resigned from the Cedarville Rancheria in March 2013, she received a check issued to Resources for Indian Student Education, Inc. (RISE) on her behalf in the amount of $29, 925," according to the DOI report. "The tribe's accountant had examined 'a number of financial concerns surrounding Knighton's tenure with and departure from Cedarville Rancheria . . . these concerns were documented in a letter to the tribe's attorney.'" The DOI did not investigate the allegation of embezzlement involving Knighton because it was being adjudicated in the Cedarville Rancheria's tribal court.

On November 18, 2016, the United States Attorney's Office for the District of Eastern California informed Modoc District Attorney Jordan Funk, Nikki Munholand, and the DOI's Office of Inspector General that it would not pursue any criminal prosecution. This was confirmed the following month by the DOI's Office of Inspector General—three years after Rurik Davis and Sheila Russo first aired their suspicions that Rhoades had embezzled federal monies.

Funk agreed with the DOI's Office of Inspector General.

"I believe there is an argument to be made that the tribe did not treat Cherie Rhoades and Jack Stockton as well as perhaps they should have. Ultimately we found no evidence Cherie was involved in the embezzlement which may have been committed by Jack Stockton's wife."

Less than two months after his wife's murder Phil Russo launched a multipronged campaign to honor Sheila. He used major internet media sources to spread his message. He said both the BIA and the Department of Justice had been notified of the allegations that Cherie and her son were suspected of embezzling federal funds. He implied that an allegation of embezzlement was a motive to kill Sheila and the three others. Intentional or not, Russo unraveled the collision of circumstances that led Cherie to kill his wife and three others.

There was no show of concern by law enforcement as to whether the two handguns were legal or how Cherie came to possess them. In this isolated Northeastern California county, the local militia trains in the adjacent national forest. Ranchers carry small arms and rifles in their trucks. A former member of the board of supervisors held a concealed weapon permit and carried a pistol in her purse. Funk later said there was no evidence that Cherie's weapons were obtained illegally. One of the pistols was a Mother's Day gift from her husband. She bought the second pistol from someone at Strong Family Health.

15

LLOYD HAD A DREAM the night before Glenn Calonico's funeral. Glenn was pulling him down into a black box. He fought with Glenn. They wrestled, punched, kicked. Lloyd pushed his way out and shoved Glenn back down into the box. Lloyd woke up sweaty and breathless, remembering it was the day of Glenn's funeral. He arranged the memorial at the family's request and would speak on Glenn's behalf. Lloyd knew Glenn's dark side: the drug abuse, robberies. But he knew Glenn was more than that. Today he wanted to share the good memories of Glenn. He tried to toss the dream aside.

The service was held at Kerr Mortuary, a large wooden house in a downtown Alturas neighborhood. The chapel is simple: white walls, white drapes. Two tall floor lamps with thin gold stems stood on either side of Glenn's casket. Dark wood folding chairs filled the small room. On each side of the casket were posters with pictures of Glenn surrounded by his children.

"Kandi stayed home from the service; she was on medical leave," Lloyd said. "I told her about the service when I returned home." How Cherie's son Jack showed up. How Brandi, Jack's cousin and Glenn's sister, arrived late. How she headed straight for Jack and screamed in his face, "You shouldn't be here, get the hell out." How Jack held back tears, but his eyes betrayed him. How Brandi continued her verbal assault until police officer Tex Dowdy stepped in and Brandi reluctantly backed down. Jack's other cousins were more welcoming and hugged him. Jack wrapped his arms around Lloyd, squeezed tight, lost control, shook, and sobbed. Lloyd reassured him. "It's not your fault." He started the service.

"I didn't want to help at the funeral, but Glenn's wife asked me to. I couldn't say no, so I spoke of the good things I knew about Glenn, how he spent time with his kids and other children on the Rancheria. Glenn was attentive. He made sure the children ate before he did, even if it meant he went hungry." Lloyd said Glenn was always respectful to him. He never raised his voice, even when Lloyd caught him in some mischief. He told the mourners, "He took his punishment like a man, and he never held a grudge." At home Lloyd told Kandi that at times, Glenn liked Cherie. He understood her because they were raised with the same shit. But Cherie could not intimidate Glenn and she hated him for that.

One of the last times Lloyd and Kandi remember seeing Glenn was four months before the shooting. They were selling crafts at a farmers' market in the parking lot of Rabbit Traxx, the tribe's gas station. Glenn told them, "I'm working now, out at the goat ranch cleaning stalls. It's hard work, but I'm making some money. I'm staying clean. My family is well. My youngest son, he's a singer." Glenn admired one of Lloyd's turquoise necklaces. "I'd like to buy that one," Glenn said, "but I don't have the money on me." Lloyd told Glenn he'd put the necklace aside and save it for him.

"I'm glad you're doing well," Lloyd told him.

"I'll be back to get the necklace later," Glenn called back over his shoulder as he walked away. They didn't see Glenn again.

At the memorial service Lloyd told how Glenn had hoped to become a motivational speaker for Native American people. Glenn wanted to share how the violence, the abuse, and the anger he grew up with had affected him, his children, and his family. He wanted to move beyond the trauma.

16

THE POPULATION OF MODOC County is less than 9,000, or 2.3 people per square mile. New York County, for comparison, has 71,999 people per square mile. Some people living in this unoccupied northeast corner of California near the Nevada line joke and say they live in Nevada. People near the Oregon line say that's where they live. There are approximately four hundred Natives in four federally recognized tribes in Modoc County. The number of Native American–owned businesses in the county is so low they were not recorded by the last U.S. Census. About 70 percent of the land is federally owned. The board of supervisors laments that lost land, lost wages, and lost enterprise are the federal government's fault. On the other hand 75 to 80 percent of the county's $42 million fiscal budget comes from state and federal programs. A few years ago the Modoc County Board of Supervisors unanimously voted to secede from the state and form a new State of Jefferson. Actually the Modoc leaders sidestepped what could have led to a contentious political issue. State of Jefferson advocates outside the county were stirring up support for seceding from California. To appease them and avoid debate, the board of supervisors agreed and then went back to conducting routine county business. The outside agitators went home. There are more registered Republicans in the county per capita than in any county in California. The last Democrat to win a majority in Modoc was Lyndon Johnson in 1964. In 2017 Modoc County led California with an opioid overdose death rate five times greater than the state average.

Alturas, with a population of fewer than three thousand, is the Modoc County seat and the only incorporated town. A scattering of retail businesses and federal, county, and city jobs provide most of the employment. There is a loose mingling of the incompatible, giving the town the feel of American bland: ranchers come to town for whatever they don't grow, raise, or make, and welfare recipients who emigrated to Modoc County in the 1970s and 1980s, mainly white, are there because of the low cost of living. At the county fair or curbside for the Fourth of July parade the ranchers, government employees, and welfare recipients come and go under the interchangeable banners of "Where the West Still Lives" and "The Last Frontier." Galvanizing rarely occurs. The exception was the Cedarville Rancheria mass murder, when the Main Street talkers wondered, why there?

"Why our town?" asked Alturas mayor John Dederick. "Modoc County is a large county, but there's not many people. They (the tribe) were a part of our community and that's a big loss. I guess our little community lost its innocence." Overnight the Empty Quarter murders flooded social media and dominated national print and television news. Mayor Dederick and the City of Alturas did not offer the tribe official condolences. Nor did the Modoc County Board of Supervisors. California Governor Jerry Brown, keenly aware of Modoc County because of its ultra-conservative views on taxes, didn't send condolences either. President Obama did. All the victims' families heard from him. Does the magnitude of the killings make people silent? Is it too much to talk about four people murdered at one time in the middle of a small town like Alturas? Life went on. The Cedarville Rancheria didn't exist for the white culture of the Modoc community-at-large.

The day after the murders the National Congress of American Indians (NCAI) issued its statement of condolence and support: "A great sorrow stretches across Indian Country for the heartbreaking tragedy in the Cedarville Rancheria community," said NCAI President Brian Cladoosby. "I know that the country is joining us in prayer for the victims, their families, and the tribe as they gather their strength to walk together during this time."

Eight days after the murders the U.S. Department of the Interior, Office of the Assistant Secretary for Indian Affairs, Kevin K. Washburn, sent out a press release announcing the killings and added: "Our thoughts and prayers continue to go out to the survivors, family members of the victims, the Cedarville Tribe and the surrounding community at this difficult time." As if to assure the press that the Department of Interior was on the job, condolences were added: "The Bureau of Indian Affairs had people on the ground in Alturas the day after the incident and has assisted the tribe with continuity of government operation."

17

IN JUNE 2014 A mixed-tribe staff of board members from the Native Wellness Institute in Gresham, Oregon, came to Modoc County to lead a three-day healing session for the surviving victims, their families, and friends. Flyers were posted on the bulletin board at the Alturas Post Office. An advertisement in the weekly newspaper invited the public. Few attended.

The day-long sessions were held at the Strong Family Health Center in Alturas. Strong Family is a federally recognized Native agency managed by the Cedarville Rancheria, with net assets of approximately $1.5 million annually. The health center's mission is "to establish and implement systems of care that will provide culturally appropriate services," meaning Native American values, traditional ways, and spirituality. The center counsels three Paiute tribes in Modoc County: the Pit River Tribe, Alturas Rancheria, and Cedarville Rancheria. Counseling includes anger management and domestic violence. Three of the murder victims were either current or past members of the center's board of directors. The same three held similar or equivalent positions on the Rancheria's executive committee. Rurik was the center's past chairman, Sheila was a director, and Angel was an alternate. Rurik's daughter Melissa was board chair and his other daughter Monica was a director.

The atmosphere was tense in the Strong Family Health Center's large meeting room. Charlie Tailfeathers Sr., the elder of the Native Wellness Institute trainers, said generational trauma was at the core of the therapy gatherings. People were suspicious. Did they want to expose themselves to strangers? The trainers weren't Northern Paiutes. That made them cultural outsiders. About thirty people attended the healing session, Natives sitting next to non-Natives, strangers among strangers. The Davis sisters were there, and so were Phil Russo, Brandi Penn, and Lloyd Powell.

They sat on metal folding chairs in a wide, open circle. Rotating from the left they were asked to say their name and give an assessment of how they were doing mentally and emotionally. A half-dozen people were still waiting to speak when there was a banging on the door. It was Tina Penn. No one had suffered greater personal loss in the killings than Tina. Rurik was her brother. Angel was her daughter. Glenn was her son. Cherie was her half-sister.

She was oblivious to the session underway. Everyone was silent as she entered the circle of chairs. She had a purpose. One of the therapy leaders said, "We will go from Plan A to Plan B." Tina made her way to the center of the circle and faced Charlie Tailfeathers Sr. She stood before him and started to speak. Tina was drunk.

"I live in a world of confusion. I don't know what to do with myself. I want to . . ." and she mumbled incoherently. "We don't kill brothers and sisters. We live with each other, we help each other." Someone began tapping lightly on a hand-held drum. Softly, rhythmically. "I forgive, I forgive because I have to," she began again and hugged Tailfeathers, who stood awkwardly in front of her. The drumming continued. Then all the women in the circle got up from their chairs and formed a tight huddle around Tina, completely shielding her. She moaned and wept. "I lost my family! Oh my God!" People tried to keep from crying. A young girl started to cry and ran outside.

"Just love each other," a woman said after a long self-conscious quiet. An older woman who had previously identified herself as a Cherokee from Oklahoma consoled Phil Russo. Speaking quietly, she leaned over him and rubbed his shoulders. He was impassive and had a white eagle feather in his hand. He sat across the circle from where Tina was standing. There was a stillness in the room and Tina was guided to the front door.

A lead trainer broke the silence.

"When in doubt we rely on our traditions," she began. "We show love, compassion, kindness. They're going to take her to ER. Alcohol is a coping mechanism. She brought it to the surface that the shooting wasn't right." An older Native woman sitting across the circle spoke for the first time. "They come by who they are by the way they are raised," she said. "The film's been played before and I ask when will it ever end? I'm not angry, I'm so sad. You have to have an understanding of our history."

"They want you to move away, drink alcohol. They want you out," the trainer added.

Phil Russo said something unintelligible and then spoke of his own doubts in attending a public group therapy session. "Unlike her I can't forget," he said, referring to Tina. "I know my wife wouldn't want this as a destiny for me. I was bound and determined to do this by myself, but I came to a realization that the only way people can get through unspeakable tragedy is to come together." Choking with emotion, he said, "I have bad days and worse days, never good days." A Wellness Institute trainer asked about Sheila, and Russo's emotional floodgate opened.

"She was an activist in every way. A diehard Democrat and a kick-ass liberal. She'd go toe to toe on behalf of women, civil rights, equality," he told the group. "She knew rivers, streams and where they started, where they ended. She knew what it means to care. I miss her more and more every day. I have such a hole in my life." He said she was appalled at the state's genocide of Natives. He said he would push forward, compelled to taking up the torch to make the world a better place.

The trainer probed again. Did he dream about her?

"In the dream I knew she had gone and come back, but she didn't know that," he answered. "It's my sincere hope this incident doesn't smear this town."

18

A BARING OF THE soul, a release of sorrowfully deep emotions, a
nakedness of the most intimate kind. A circle stage of folding chairs,
mostly strangers mourning the dead in their own way. What did it
mean? Tina and the women around her? The circle? The drumming?
The woman consoling Russo? An out-of-state mixed-tribe team trying to bring healing to the Northern Paiutes?

"It was a scene in a play, a ceremony," explained Lloyd. "That's
how they worked it out, by acting out the parts. Had to be done. The
women come in and pray, lay hands on the hurting woman. They
take her around in a circle. They say that women teach women, and
men teach men. So the wellness team allowed the women to circle
around Tina for quite a long time."

Only Lloyd knew Tina was coming. Brandi Penn made the decision to bring her to the meeting. Brandi told Lloyd she thought the
healing session might help her mother. Ease her grief. But Tina was
drunk to the max. She didn't know why she was there or the purpose of the gathering. Tina kept repeating, "Who are these people,
what's going on?" She was loud and obnoxious. She said something
like, "Is this an intervention?" Because of Tina's behavior, the mood
quickly changed from a grief session to what felt like an intervention. Lloyd knew that wasn't the time or place for an intervention,
but what choice did they have?

"I thought the staff allowed it to go on too long. When Tina's emotions settled down, the women continued to circle around her and
then Tina would escalate again. I thought, 'What are you doing?' As
soon as she calmed down the first time, they should have walked her
around the whole circle, and formed a line behind her. They could

have done their walk and walked Tina out the door. There's a ceremony for that, but no one knew it. Tina would have gone with it, with the flow of it, because it's natural. But Tina was so drunk I didn't know if she'd remember what took place. She could not find healing in her inebriated state."

Lloyd thought the trainers did go with the flow, but they were outsiders and didn't know the dynamics of the family. Tina was in pain, and rightfully so, but she was emotionally charged. He noticed she sought comfort from the elder who could offer her spiritual guidance, to relieve her pain. She was saying to Tailfeathers, "Make it stop. You're an elder. You should know. Make it stop." Tailfeathers was out of his field. He wasn't there to provide spiritual guidance. He wasn't a counselor or a medicine person. He worked in tribal court systems and family wellness court.

"I spoke with Tailfeathers," Lloyd said. "He didn't really have a background in psychology or healing. He was a man who saw a need and came up with a program. He was there to support that program." Tailfeathers relied on other professionals to make the program therapeutic. He didn't interact with the participants. His role was more of an advisor to his staff. Tina's behavior caught him off-guard.

One of the people who came with Tina was a driver for Strong Family Indian Health Center. Lloyd assumed the man knew Brandi's unannounced plan. He was there to catch Tina if anything went sideways. Looking calm, Lloyd made eye contact with him, signaling he was ready to jump in. Tina was unpredictable, but as far as Lloyd was concerned, he and Tina's aide knew what they were doing, and that was to watch her body language and make sure she didn't escalate out of control.

Once one woman got up, the others knew that somehow it was the thing to do. Lloyd felt it was like blood DNA. Like when he worked with Native men in the prison up in Lakeview, Oregon. "It's a knowledge they don't know they have. It comes out through ceremony or therapy sessions. It just takes one person to set an example for them to see what they need to do." Lloyd guessed the older Cherokee woman who consoled Phil was probably answering the grandma in her. Maybe she felt as an elder her role was to comfort Russo. Native women don't typically approach Native men and touch them.

"The grief group at Strong Family was small and not many of the participants were connected to their culture," Lloyd explained. "With a larger group, there's a greater chance there will be women with spiritual and cultural experience who know what to do. One time I went up to Pendleton, Oregon, and they had a grief ceremony there and many women had cultural knowledge and experience. They knew what to do next. When things went sideways, they knew how to bring things under control."

When Lloyd saw Tina escalating he signaled *drum* to one of the facilitators who held a hand-drum. *Your drum.* Lloyd was trying to signal him to sing. "The drum is our heartbeat." They needed a heartbeat to bring the scene into control. *Boom . . . boom . . . boom.* That was when Tina began to settle. The man handed off the drum to one of his daughters, who continued to drum. They needed to change the mood. Otherwise Tina was going to start wailing again. She was also angry; she needed to de-escalate. "The girl continued to drum and Tina let the spirit of her pain go. She was moving her body, sending all that sad and angry energy to the creator. You know, take this, take this from me. Take it. And then you could see her go weak. That's when something was happening. She did that intuitively. It was a surrender. Tina needed the space to do this herself."

When they started the meeting, they opened the circle with a song and a man blessed the circle, smudged it with sage. That meant no one crosses the sacred circle. Walk around it. When Brandi came in, she cut straight across the circle, dragging her kids with her. Some people would be more observant. They would know by the smell of sage or the tight circle that this was a ceremony. Because of Brandi's lack of cultural experience, it would not be in her mind to know this was a ceremony. Don't cut across the elders. There was little attention to culture or Native traditions.

"Before the session started Tailfeathers said 'Generational trauma,' because traditions and ceremony were taken away from them. That's why I worked with Native youth, trying to help them connect to their culture, to build some foundation underneath them to help in times like this. What the participants in the grief circle saw was a sampling of Tina's life. She was intoxicated and that was her history. These missing pieces were the things that led up to the shooting at the Rancheria."

To Lloyd, Cherie's anger, building to where she actually killed her family, showed her complete loss of culture and spirituality. She was missing that connection. Could Tina have turned violent? Possibly, but not like Cherie's premeditated murder. Heavily intoxicated, Tina had been in jail for drugs and alcohol, meth and heroin. She could have been violent or could have gone into a seizure. Lloyd said he didn't know Tina's personality. He knew Cherie's, and Cherie's penchant for violence was always there. The trainers wanted to pull together the energy that was going on in the town—to do something.

"The facilitators opened a conversation, a dialogue. Brandi said that was the first time she cried. She was so angry. There were a lot of theatrics. In many ceremonies that's what it's all about. Even when you go to the Catholic Church, you know, it's theatrical. In Native American spirituality we're not looking for converts. It's who you are. It has nothing to do with money or anything. You don't have to go to churches, it just happens, it's who you are, how you live. So that's the big confusion. There's an absence of understanding."

"They took Tina to ER. Got her something to calm her down because she was just going to go for more alcohol. Frequently, at powwows or other events, a drunk person might come in. So we let it go. But this was why we were there. We don't want it to be like this, but the sessions were a good example for our children. The staff did a few things afterward to lighten things up, balance things out. They did a dance, a stomp dance, which is actually my tradition, Chicka-saw. But it was a Choctaw dance, so it was similar. The children did not show emotion at Tina's outburst or by anything at all. They often see similar behavior at home. It comes from alcoholics. The deaths, drugs and alcohol. It's in the family, the community. Many people, of all races, have someone in the family with drug or alcohol prob-lems. You just become numb."

After Tina left, the group continued. They introduced themselves to one another and talked about how they were dealing with drugs and alcohol and how it affected their lives. They talked about how grief affected the community, but the community-at-large wasn't there.

"It was hard, because it seems like we are always in mourning," Lloyd said. "We have lost teens to suicide, others to drug overdoses. Many California Natives are in mourning. And what happens is that a lot of our ceremonies get put away during mourning periods. You can't do them, and so they get lost because there's so much mourn-ing, so much death."

19

TWO HOURS SOUTH OF the Cedarville Rancheria, at the isolated intersection of Nevada Highways 447 and 446, there are a general store and gas pump. The Nixon Store serves seasonal fishermen from Reno and the Paiute people of the Pyramid Lake Indian Reservation. Inside, thumb-tacked above the ice cream freezer is a poster, on it a painting of a young Native woman in full ceremonial dress. Her headdress is turkey feathers. The otter skin band across her forehead is worn by Pomo women in the feather dance. The small charms on the band represent the spirits of ancestors. She is wearing a shell necklace. Her dark hair is cut to the shoulders. She has a wistful but sad look in her eyes, seeing something we are not seeing. Beneath the picture in bold letters is "Violence Against Native Women Is *Not* Traditional." A second line reads "Ending Domestic Violence Is a Tribal Responsibility." The message is part of the Inter-Tribal Council of California's generational trauma awareness campaign.

Ask Natives about the genesis of generational trauma or ancient grief and their answers will differ. There are hundreds of tribes, and each tribal group has its own historical event that haunts it: the Massacre of Wounded Knee for the Lakota, the Trail of Tears for the Cherokee, the Long Walk to Bosque Redondo for the Navajo, the Seminole War for the Seminoles, the Pequot War for the Pequot, the Modoc Wars for the Modoc, and the worst slaughter of Natives in United States history officially carried out in California in the mid-1800s that has no name other than mass genocide. These are only a few of the historic and tragic trials Natives have endured. Forced relocation meant the loss of land, and the loss of land meant loss of cultures, languages, religions, and traditional life-supporting foods—resulting in a devastation of Natives at the hands of Christian whites.

Generational, trans-generational or multigenerational trauma is transferred from first generation survivors to second, third, and future generations. Examples are children of an abusive or neglectful parent or parents. The children can develop post-traumatic stress disorder, a psychological condition associated with Holocaust survivors, prisoners of war, concentration camp survivors, and war veterans. Among Natives it reveals itself in suicide, alcoholism, domestic abuse, depression, substance dependence, diabetes, dysfunctional parenting, and unemployment. Not all Natives should be grouped under any of these examples. However, rates for alcoholism through dysfunctional parenting among Native adults and children are higher than the national average. Suicide is one of the leading causes of death for Native Americans between ten and thirty-four years of age—or one and a half times higher than the all-inclusive national average for that age group. Individually, Native Americans have the lowest income and least education of any demographic group. One out of every four live in poverty.

The fight to overcome generational trauma and regain the loss of Native land and Native traditions continues. The fish-in demonstrations of the mid-1960s are one of the most important civil rights issues for Natives in Washington State. It wasn't until 1974 that a federal court ruled that the tribes' treaty rights had been violated and they were entitled to half the salmon in Western Washington. The 1969 occupation of Alcatraz by Indians of All Tribes set a precedent for Native activism that continues today. Four years later, in late 1973, the American Indian Movement (AIM) drew global attention to the corrupt tribal government on the Oglala Lakota Pine Ridge Reservation and to unsafe living conditions and generations of mistreatment from federal and local agencies. In 2015 the Keystone XL pipeline was declared an act of war by the Rosebud Sioux and resulted in President Obama vetoing the pipeline project. And in 2016 the seven-month resistance to the Dakota Access Pipeline ended in a tenuous but temporary victory for the Standing Rock Sioux. Hundreds of tribes came to oppose the Keystone XL pipeline. The demonstration was a generational descendent of the fish-in protests, the invasion of a federal prison island, and the violation of salmon treaty rights—all before a national television audience.

During that early summer wellness session at the Strong Family Health Center Natives came together to grieve their loss of family and friends. "It's about generational trauma," said Charles Tailfeathers.

20

"IT WASN'T OLD NEWS for the rest of us. It was raw," Lloyd said, thinking back on the wellness sessions. "The numbness. To me, the numbness is how you become a Cherie. How you can pull something like this off with no conscience? It's because of the disconnect from reality. Then sovereignty comes along. A person who is a cannon or a loose gun believes they have the protection of sovereignty. They call it sovereignty to get away with doing these things."

To Lloyd, it's endless generational trauma, the loss of Native traditions, the culture clash, the disconnect. It's a fight against total surrender to a world dominated by whites, all under the protective guise of sovereignty. Sovereignty is not a simple concept guiding the rights of tribes and their members under the authority of the government. Even though there are protections in Native constitutions, a sovereign nation—as the Bureau of Indian Affairs points out—must also abide by the laws of the United States.

"So, in reality, are we sovereign? No, we're more like a government. We're more like a state. We've lost the traditions. That's why it keeps going back to this generational trauma. Because they traumatize you by taking away your traditions," Lloyd said. "I'm not sure how to get past the numbness. That's why practitioners and people come in, trying to make things better even if it's months later. There has to be follow-up."

He gave an example. A high school program called Every Fifteen Minutes staged a drunk driving scene with a crash, a grim reaper, and a funeral. The program lasted a few days, but there was no meaningful follow-up. The schools also brought in special speakers who gave emotional talks on bullying. Lloyd said these programs were moving in the moment, but they didn't have staying power. He compared them to the wellness sessions—a few days of grief counseling without extensive follow-up are just a Band-Aid. Lloyd said he could see that if Modoc County officials were proactive they could make healing happen, but he admits that it's not easy. "Starting with the Native community and spin it out from the tragedy, spin it out everywhere."

Lloyd hears a language of hatred and violence. In the Native community generational trauma is passed down. He could name each child at the wellness sessions. They all came from anger-filled alcoholic or drug addict homes. Lloyd is convinced that to bring Native culture back, people need new tools. The old tools like tribal traditions of governing themselves are caught in a culture clash. Now they are governed by constitutional verbiage spoon-fed by the government.

"It's okay to kill your brother and sister. Or take money from somebody. Every individual Native nation must find their tools so they have something to combat the rhetoric or that horrible stuff in the news," he said. "It needs to be stopped. Let's look at our culture and what we have that's positive. That's the only way it's going to change. You can bring in all those healing people, but they're doing a pan-Indian thing. They were all from different cultures and they didn't know the people individually."

In Modoc County there is a moment in each day when Native children can unplug from the white world and learn their heritage.

"There's RISE with the kids doing the drum. When they come to our drum, it's a sanctuary. Whatever is going on at home is not going on here. This is a place where they can come and feel safe and whole," he said. Another source of Native support is Strong Family Health Center, run, ironically, by the Cedarville Rancheria. In addition to its diabetes program, the center has a K-12 tutoring program funded by the U.S. Department of Education and coordinated by the Modoc Joint Unified School District. "It's place where there's comfort and trust. That's where the healing takes place. Yes, we lose them usually in the teenage years because they want to be with their friends and they've opted out, but they usually come back as adults."

He went on. "Through our culture we have to have activities. Our cultures are so diverse and we're piled into this melting pot. So how do you maintain your culture? Now there's what we call this pan-Indian culture. The powwow, our sweat lodges, or what we call the

Red Road, our medicine wheel. These were the common denominators that all tribes had as indigenous people, and we've brought them together as one concept that has a lot of good things in it. A lot of good medicine. The drum. Our incense. We're bringing this back because that helps us have a foundation. And then having that foundation grow. It's the only thing we have."

He went further. "Mainstream society's idea of how to treat indigenous people is so wrong. All they've done is kill us off. And even today, amongst ourselves, about my being brown and someone else light. In our culture it's ridiculous that we're that way with each other. Oh, you're too brown, you're too white, you're too this, you're not. That was all given to us because in our culture we don't have that. But there's so much healing has to take place."

Two years after Phil Russo's initial internet and television campaign to honor the memory of his wife, he commented on change.org. He demanded that the video titled "Zero Minutes of Fame" be removed from circulation. The video was part of the Brady Campaign to Prevent Gun Violence. It promoted a browser plug-in that erased the names and photos of mass killers from the pages users viewed. The purpose of "Zero Minutes of Fame," according to the Brady Campaign, was to block mass shooters from notoriety in the press. Similar to government security agencies' practice of redacting public records, the software scanned headlines and article texts for the names of mass shooters and replaced them with the phrase "name withheld out of respect for the victims." It also scanned for photos of mass shooters and replaced them with photos of their typically lesser-known victims. The plug-in was supposed to work on major news sites and Google search result pages.

Phil consistently objected to the infamy given mass killers in the press. He also objected to the Brady promotional campaign for "Zero Minutes of Fame." "My wife was murdered at mass shooting in Alturas, California on Feb. 20th, 2014. I find this app to be exploitive to victims and survivors. It is just a ploy to commercialize and profit off the tragedies of victims of mass shootings," he wrote. He was not the only surviving victim of a mass murder to protest Brady's censoring tactics. On the same comment thread, survivors of the Aurora Theater and Sandy Hook Elementary School shootings—both in 2012—accused

Brady of being insensitive. Offended, they said the "Zero" campaign was having the opposite effect from what was intended, and they asked for an apology. Brady did not apologize, but the two-minute video was shortened to fourteen seconds. There was no mention by major media outlets that the Chrome extension failed, blocking photos and names of mass murderers only 20 percent of the time.

Melissa Davis was the first person to side with Russo publicly in his campaign for anonymity of mass killers. In a letter to her local weekly on August 13, 2015, she asked why it was that "we victims and citizens who try to go about our daily lives, are treated less than the person who murdered lives?" Why is it that a criminal gets publicity, but the victims are not given a second thought?

On March 19, 2019, five years after Sheila was murdered, Phil was joined in his crusade to shroud the identity of criminals following another tragic mass murder. New Zealand Prime Minister Jacinda Ardern, in her first speech to her nation's Parliament after terrorist attacks on two mosques in Christchurch, said the gunman should be denied the publicity he was seeking.

"That's why you will never hear me mention his name," Ardern said. "He is a terrorist, he is a criminal, he is an extremist. But he will, when I speak, be nameless."

Then on July 28, 2019, two children and an adult were killed at the Gilroy Garlic Festival in Northern California. At a press conference Gilroy police chief Scot Smith identified the killer, who was shot and killed by police, telling reporters, "I say that name with some hesitation. I don't believe that someone like this deserves the notoriety or the recognition."

21

KANDI LOOKED BACK ON the twelve years she taught English at Modoc High, Home of the Braves. Her classroom was mostly white kids with a few Native students. It was a casual, free-flowing setting for teenage talk. In the eerie freshness of the post-murders her students told her what they thought about Cherie and the murders.

One student, a former girlfriend of Cherie's son Jack, loved Cherie. She loved that Cherie was a badass. This girl's mother took her out for ice cream after she beat the shit out of another girl at school. Later Jack Stockton's stepson was one of Kandi's students. He told her he believed Cherie acted out of love for her family, not that murder was right, he said. He understood Cherie's fierce loyalty to her son and his family. He said he believed Cherie was the one who was treated unfairly. The son of Rurik's girlfriend was also in Kandi's English class. They talked freely about music, Rurik's love of cars, and a planned trip to Hawaii. The boy liked Rurik, looked up to him as a father figure. Angel was an attention-getter. She had both friends and detractors in Kandi's classroom.

"The students told me when Angel got pregnant with her first baby. Some of the girls said she was a neglectful mother," Kandi said. "They told me where Angel was living, who she lived with. I remembered looking out my classroom window and seeing Angel stroll her first son down Main Street. She was with the local bad boys."

And the students told Kandi about Brandi, Angel's older sister, who was temporarily the Rancheria's tribal leader after the murders. "They told me who Brandi lived with, when she had her first child, that she was doing meth. Brandi had been in my class. She was a good artist and articulate writer, but she was angry and I never could break through the anger. I often spoke with Brandi about her future, and Brandi always replied, 'I will get free money. I don't need to work.' She was referring to her share of 'casino money' that was doled out quarterly."

Kandi invited Brandi to after-school events organized by RISE, but she never attended. Still, Kandi encouraged her to remain in school and get her high school diploma. "I felt college might pull Brandi out of her brushes with the law, but it was too late. Brandi was already into drugs. She was placed in a foster home and finished at Warner High, the on-campus continuation school."

Both Kandi and Lloyd volunteered as tutors at RISE and took students on trips outside Modoc County. Lloyd was a county health counselor and confidant on call twenty-four hours a day. Once Kandi took two Native teenage girls to Ashland, Oregon, a half day's drive from Alturas. The three explored hippie shops filled with incense and candles and wandered down the aisles of trendy dress shops. They ate salty hot French fries and burgers at an outdoor patio restaurant. The girls told her, "This is the best day of our lives."

Kandi felt a close bond with her Native students. Modoc High was moderately small at 250 students, and personal relationships with most of her students came easily, but the bond was a transient one. Most of the teenagers were in her classes only one or two years, but she knew her Native students and their families years after they left her classroom.

"I saw this as a blessing and a curse. It was difficult to watch students fail in their lives, and I often felt inadequate. There was so little I could do to fend off their demons. But I listened. My most cherished memories are the students' life stories. They never sugar-coated the truth, and even as my heart broke when I heard 'mom burnt my face with the curling iron,' or 'my uncle raped me,' or when they told me about Cherie and her victims, I knew they were sharing; they were trusting their lives with me openly and honestly. I'm thankful for the Native students I worked with, those who triumphed and those who broke my heart, because they had let me in. They let me enter their world, and that was no small thing. Through it all there was resilience, a strong sense of Native community, even in tragedy."

22

"WHY ARE WE READING about other races if this is American Lit?" "Why aren't we reading about Americans if this is American Lit?" "Why are we wasting time reading about Indians?"

Kandi gave her American Lit students multicultural reading assignments. They vented their resentment and followed up in their written assignments. One student wrote a paper arguing it was wrong that the Pit River Tribe could hunt on their own land, when he couldn't hunt there without a permit. When her students studied the loss of the Mexican American history program in Arizona, a student wrote a rant against Mexican Americans. The reading assignments were conforming to California's common core standards: students were asked to use their critical thinking skills and supporting evidence to form an opinion. To write persuasive essays on an assigned subject, the students were given material covering both sides of an issue in order to form their argument.

When students wrote racially biased papers Kandi asked the parents to come in and discuss the work. Typically it was the student's mother who came. The student who complained about a permit requirement to hunt on tribal land had to rewrite his paper when his mother required this. However, the mother of the student wrote the anti–Mexican American paper sided with her son, saying Kandi shouldn't make students write about those kinds of topics.

"When I asked the mother what she thought students should write about, she told me, 'Well, in the middle school, they argued about whether or not gum should be allowed in school.'" Dumbfounded, Kandi said, "'This is high school.' The pattern was set. If a student wrote a paper filled with racist shit, I called in the parents. Some parents didn't bother meeting with me."

She wanted her students to know about current Native issues. She used Native American sources, writers like Sherman Alexie and websites such as Indian Country Today. The students complained anyway. It wasn't apparent to them that high school literature textbooks are filled with writings from other cultures. Native American lit was included in the state's American Literature standards, but the literature of other cultures was always questioned by racist students throughout her ten years in Modoc County.

"The racism was not always so blatant," Kandi said. "Most of the time it was subtle, but endless." Are students in Modoc racist? "They will tell you 'no,' then turn around and call one of my Mexican students a 'beaner.' Yes, many students in Modoc were racist, especially the ranch kids I had in my last few years of teaching. To support my multicultural program I used the Southern Poverty Law Center's "Teaching Tolerance" guidelines. But the Tea Party movement and nationalism were taking hold. That was about 2010 to 2014, the year Cherie killed."

Kandi said she felt she was battling for the soul of democracy for all, especially Native Americans. The students no longer used sports slogans like "wagon burner" at football games, but they still did the war whoop and a fight song that stereotyped Native people.

"In this era of Trump, I doubt that I could teach in Modoc. Today I would be afraid I'd be fired for using a curriculum that included civil rights for all. I would refuse to bow down to parents who wanted a watered-down curriculum. The fight against it and me would be stronger. It angered me that the world has embraced such racist values and Modoc students will stand with Trump. Teachers today are in a real tricky spot. You can tell the truth and lose your job. In this age of Trump, I don't know if I would have the support of the parents."

Kandi retired just before Trump was elected.

When Obama became president, she had a poster on the wall with a photo of him and the word "hope." Her tenth graders read *To Kill a Mockingbird*, Elie Wiesel's *Night*, and other books about racism. Often students would demean Obama. They didn't like his picture on the wall, and they openly questioned why she had it in her classroom. When she told them the poster represented hope for people who were oppressed, they didn't see the connection to the literature. They felt empathy toward the injustices of Tom Robinson and Elie

Wiesel, but they could not connect their own racist behavior to their attitude toward Obama.

"I don't think they even knew why they had such anger against him. It was generational. Handed down. A belief that people of color were somehow not Americans. I definitely saw a progression of this racist attitude and the assumption that the students could freely speak racially inflammatory words when the Tea Party movement began."

Attitudes against other races and liberals became more integrated into students' talk. Students used racial slurs more often. Democrats were seen as scum. The year before Kandi retired, she had an exceptionally bad bunch of eleventh grade boys. Many were from local ranch families, and they constantly challenged Kandi and the literature she assigned, as if she were changing their history by reading Frederick Douglass's slave narratives or Lorraine Hansberry's *Raisin in the Sun* or *Esperanza Rising* by Pam Muñoz Ryan. It went back to their complaining, "When are we going to read about Americans?"

"What they meant, of course, was why aren't we reading about white people? I thought it was awful then, but I can't even imagine it now. Parents will support their students' rights to express their beliefs, whether they are hurtful, inaccurate, or untruthful."

She paused. "I think many Modoc students and Modocians in general felt that degrading a president of the U.S. was appropriate. This was fueled by the fiction that Obama was not born in the U.S. and that Obama was a Muslim, ideas perpetuated by Trump and the Tea Party. Once these views were established, students felt they had a right to demean and disregard Obama as president. They saw Obama as an outsider. And yes, this prepared the students to jump onto the Trump bandwagon. So much for college or life preparation."

By the start of school year in 2019—two years into Trump's presidency—there were no complaints heard from students like the ones Kandi heard five years earlier. The refrain "Why are we reading about other races if this is American Lit?" is a faint echo in the school halls. The silence may be by chance. Today there are no teachers at the high school of Native ancestry. At least none recognized in Indian Country. There is not a single Native teacher who can act as a social conscience in defense of reading literature by non-whites. Left in Kandi's absence is the thought that non-Native teachers are less likely to be sensitive to undercurrents of racism.

23

FOR NEARLY A YEAR—JULY 6, 1872, to June 4, 1873—the small Modoc tribe held off U.S. Army troops in one of the costliest "Indian Wars" fought in California—the only major one. Today there are few if any Modocs in Modoc County. The survivors of the Modoc War were taken by box car to the Quapaw Agency in Indian Territory, Oklahoma, where they were held as prisoners of war—39 men, 64 women, and 60 children.

"Home of the Braves" is Modoc High School's nod to the Modocs who lost their home ground and were taken to Oklahoma. If honor was the sentimental intent behind the school's depiction of Native bravery, it has been lost to history, like the Modocs of 1873.

Professional sports franchises and university athletic departments set controversial examples by using racial nicknames for their teams— Cleveland Indians, Washington Redskins and Florida State University Seminoles among them. The Braves of Modoc High kept to the trend by performing mocking rituals on the field. Before Kandi's arrival Native teenagers in the high school's leadership class protested to the administration about homecoming, when a white girl dressed as a Native boy rode horseback onto the football field and drove a spear into the turf to start the game. Adding fuel to the insulting myth of the Native, the school's mascot is actually a depiction of a Nez Perce, not a Modoc or even a resident Paiute. The image is the result of a student-faculty compromise with school authorities.

April Lea Go Forth taught at Modoc High School in the late 1980s and early '90s. She later received a master's degree from California State University, Chico, and then earned a doctorate in education from the University of Nevada, Reno. She is a member of the California Indian Education Association and has twice been honored as California Distinguished Indian Educator.

"When I first taught at Modoc High School I requested some repairs to my classroom and the custodians vandalized it with drawings on the poster boards of tomahawks and penises. That was in 1984.

"Mostly I was introduced as 'our Indian teacher,' meaning I was the only Native teacher in the school and for a long time the only Native teacher at any of the schools in the district. The principal called the Native boys 'wagon burners' and it took more than five years to end the homecoming float theme of burning the opposing team at the stake, spearing or scalping the players, and all manner of negative depictions, phrases and name calling."

The high school principal, whom April described only as a 'non-Native woman,' "wouldn't hear the protests or reasons, and completely trusted the boys' coach on all decisions—including kicking a Native student off the football team during practice because the student refused to 'obey' when the coach called for the wagon burners to get on the field and scalp 'em."

The coach sent the student back to the locker room, but the boy left and in frustration took a locker lock with him. He narrowly avoided suspension for stealing, but the implication was that he was a "thievin' Indian." The principal supported the coach's decision to suspend the student and refused to accept the student's version of what caused the incident. Avoiding suspension came with a stiff price: the boy agreed to transfer to Sherman Indian High School in Southern California. When he later returned to Modoc High School, specifically for the baseball season, the coach would not allow him to play sports at the school.

April told how the next principal and his wife, who was dean of students, were refreshingly neutral about race. He was hyper-vigilant about gangs. The new principal decided there was a gang problem at Modoc High School. The Native students and a few of their friends wore black all the time. April knew the Native students found it humorous that they were regarded as a gang. "They laughed about the teacher trainings and assemblies that the principal called because he believed there was actually a gang."

Though he was mistaken about the "gang," the new principal was sympathetic to the debate over the offending mascot. He met with

April a number of times to discuss the controversial team logo, stereotypes, and racial slurs in high school sports.

"He was the reason the football coach had to change his style and clean up his tactics. And one of the teachers had to show just cause for her consistent failing of Native students."

She said it was 1988 when the principal brought a commercial catalogue of school sports logos to her classroom. He asked her to pick a new logo. There was growing dissatisfaction with the school mascot, the stereotyping of "Brave" and of Native culture. The principal wanted to introduce a more acceptable logo for the school mascot. He said the logo would continue to be a Native male as a brave but asked April to find something that better represented the Modoc Nation.

"I pointed out the Modocs no longer lived in California. Despite telling him that human beings are not mascots, I accepted the task of getting a consensus on a new logo that would be an image of a Native male."

A majority of her students were Native boys, the ones who had been labeled as a "gang" by the principal. April turned to them for their opinion on what the logo should be. Flash forward. The current Modoc High image of a Nez Perce was a compromise. Why? Because it was the least offensive in the catalogue of logo choices. The principal was thrilled, and a change was made from the old stereotyped Lakota headdress image to that of an Idaho-region male with two feathers tied in a downward position in his hair, which was gathered and tied back. The image did not resemble a Pit River Native person. Paiute elders were unhappy because traditionally hair is not tied. The new logo was not a Pit River profile nor even Modoc.

"Also, the principal told the 'gang' of Native students in my classroom that they could design a Native image and they could paint it on a wall. He said he thought it would give Native students recognition with a positive school identity. In 1989 two of Native male students designed an image of a Native person, not a logo, with outstretched arms surrounded by a medicine wheel. They were told the art could be painted on a dugout at the school's ball field. The leadership teacher prevented the students' image being painted on the dugout. The principal instead approved the painting to go on the cement at the school's front entrance. It was walked on every day by everyone going into the school. The principal did not understand how Native people could feel that was a negative outcome, a disrespect."

There was a growing racist group of white youth in Alturas. By 1990 they were strong and threatening. One was convicted in the shooting death of a local teen girl. The girl's sister was in April's class.

"The white kids made up opportunities to attack youth of color. My son played football. His circle of friends were diverse or 'of color.' One was a white boy, two were Native, there was an Islander, and one black whose father worked at the prison camp outside Alturas. The fall of 1990 my son's friends were jumped after a game and the black student was beaten up. The next spring in 1991, a Native student was severely beaten after a basketball game. And in the summer of 1992 my son and his friends were attacked in the street downtown. His nose was broken by a flashlight across his face.

"At a courthouse hearing, a non-Native woman from the school approached me and asked me not to continue saying it was a racial matter because 'there were no racial incidents in Modoc County.' I told her to look at my son with his group of friends, all of color, then look across the hall at the group charged with assault, all white and calling themselves skinheads. I asked her what was not racial about it and she walked away from me."

In the mid-90s there was a change in school administration and April brought a civil class action suit against the school district and Modoc County for harassment. The plaintiffs were April and the Native students. They won. When the assistant principal at the high school was told that cultural sensitivity would help the students feel connected to the school and perform better, he told April, "They can't live on the reservation forever."

"At that time only one family lived on the XL Reservation, but that's not the point. The high school administration teamed up with one of the longtime teachers. Those days were sad with constant accusations and witnessed attempts to provoke Native male students to react so the school had an excuse to suspend them. I literally began coaching students on how to roll their shoulders, look meek without eye contact and to request that I be called until their parent arrived. The parents agreed to that. The boys had to be protected from being accused of hostile behavior.

"And Native parents were told they couldn't powwow while they were waiting for their children after school. Teachers were sent to tell me how I needed to be a team player because the school was looking at the Distinguished School Award. That was the year I was not included in the Western Association of Schools and Colleges report and was told not to speak with the accreditation team on campus.

"It was all building and at the time I did not realize that it had to do with the award. One day the principal told me things could get better for me if I was a team player. I told my husband and my husband visited him at school with a poor outcome."

All students were required to take three exams to graduate: math, reading, and a written component. Math and reading were timed and structured. Writing was subjective and graded by a teacher who April said was well-known for failing Native kids. Students could get extra time on their writing in April's class. She read their work and felt confident, but the students still failed.

"This went on and on. I asked to see some work that had passed and was shown examples. Nothing remarkable, nor much better than the Native students' writing who were failed two and three times. Yes, I wrote three written tests. Actually, I typed what the students told me and they copied what I corrected. All three failed. I was stunned because I had failed.

"I could pass university courses and I was in a master's program at the time, but I could not pass a high school writing exam. I finally pointed out some punctuation, restructure of sentences for a better-than-high-school product, and they did pass. It was a total cheat."

April objected to what she saw as the unfairness in grading Native students, but she was told the teacher had tenure and her husband was "Modoc." The implication was not that the teacher's husband was a Native. He wasn't, but he was full-fledged influential member of Modoc County's white community. The last year April taught at Modoc High the school was awarded a California Distinguished School Award. That was in 1994.

Twenty-five years later, in the fall of 2019, Modoc Joint Unified School District was ranked number one in California for suspending both Native American boys and girls. A new report said that in Modoc County Native boys are suspended from school five times more than Native boys statewide. Nearly four out of every ten Native American boys are suspended in a given year in Modoc County. Native girls are suspended nearly four times more than Native girls statewide. In Surprise Valley, where children from the Cedarville Rancheria attend school, the suspension rate for girls is three times the state's average. No figures are available for boys in the Surprise Valley school district because there are fewer than ten in the schools, and the data include only Native enrollments of ten or more. The rates reflect students who were suspended at least once. They do not include students suspended multiple times. The California statewide suspension rate for Native Americans kindergarten through high school is 7.2 percent, or twice the suspension rate of non-Native students.

There are more than 30,000 Native American students attending California public schools. Across the state, nearly 50 percent of suspensions are for a violent incident where no injury occurred. This is followed by suspensions for "perceived" defiance. Rural school districts are a particular problem. "One noticeable pattern among the high suspension districts," the study concluded, "are the relatively lower numbers of Native American children and youth in these areas. In schools where these students may already feel isolated from their community, they are also targeted by educators." The study recommended that all teachers, educators, and administrators in California undergo training in order to understand Native students. The training should be in partnership with local tribes.

Sensitivity to how the "Braves" moniker is or isn't used at Modoc High School has never completely vanished. During the 2018 fall football season a letter appeared in the local weekly complaining that a "time honored tradition was nixed." The tradition was instead of ending the national anthem with "O'er the land of the free and the home of the brave," Modocers always added the "s" as in "Braves" before the team charged the field. The rationale, according to the letter writer, was that by singing "Braves" instead of "brave" they were honoring country, flag, the school, and school spirit.

24

A SUMMER GLARE SEARS the asphalt of Tulelake's empty main street. The town is dying. From the looks of its downtown vacant store fronts it has been dying for a long time.

Now there is a plan offered by Modoc County to erect a three-mile-long, eight-foot-high fence topped with barbed wire at the town's small airport. The county doesn't own the land. The city owns it. The county, in acting as the airport's sponsor for the Federal Aviation Authority, leases the airport from the city. The theory advanced by Modoc County is that a fence enclosing 358 acres will keep deer, coyotes, and dogs from wandering onto the single-lane landing strip. The fence would also slice through thirty-seven acres of the World War II Tule Lake Concentration Camp.

Tulelake is ninety-five miles of barren landscape north of the Cedarville Rancheria and just shy of the Oregon border. It is a roadside marker of Japanese American incarceration and atrocities against Natives. It was near here, at what is now the Lava Beds National Monument, that U.S. Army troops in 1873 defeated a small band of Modoc Indians. They killed babies, children, and women and kicked severed heads around like soccer balls. The 1873 victory over the Modocs influenced President George W. Bush after the terrorist attacks of September 11, 2001, to rationalize the torture of prisoners at Abu Ghraib and Guantanamo Bay. It was also near Tulelake where thousands of innocent Japanese American men, women, and children were unjustly imprisoned during World War II. Modoc County's fencing plan set off a racial debate and resurrected the past.

Tulelake is named after Tule Lake. Because of a hiccup in the north-south county dividing line, the town of Tulelake is in Siskiyou County.

Tule Lake, the prison camp, is in Modoc County. Merging the two names into one township moniker has gone by without explanation. The Japanese American prison camp lies in Modoc County. The Lava Beds National Monument, site of the Modoc War, is in both counties. As for Tule Lake, an intermittent body of water that was drained so that veterans returning from World War II could farm the reclaimed land, it is in both Siskiyou and Modoc counties.

The prison camp held over 18,000 Japanese American men, women, and children during the war. Today it is recognized as a California Historical Landmark and in 2008 was designated as a national monument. Tule Lake Concentration Camp rests on flat treeless land within a volcano corridor formed by the Cascade Range. Like a wall, the fence would dissect what remains of the prison camp's site. However, the Modocs of Oklahoma, whose ancestors were killed, executed, hanged as criminals, or taken to Oklahoma as prisoners after the Modoc War, have exhorted the FAA to build the fence with a promise of expanding airport operations—if the dying town will sell the land to them.

Unsaid in the developing debate: Homeland Security guidelines for small, rural, and municipal airports have for the last decade provided funds to erect perimeter fencing as a precaution against terrorist attacks. In the instance of Tulelake a terrorist attack would presumably target a national monument in the middle of barley, potato, and alfalfa fields. Earlier Modoc County and the FAA considered erecting a fence that would have cut through the historic site. Thousands of Japanese Americans objected, and the site's historic resources are now being examined. That plan was dropped. But the sale of the airport and the revived plan for a fence escalated into a five-way dispute. The clash involved Modoc County, the City of Tulelake, Japanese American descendants of the World War II incarceration, descendants of the Oklahoma Modocs, and descendants of eighty-six World War II veterans who won postwar lottery rights to farm the neighboring land. Each group saw the land as sacred, with the Modocs exercising their own unique sense of sovereign jurisdiction. Even the descendants of WWII veterans who saw the land as their inheritance and legacy said they held a local outcrop in reverence.

The Modocs didn't object to the fence, Tulelake had no objection, descendants of WWII veterans didn't object, and Modoc County didn't object. Survivors of the World War II incarceration camp and their descendants did object. The Tule Lake Committee, representing Japanese American interests, said the former prison had a spiritual meaning to them. They consider the remnants of the concentration camp an American civil rights site and asked, "How does one preserve the sacredness of human life at the site of an U.S. concentration camp?" More than three hundred Japanese Americans died at Tule Lake during the years of incarceration. In a letter to Modoc County opposing the fence, nine California state assemblymen and two state senators, all members of the California Asian Pacific Islander Legislative Caucus, asked the same question.

The Japanese Americans, led by the Tule Lake Committee, reminded fence supporters that their memories are short. The Tule Lake Committee went straight to the point of racism in its effort to protect the historic integrity of the concentration camp. "All this seems to be forgotten by the locals," said Barbara Takei, representing the Tule Lake Committee. She reminded the city council and sparse audience of a history that has fallen silent. "Over the decades, local amnesia buried memory of the massive hate crime on those lands, eclipsed by a homesteader narrative that sought to erase memory of the Modoc genocide and the Japanese American incarceration." She told the council that thousands of Japanese Americans and their supporters do not understand why Modoc County continues the desecration of a place that has deep spiritual and emotional significance for Japanese Americans and all Americans. "Does Modoc County comprehend the message they are communicating with its county garbage dump site located across from where the cemetery was located—a cemetery that was bulldozed and the earth and remains used for fill-dirt on the airport?" The Tule Lake Committee offered $40,000 for the land beneath the airstrip and said it wanted to establish a center commemorating the prison's history as a unifying site for several groups. The council was reminded: "The histories of Native Americans who resisted removal programs that accommodated white settlers, and the settlers and homesteaders who benefited from government programs—are all part of Tule Lake's history." There was no public or official response.

On Columbus Day, October 9, 2017, on the Save Tule Lake Facebook page there was a sketch of the prison camp at the base of Castle Rock. Next to the sketch was a mugshot of Captain Jack staring straight at the camera before he was hanged. Next to his photo were the words, "In memory of this Nation's dark and even depraved history with indigenous people whose lives were part of the land we now call the United States, we honor the Modoc people, whose warriors resisted the U.S. Army during the Modoc War of 1872–73, and whose descendants were forcibly removed to Oklahoma where they endured cultural genocide and near extinction." Captain Jack was the Modocs' leader when they surrendered.

If the Japanese American committee thought they and possibly the Oklahoma Modocs, who are derisively known in Indian Country as the "whitest tribe in America," had the only claim on the sacredness of the prison site and neighboring Castle Rock, they were mistaken. In hostile, racist-tinged public debate, descendants of the WWII homesteaders said they too considered Castle Rock a sacred site. After all, they asked, didn't we erect the white-painted cross on top of Castle Rock and didn't we hold Easter sunrise services there? And if the Japanese American alliance thought the Modocs were simpatico with their struggle in opposing the three-mile fence, they were wrong again. The Modocs, the first to make a bid for the airstrip land, offered $17,500 and said they would keep the airstrip. This put the construction of the eight-foot-high, three-mile fence in little doubt.

If a misuse of sovereignty posed a problem for tribes in California during the disenrollment epidemic, the Oklahoma Modocs were caught in a misuse of their own sovereignty. The Modocs recently forfeited $4.2 million in New York and Kansas in federal court non-prosecution agreements. They were tied to a payday lending scheme known as Red Cedar Services that defrauded borrowers. The forfeiture and the tribe's fraudulent use of its sovereignty was never mentioned throughout the fence debate before the Tulelake City Council—at least not in open session—and the tribe's business credibility was never questioned. The Modocs weren't the only tribe. The Santee Sioux Tribe of Nebraska, where a payday lender called Santee Financial Services operated, forfeited $1 million. The U.S. attorney for the Southern District of New York said the two tribes admitted that despite the payday lending schemes operating on tribal lands, the tribes didn't play a significant role in the business. However, the tribes admitted they knew the payday lending was used to skirt state usury laws. The company behind the payday loan sharking, Tucker Payday Lenders, unsuccessfully contended that it could not be sued because it was entitled to the protection of tribal sovereign immunity, a legal doctrine that generally prevents states from enforcing their laws against Native American tribes. But in 2017 in the US. District Court, Southern District of New York, a federal grand jury disagreed. Two of the business principals in the payday ploy, former American Le Mans Series race car champion Scott Tucker and his accountant, were indicted on charges of conspiracy to collect unlawful debt. Both were sentenced to federal prison terms. By the time the payday scam was fully exposed, news reports said U.S. Bancorp, the holding company for U.S. Bank, agreed to pay $613 million to the federal government as a result of its lax anti–money laundering protocols, which were exposed by an investigation into Tucker's business. Back in Modoc County the Tule Lake Committee made an all-out effort to have the Modocs' illegal use of its business practices openly examined by the Tulelake City Council. They called the payday lending schemes "predatory," "rent a tribe," and an "abuse of sovereignty immunity." Who would do business with them?

Modoc County came in with a verbal offer of $17,500, but only after learning that Tulelake had been in negotiations with the Modocs of Oklahoma. This indicated the county was prepared to compete with the Japanese American committee for the site. In open session, the Tulelake council listened to Michael Colantuono, their hired outside attorney, call the prison site "just dirt." Colantuono, president of the California Bar Association, ignored the prison's historic importance and called the site "dirt" three times during his short report. The prison site may have been dirt to his legal thinking, but that dirt was sacred to the Japanese Americans, and calling it dirt was perceived by them as disrespectful.

"Survivors and descendants of the incarceration seek healing pilgrimages to the incarceration sites," the Tule Lake Committee argued. "The trauma experienced at Tule Lake makes this historic site hallowed ground to Japanese Americans. Tule Lake's preservation is part of the healing made possible when the government acknowledged what President Reagan described as a 'great wrong.'" Four-day pilgrimages to the site are conducted every two years. The Modocs, claiming the property was their homeland, said they wanted to return to it. Comparing the Modoc War to the Tule Lake prison camp, they said: "The Japanese Americans had it much better than we did."

While the Modoc War is history, and the imprisonment of the Japanese Americans is a more recent suffering, the two persecutions were only seventy years apart. Both injustices were the result of wars—the Modoc War and World War II. Both involved men, women, and children. Both had their defiant and stigmatized members—Captain Jack, the Modoc leader, who was considered a murderer, and the "No-No Boys" who refused to answer the U.S. government's skewed "loyalty survey." Both groups were official U.S. Army prisoners of war and both were displaced and taken to bleak and strange lands. Today both are staking a claim on the airstrip land. Both bear the weight of generational trauma. During a plenary session at a Tule Lake pilgrimage a Japanese American said, "We (Tule Lake internees) never had a crisis of loyalty . . . we had a crisis of faith in our government."

The Tule Lake Committee asked: What about the $4.2 million in federal penalties against the Modocs? Shouldn't that be a consideration? But the dying town's city council said nothing publicly about the tribe's standing with the U.S. government. Instead, on July 3, 2018, exactly five days after it became public that the Modoc tribe had settled with the federal government for $4.2 million, the city council proposed an ordinance to sell the land beneath the airstrip to the Oklahoma Modocs. The deal was all but sealed. Apparently willing to chance its survival on the vague promise from the Modocs to keep the airstrip alive, the council of four men and one woman, all white, voted unanimously—without a word of regret for Tule Lake's infamous history—to accept the offer from the Modocs. Neglected without comment were the $40,000 counteroffer from the Tule Lake Committee and the $17,500 from Modoc County. The county's offer, it was later learned, was made partly because of fears that the Oklahoma Natives might eventually close the airport, which would leave the county liable for millions of dollars of federal grant money spent on the airport under the county's ownership.

When the deal between the Modocs and the Tulelake City Council was announced, public animosity and racism was palpable. An alfalfa and beer barley grower said he believed the Modoc tribe would bring "positive ideas" that would boost the region's economy. "I would like to welcome the Oklahoma tribe back to this basin," he said to the applause of the audience. This in spite of a Klamath Tribe woman informing the council and the beer barley grower that when the Modoc Tribe was officially "created," meaning federally recognized, there was no mention of the tribe having connections to the Tule Lake and Klamath basins. This land purchase by the Modocs was not its first in the region. It bought ranch and sage acreage near the lava beds war site and was reportedly negotiating the purchase of a former elementary school adjacent to the Tule Lake Concentration Camp. In explaining why the tribe is buying the land, an attorney representing the tribe said, "The tribe can conduct business wherever it chooses. The tribe is returning home and part of that involves buying land." As for the Modocs' $17,500 the City of Tulelake bargained for? It went to attorney's fees.

The Tule Lake Committee got a temporary restraining order and injunction to halt the sale of the land. The committee took its case to federal court, arguing: "Based on the tribe's previous statements about the World War II history, abusive business model and extralegal behavior, one might expect the tribe to push the legal envelope, using its tribal sovereignty to try to avoid regulation by the environmental and historic preservation laws that have protected the historic Tule Lake Concentration Camp."

Continuing, the Tule Lake Committee said, "One wonders that a small and self-described 'dying community' such as Tulelake might re-gift an irreplaceable historic property to a tribe that takes pride in promoting activity at and beyond the fringes of legality. Although the mayor and city council had two other and quite sensible options, they seemingly went out of their way to avoid fair examination of those alternatives. The question that arises in reasonable minds is Why?"

It's not clear when the question of "why" will be answered. After a series of appearances before a federal court judge in Sacramento there was a settlement between the Tule Lake Committee and the City of Tulelake. The case was sealed and no details of the agreement between the Tule Lake Committee and the town's council have been made public.

To the west of Tulelake and the Tule Lake prison camp is the Lava Beds National Monument. The monument was signed into law by President Calvin Coolidge in 1925. Its designation only recognized the extraordinary lava caves and not the Modoc War of 1872–73. To wrap up its victory the U.S. Army declared Captain Jack, the Modoc leader, and three of his followers guilty of murder. They were hanged at Fort Klamath, Oregon, and buried in unmarked graves not far from the gallows. In a nineteenth-century version of the U.S. government's "Native relocation" program the remaining Native survivors were moved to Oklahoma. Cheewa James, an enrolled member of the Modoc Tribe of Oklahoma, tells the story.

"After Captain Jack and three other Modocs were hung at Fort Klamath, some 150 or more Modoc men, women and children associated with the Modoc War were placed in 27 wagons for transport to Redding, California. They left Fort Klamath on October 10, 1873." Many people wanted to see the Modocs as they traveled southward, James tells, but high sides were built on the wagons to shield them from view. Twelve days after leaving Fort Klamath, the wagons arrived in Redding. The evening of October 23, 1873, the Modocs left the Redding Central Pacific Station. They lived and slept in three emigrant rail cars. The men, with a couple of exceptions, were chained the entire trip. Twenty military men lived in two cars in front of and behind the Modoc cars. The Modocs were sparsely clothed; it was the dead of winter. In Ogden, Utah, a change was made to Union Pacific cars. They arrived in Baxter, Kansas, on November16. The women and children were housed in the Hyland Hotel there while the men were transported to the Quapaw Agency, which is located near the town of Miami, Oklahoma, to build barracks for the POWs.

"The Modocs were to remain prisoners of war into the 1900s," she said.

Today Fort Klamath is on the National Register of Historic Places. There is no indication in the 1971 application for registration that Captain Jack or the Modoc War carried any historic merit. Since 1971 markers have appeared on the grave sites—a convenience for the curious.

In 2002 the U.S. government found a usefulness for Captain Jack, his followers, and the Modoc War of 1872–73. Immediately after the 911 attacks a series of human rights violations known as the Abu Ghraib torture scandal forced President George W. Bush and his staff of White House lawyers to find legal justification for the use of torture when interrogating al Qaeda and Taliban prisoners. An opinion written by George H. Williams, attorney general under President Ulysses S. Grant, said that Captain Jack and his followers could be executed.

They had committed murder when they shot and killed Major General E. R. S. Canby during white-flag peace talks. Classifying them as combatants, the U.S. Army could hang Indians because the army had the law behind it. The Indians were outside the law by decree of the United States attorney general. In 1873 Captain Jack and the others were not legal war enemies—instead they were criminals.

What was good enough reasoning 130 years ago was good enough for President Bush and his staff of lawyers. Williams's 1873 opinion found its way into what became known as the War Memos. The War Memos' rationale was that President George W. Bush had legal authority to authorize and impose torture on so-called detainees—and there was no provision for due process. The president declared the detainees had no rights under the Geneva Conventions of 1949—war rules made to protect those who were no longer in battle, such as prisoners of war. The War Memos became a controversial stretch of the law.

A few miles south of Tulelake is a popular local restaurant called Captain Jack's Stronghold. Down Highway 139 heading back to Alturas is a small town named after General Canby. Today some younger members of Tule Lake Basin families call the Japanese American men, women, and children interned as World War II prisoners "Japs."

Lookout, south of Tulelake, has a population of about eighty. Legend credits the name Lookout to Native Americans using nearby hills as observation points. Looking back to 1901, all-white baseball goes major league, J. P. Morgan creates U.S. Steel in a billion-dollar deal, Booker T. Washington is a guest at the White House, the South erupts, and Alabama conjures up a law requiring voters to pass a literacy test. In Lookout there is a mass murder.

Four men and a sixteen-year-old boy were hanged side by side from the Pit River Bridge. Three of the victims were half-breeds. Their mother was Paiute. Their crime? The five, all related except for one, were prime suspects in a series of robberies and acts of livestock rustling, stealing, vandalizing, and petty larceny. They were being held by guards in a local hotel overnight before being transported to the courthouse in Alturas for trial. An all-white vigilante mob, using brand new ropes for the lynching, was impatient. There was a grand jury indictment and a trial. The vigilantes were acquitted by a male all-white jury.

Less than a twenty-minute drive south of the Cedarville Rancheria is the little settlement of Eagleville, today's population estimated at fifty-nine. In 1911 the then bustling town-in-the-making became the center of attention—and has remained so in history—for what is known variously as Shoshone Mike, the Battle of Kelley Creek, and the Last Massacre.

Four stockmen were found murdered at Little High Rock, a remote canyon across the state line in Nevada. A sheriff's posse was formed in Eagleville, and the men set out to track a small band of marauding Shoshone they believed to be the killers. The band was led by Mike Daggett, who after his death was known as Shoshone Mike. The band defiantly left its reservation in Idaho when white settlers claimed ownership of the land. The vigilantes' chase played out at Kelley Creek in Northern Nevada. Eight Shoshone men, women, and children lay dead in the snow. One member of the posse was killed. Back at Little High Rock, the frozen bodies of the stockmen were pried from the icy snow and placed on a travois. They were taken back to Eagleville and laid out in the town church. As the bodies thawed, blood stained the plank floor. There had not been a massacre of American Indian men, women, and children in twenty-one-years, not since the Wounded Knee Massacre of 1890 on the Lakota Pine Ridge Indian Reservation.

History is vividly alive in Modoc County. To bring up the Lookout mass lynching murders is to invite glaring silence from the mob's descendants or allies, who believe the victims had it coming to them. Mention Shoshone Mike, and distant relatives of the stockmen will say the same. The Modoc War? Well, the U.S. Army won, didn't it? And, the Japanese Americans' Tulelake embroilment with the Modocs of Oklahoma is so fresh that the Alturas street talkers haven't had time to process it. "Where the West Still Lives" is a reflection of a deeply inbred sentiment residing in the county.

25

QUESTIONS ABOUT MODOC MASS murders linger and renew the age-old clash between morality and legality. Was it morally acceptable for a local posse to track down and deliberately attack and kill a Native family of men, women, and children? Was the posse invested with the legal right to do that? Was it morally acceptable to declare Natives legally criminals rather than war enemies so that the U.S. government could conveniently hang them? Was it morally and legally acceptable to declare the Modoc War survivors prisoners of war when Captain Jack and his men were adjudged the opposite? Should we ask why the Modoc War was called a war in the first place? Were the Lookout vigilante gang within their legal rights to hang the five from the Pit River Bridge when they took the law into their own hands? Where was the ethical-moral standard when President Roosevelt signed the paper making it legal to put every Japanese American in a concentration camp? Did the desperation to find a legal right to torture prisoners at Guantanamo actually make it legal or did it make President Bush an amoral leader of the free world?

Can we rationalize that legal rulings outweigh moral beliefs? This question goes unanswered among students at the three high schools within Modoc County's unified school district. There is no platform for discussion of this kind in the classroom. Ask students what they know of these notorious episodes in Modoc County's history and the answer will most likely be little or next to nothing. Local history—under California's modified version of the Common Core program—is not a required subject in any of Modoc County's schools. Common Core is not mandatory. However, it is strongly recommended by the state board of education and takes precedence, requiring social studies primarily in U.S. and world history. To learn their local history Modoc County students need a teacher willing to take the time and interest to shoe-horn it into an already over-burdened teaching "hour" of fifty minutes. An exception is Tulelake High. There local history is slipped into the curriculum on a limited basis—in this instance the focus is on the history of the Japanese American concentration camp—by walking across the street to the fairgrounds, where there is a display on the topic in a corner of a small museum.

RISE has an ambitious off-campus summer program. Its goal is to provide educational and cultural support for Native students, effectively augmenting the state's more general Common Core requirements. One summer Kandi worked at a music camp with Irene Bedard, daughter of Inupiat Eskimo and Cree–French Canadian parents. She played Susie in the movie *Smoke Signals* and was the title voice in the animated film *Pocahontas*. Another summer Kandi and the girl students camped at Medicine Lake. The girls made traditional crafts, sang drum songs, and learned about Native environmental practices. Another memorable summer Jack Kohler, actor, screen writer, and the executive producer of *On Native Ground*, was hired by RISE to give Native boys a guided camp-out field trip through the Lava Beds National Monument—site of the Modoc War and Captain Jack's stronghold.

Kohler is from California's Hoopa Valley Tribe. He played the lead role of Captain Jack in a production about the war. He and Kandi led the boys through the stronghold, describing each place and how the Modocs used the topography of the land to hold off attacking U.S. Army troops. Told by a Native man to young Native boys, the story of the killings, the deceptions, and the hanging of Captain Jack, made for a compelling moment. That night the boys got into a fight. There were intense, angry words and at dusk one of the boys, a tall, lean twelve-year-old with dark intelligent eyes, ran off. Kandi went after him, afraid she would lose him in the same volcanic landscape that successfully hid Captain Jack and his people. She found the boy sitting alone at a picnic table.

"Can we talk about this?" she asked.

"It won't help. Nothing helps. I hate those bastards."

They returned to the campfire and the tall, lean boy's cousin, a natural storyteller, entertained them with tales of adventure—an evil teacher, a hidden closet, and an army of middle schoolers armed with rubber bands. The boy's angry tension gradually subsided, but in the middle of the night Kandi heard someone weeping. It was the boy's younger brother.

"What's wrong? Do you need something?"

The boy crawled out of his tent and he and Kandi sat by the dying camp fire. The other boys heard his sobbing and came and sat with them. All three boys were in tears. He left us. Drunk again. Punched mom. Won't listen. Off drugging. When he was twenty, the tall, lean boy with dark intelligent eyes hanged himself. After the funeral Kandi and Lloyd prepared a sweat lodge. Water was poured over the hot rocks. Steam rose in the darkness. Emotions held tight, afraid to unleash the anguish inside, the young people prayed in silence. It was an elder woman who spoke.

"Grandfather. Help these children let go of anger and find their way. Help us give them guidance so they may live life without harm."

The elder was the mother of another RISE student who had committed suicide when he was twenty.

Modoc County's historical relationship with Natives may be no different from that in similar regions in the U.S. This does not excuse it. Over time this history, because it is not commonly acknowledged either on the street or in the classroom, has vanished into Modoc memory, a place where whites refuse to remember and Natives cannot forget.

26

CHERIE WAS ARRAIGNED FEBRUARY 24, four days after the murders, and held without bail on four counts of premeditated first-degree murder and two counts of attempted murder. During those four days she went from the sovereign privacy of the tribe's court into the public glare of California's Superior Court in Alturas. The eviction hearing was under the tribe's authority, but murder put her in the jurisdiction of the state. In 1953 Public Law 280 transferred most criminal Native jurisdictions from federal to state. California was one of the first. Because the two Modoc County judges, Dave Mason and Francis "Fritz" Barclay, had no experience in capital trials, Judge John T. Ball of Santa Clara County was assigned the case. Mason and Ball took turns on the bench during the relatively routine early proceedings. DA Jordan Funk was the prosecutor and Antonio R. Alvarez, an attorney from outside Modoc County, was appointed to represent Cherie. Now, instead of being before a three-member tribal executive committee with no avenue for appeal, Cherie's case was to be heard by either a judge or a jury. It was her choice—if she went to trial. She was to enter a plea in two weeks.

District Attorney Jordan Funk was imposing, as fit as when he played high school football, even though he was carrying an extra thirty pounds. He looked as if he might be wearing a bullet-proof vest. If he took one extra-deep breath, it seemed the buttons would pop off his shirt. He arrived in the courtroom with files and law books under his arm. In contrast to his overbearing physical appearance, he addressed the court in a toned down voice. He had campaigned for district attorney as a conservative Republican. Most of his long career in Modoc County was in that office with an interlude in private practice.

Funk and Alvarez were opposites. Alvarez exemplified the professional, with no theatrics, no posturing, no distracting lawyer games. He was consistently smooth in getting down to court business. Sometimes he brought his eleven-year-old son with him to pre-trial hearings. He had a quiet bearing, always in control, efficiently avoiding any attention in and out of the court. He was the chief defense attorney at Richard A. Ciummo and Associates in Fresno, which contracted its legal services with various Northern California counties, including Modoc.

Cherie returned to Superior Court, which is in the justice center, in early March. The actual courthouse is next door. It's a 1914 dome-topped Neoclassical building with interior marble and brass rail stairway. At the top of the stairway is the original courtroom. It's used when there is a crowded court calendar. Secretaries in the district attorney's office down the hall swear they've seen ghosts in the old court room. Certainly not the ghosts of the four men and boy who were hanged from the Pit River Bridge: the Lookout lynching happened thirteen years before the courthouse was built.

Cherie entered the courtroom in a black bullet-proof vest, handcuffed, with a chain around her waist. She was there to enter her plea to charges of multiple murders. She arrived through a side door, a secure route to move inmates from the jail to court. Press photographers had to be in position ahead of time to grab a shot before she was inside the building. A bailiff unlocked her handcuffs at the defense table. She swiveled around in her high-backed chair and looked at the audience of mostly women in the back row. It was a look of malevolence, but there was something else: an animal in a hole. Still burly, Cherie wore her graying hair in a well-groomed tight ponytail. Gone was the reddish-to-orange dye. Gray and black jail stripes replaced her all-season tank top and hid her tattoos. She was in higher spirits than at her previous court appearances, easy in her step, light in her brief answers to the judge's questions—even Alvarez noted the change. Judge Mason, sitting for Judge Ball, ruled that there was probable cause to try her under special circumstances: the multiple killings were apparently premeditated. She pled not guilty and bail was denied.

Four months later, in early July, when she waived her right to a speedy trial, the bloody murder scene was replayed; as earlier noted, it had been captured by a live digital recorder in the room. There was the pleading voice of Glenn, the baby's crying, and the women's screams at high volume through the courtroom's speakers. Everyone was stunned by hearing a mass murder for the first time.

"Holy sh . . . hold on, Cherie . . . aw fuck . . . Cherie, Cherie . . . Oh my God . . . Cherie . . . not till you're dead . . . oh . . . Cherie please stop, please stop, please stop Cherie, stop . . . I'm not stopping until you're all dead . . . No, no . . . fucking bitch . . . Fucking . . . move . . . aw, aw, aw . . . bullshit . . . aw . . . aw . . . aw . . ." And then it was over. Through it all Cherie sat looking straight ahead, impassive.

At the July preliminary hearing Funk asked Judge Mason for a holding order on attempted murder for each of the persons present in the conference room when Cherie started shooting. His theory was that she intended to kill everyone in the room. In California the law permits an inference of intent to kill every person in the "kill zone" of a mass shooting event. "Obviously, she intended to kill the people she actually did kill or shot at, but what about those who were present when the shooting started who got away?" Funk argued. "Who she did not shoot or shoot at?" Cherie told the victims she was not going to stop shooting until everyone was dead. He contended Cherie also had a motive to kill Bogda because she was the tribe's attorney. Bogda had been the tribe's adviser in bringing the eviction action against Cherie and Jack, and it was Bogda who was instrumental in setting up the tribal court with Judge Lenzi at the bench. "The only thing saving Bogda's life was probably the fact that Shelia Russo lay on top of Bogda and was then shot and killed, concealing Bogda's body from Rhoades," Funk said. Bogda did not move a muscle during the entire shooting spree, expecting that any second Rhoades would discover and kill her. Judge Mason, even though he had never presided over a case of this magnitude, denied Funk's request.

When Judge Mason refused to find probable cause that Cherie intended to kill anyone who was not actually shot at, as the law permitted, Funk followed with an "information" filing in Modoc Superior Court. His intent was to have the filing reviewed by Judge Ball. He repeated his argument about the "kill zone" in California law. Alvarez made a counter motion to dismiss the additional attempted murder charges. He argued there was insufficient evidence to show probable cause that Cherie also intended to kill or attempted to kill others in the room when she started shooting. Funk disagreed, but later he shifted his strategy. Judge Ball never made a ruling either way.

"After filing my response to Alvarez's motion and after consulting with other capital case prosecutors, I made the tactical decision to concede the motion," Funk explained. If the goal was to obtain a death verdict against Cherie, then there was nothing to be gained by adding further victims of attempted murder. Verdicts on those attempted murders would not add anything to the strength of the evidence or argument for the death penalty, though there was evidence Cherie had a motive to kill everyone. The facts and the law on which attempted murder charges depended held the risk that she could be acquitted on one or more of those additional charges. If she was convicted on those charges, she would not be more eligible for the death penalty than she already was. That would have played into the hands of the defense not to execute the defendant. Funk's goal was to optimize the possibility of achieving a death verdict. He didn't want the jury deliberating on the possibility of death if they were under the psychological impact of acquitting Cherie of several attempted murder charges.

He didn't know if the tribe officially wanted death for Cherie. He was certain the tribe had not voted. He would have been told if a vote was taken. He did know the witnesses or victims with whom he was in contact during court proceedings, and all of them—Bogda, Monica and Melissa Davis, Brandi Penn, and Munholand—wanted the death penalty.

Bogda and Munholand were upset. They would not be named as victims of attempted murder after Funk conceded the defense motion and Judge Ball agreed. "I'd had problems well before the preliminary hearing with Bogda and Munholand in other respects," Funk said. "They seemed unable to accept the wisdom in not "gilding the lily" with additional charges that might lessen the possibility of a death verdict." He said the witness hostility came from Bogda, Munholand, and two of Rurik Davis's daughters, Melissa and Monica Davis.

After the preliminary hearing Funk said Munholand was angry that she had to identify the audiotape as a true recording of the shooting. She had to listen to the first few minutes of the audio recording of the tribal court session, but she was not required to listen to the shooting portion.

"I didn't understand why she would be incensed over having to testify that the audio tape was in fact an audio of the actual court session during which the shooting occurred," Funk said. "I understood how she might be upset at recalling the event, but not incensed. So I thought Munholand and Bogda were upset over a trivial issue—being called as a witness to lay the foundation for an audio recording of a court session at which Munholand was present."

This confirmed for him that they wanted to criticize the prosecution. Looking back, he admits he probably said or did some things they found off-putting. At an early hearing he couldn't recall the names of the two Davis sisters. That angered them. He'd seen them a few times and been introduced to them. Because he couldn't recall which name belonged to which sister they were offended.

"Bogda was haughty and condescending toward me. She was hypercritical of the investigative work of the police and the sheriff," Funk said. "She insisted everyone needed to be re-interviewed and wondered why they hadn't been." The initial interviews were perfectly adequate for Funk's purpose. The shooting was captured on audio and video. Bogda also felt he hadn't done enough witness preparation before preliminary examination. She and Munholand were upset that he hadn't spent more time preparing Munholand to testify. "I wasn't sure if I was going to call Munholand at the preliminary hearing and it was only at the last minute that I decided I needed her testimony on a foundational issue."

Funk said Bogda, Munholand, and Melissa and Monica Davis were upset because he didn't charge Richard Lash. Lash had left the conference room just before the shooting. The timing of Lash's exit seemed suspicious to them. They were also unhappy that Funk wasn't prosecuting Jack Stockton. Their unhappiness and dissatisfaction resulted in two contentious meetings with the U.S. Attorney's Office in Sacramento, its Native American liaison, and the FBI.

"My assumption is that these government entities had become aware of the tribe's dissatisfaction and wanted to assure Bogda and others that the tribe had the full support, concern, and attention of law enforcement at all levels of government. I attended both meetings," Funk said. Bogda's dissatisfaction and that of some of other tribal members was evident during the two meetings. The federal and state government representatives assured the tribal members that this case had their full attention.

"I found myself wondering why some members or affiliates of the tribe were so quick to fault those who were working hard to obtain justice for them. Monica and Melissa and Bogda had endured a horrifying event. The Davis sisters had suffered severe, life-threatening gunshot wounds and were witnesses to their father's murder, and Bogda had lain motionless under the body of her dear friend, Shelia Russo, knowing that at any second she could be discovered and killed—all while Russo's blood was dripping onto Bogda's face and mouth. But those horrifying facts did not constitute a basis to criticize the investigation or prosecution."

Funk said the thrust of the second meeting was the same as at the first—to answer questions from the tribe, assuage them, and convey support and concern for the tribe from the state and federal government. Again, he said, Bogda and the others "seemed unhappy" with how the case was being handled. He felt it would be difficult ever to satisfy Bogda and Munholand. Following the two meetings—when Funk explained why there was insufficient evidence to prosecute Lash and Stockton—he also held a separate meeting with Bogda, Munholand, and, he believed, possibly one of the Davis sisters. Alturas Police Chief Ken Barnes, the prosecution's lead investigator and a key witness, was also present. Bogda and the others still wanted to know why he hadn't charged Lash and Stockton.

"I again explained that if Lash and Stockton were to be prosecuted at all it would have to be under the theory that they aided and abetted Rhoades's killing spree," Funk said. "This meant there had to be proof beyond a reasonable doubt that Lash and Stockton knew Rhoades was going to attempt to annihilate her tribal government. Evidence was needed to show that they did in fact aid, abet, assist, or encourage Rhoades in the commission of her crimes."

Funk didn't have the evidence. Lash left the room before the shooting began in order to check on his child, who was playing in the back yard. There was no way to disprove his claimed intent, even though one could assume he was lying. Even assuming Lash left the room because he knew Cherie was going to kill everyone, Funk's opinion was that Lash's leaving the room did not seem to aid, abet, or encourage Cherie or facilitate in the actual shooting.

"If Lash had stayed in the room, arguably Rhoades would not have shot him because Lash had been either neutral during the banishment process or mildly supportive of Rhoades. Lash had no legal duty to stop Rhoades—whether he had remained in the room or not," Funk said. "The assumption that Lash was sympathetic with Rhoades did not, as a matter of law, make him guilty of her crimes as an aider and abettor."

Funk said Stockton, months before the shootings, had allegedly made a statement to Shelia Russo's husband Phil Russo that Stockton wanted Russo to kill Rurik. Russo did not take Stockton seriously. Even though he was a correctional officer for the sheriff, Russo was not concerned enough about Stockton's statement to report it. As a matter of law, the statement did not constitute a solicitation to murder. "Moreover, after the shooting Stockton denied knowing anything about Rhoades's intent. He said he had no idea his mom planned the shooting. He saw no change in her demeanor or anything else suggesting she intended to kill anyone," Funk said.

"He expressed utter shock, disbelief and horror at the event. Stockton's rhetoric several months before in Russo's presence was concerning, but Russo himself seemed not to have taken it seriously. It was a mere expression. If you say you'd like someone to kill someone else, without more, it's not sufficient to prove a crime," Funk added. Stockton never followed up with Russo on his initial request or suggestion.

"Jack Stockton was polite and civil to me in all our interactions in and out of court," Funk said. "I knew he was heartbroken at what I was attempting to do, but he was never hostile, rude, or uncooperative. He made himself available as a witness and I thought testified truthfully. He stated under oath he had no knowledge of his mother's plans. He loved his mother. He was not an uncooperative witness and treated me with civility. He told me, 'I know you're just doing your job.' Jack Stockton was more civil to me than Bogda or Munholand. I was rather struck by that dichotomy."

In mid-August, six months after the killings, Alvarez offered a plea of guilty in exchange for life in prison without the possibility of parole. Funk said he would consider the offer, but on November 10, three months after the plea deal was offered, Funk announced in a press release that he would ask a jury to sentence Cherie to death. It didn't take long for the news to hit the Main Street of Alturas.

27

"THEY'RE JUST INDIANS, WHO cares if they kill each other. It's certainly not worth the cost of a death penalty trial."

There was a familiar ring to these complaints. They were echoes of complaints Kandi heard from her students at Modoc High. "Why are we reading about other races if this is American Lit?" "Why aren't we reading about Americans if this is American Lit?" "Why are we wasting time reading about Indians?"

The grumbling was loud enough to reach the district attorney. For nearly a year before Cherie's case went to trial—and well in advance of the change of venue that Funk eventually agreed to—he was aware of the antipathy between the Native and white populations in Modoc County.

"In the course of the case a few people said to me, 'Why are we spending the money to prosecute an Indian who killed other Indians?'" Funk said. He heard that people were hearing the same complaint from others they knew. The message was clear to Funk: "If she wants to plead to multiple life terms, that's good enough." Why waste white taxpayers' money to execute an Indian? Indians weren't worth it. After the trial, he admitted he had encountered a "fair bit of virulent racism as push-back against seeking the death penalty for Cherie Rhoades."

"I heard the argument. I understood the argument. But the bottom line was it was a cold-blooded, premediated mass shooting perpetrated by ambush. The crime deserved the death penalty if a jury would render it. It was that simple," Funk said. It wasn't that the grumblers were opposed to the death penalty. Most of them, according to Modoc County voting statistics, favored lethal injection.

Funk knew some of the victims and their families because he had either prosecuted them as district attorney or defended several when he was in private practice. However, their brushes with the law didn't mean they weren't entitled to his pursuing the death penalty, which was what they wanted.

There were two reasons for imposing the death penalty. One was the severity of the crime. The other was that surviving members of the tribe wanted Cherie executed no matter the cost to taxpayers. Tribal dynamics could not be ignored. As Funk later explained, Cherie's crime was a cold-blooded, premeditated killing. At the same time there was a lot of passion behind it. She hated her brother and the tribal government for their treatment of her. What didn't help in preparing his case—in Funk's opinion—was that the tribe was tragically dysfunctional.

While Funk was deciding whether he would accept Cherie's offer of a plea deal or seek death, California and the nation were debating the moral, legal, and economic merits of legally killing someone. On July 16, 2014, U.S. District Judge Cormack J. Carney ruled California's death penalty unconstitutional. His decision pivoted on a petition by death row inmate Ernest Dewayne Jones, who had been sentenced to die nearly twenty years earlier for the rape and killing of his girlfriend's mother. Jones's attorneys argued that California's dysfunctional death penalty system caused delays in carrying out a backlog of executions. They said the death penalty was arbitrary and unconstitutional under the Eighth Amendment. Judge Carney agreed, saying that California's death penalty system was so plagued by inordinate and unpredictable delay that the death sentence was actually imposed only against a trivial few of those sentenced to death. "No rational person," he wrote, "can question that the execution of an individual carries with it the solemn obligation of the government to ensure that the punishment is not arbitrarily imposed and that it furthers the interests of society." It was the first time a federal judge had found the state's current system unconstitutional, but Carney's ruling had its limitations. It applied only to the specifics of Jones's petition—the issue of undue delay.

California's then Attorney General Kamala D. Harris was running on the Democratic ticket for a U.S. Senate seat. She joined other state agencies and appealed Carney's decision to the U.S. Ninth Circuit Court of Appeals. The argument she joined was that Jones had failed to seek a review first before California's Supreme Court. Was Harris ignoring her fundamental duty to serve justice in the face of an unjust law? Or was the law bad public policy—especially when she was known to oppose the death penalty personally? She said: "I am appealing the court's decision because it is not supported by the law, and it undermines important protections that our courts provide to defendants." She did not elaborate on what she meant by "undermines important protections." There was a second option. She and then California governor Jerry Brown could have conceded that the death penalty was unconstitutional and ceased defending it in federal court.

In February 2016 Pope Francis took the death penalty debate to the international level when he called for its worldwide abolition—at least temporarily—telling tens of thousands of people in St. Peter's Square that the commandment "You shall not kill" was absolute and equally valid for the guilty as for the innocent. And he asked that Catholic politicians "make a courageous and exemplary gesture" by seeking a moratorium on executions during the Church's current Holy Year, which ended that November. The pope's words reached attorney Alvarez's parish in Fresno following that sermon. Alvarez was pragmatic. "I don't think Pope Francis' call for a moratorium will have any effect on Cherie's case," he wrote in an email. "I just do not think that it will have any influence on Jordan. I don't know if he is a Catholic or not, but regardless I just do not see it factoring in his decision." The pope's call for a suspension on the death penalty did not reach parishioners at the Catholic Church in Cedarville. One Cedarville parishioner said the pope's message was not actually new—that the church had never officially said enacting the death penalty was a mortal sin, but in effect, the pope's timing brought the issue to public attention during 2016, the "Year of Mercy and Forgiveness."

As for California's Catholic population, Alvarez thought the pope's plea would simply reinforce the beliefs of those against the death penalty. And for those favoring it, he doubted if his words would have any significant impact on their conviction. The pope had already been on record as against the death penalty. His call for a one-year moratorium wasn't going to persuade those who favored death to change their minds. But it was another voice against the death penalty, and it added to the momentum to rescind the death penalty in California and elsewhere.

"My personal and public position on the death penalty mirror each other. I believe we as a society need to be above taking a life," Alvarez said. "If the issue is protecting society, locking someone up forever serves that purpose. If it is about vengeance, my position is the government should not be in the business of seeking vengeance."

Funk, a classical liberal and non-practicing Mormon, declined to say if he agreed or disagreed with the pope. However, he did candidly dismiss the pope's call for the worldwide abolition of capital punishment. "I'm not very impressed with Pope Francis. Is he a religious leader or a politician?" The Mormon Church does not take an explicit stance on the death penalty. It is neither for nor against executions. Its official website states that it "regards the question of whether and in what circumstances the state should impose capital punishment as a matter to be decided solely by the prescribed processes of civil law. We neither promote nor oppose capital punishment."

The State of Utah offers the occupants of death row two choices for execution—both carried out in the death chamber at the Utah State Prison in Draper. One is by lethal injection, the other by a firing squad of five anonymous volunteers trained by police officers. The decision is solely the choice of the condemned, but the firing squad is also a backup method in case the chosen lethal injection formula doesn't work or is unavailable.

To impose or not to impose death for Cherie fell solidly on Funk's shoulders. Later Funk said he never felt any pressure from his church—one way or the other—when it came to the death penalty. "Not one single bit, and I could have cared less," he said later. "I diverge from my church on a lot of issues. That's why I think religion's a non-issue. I've always believed in the death penalty. So I didn't have a crisis of conscience over this at all."

While the Carney decision was pending before the federal appellate court in San Francisco, Funk declared he would seek the death penalty in the Rhoades mass murder case. As the U.S. Ninth Circuit Court of Appeals reviewed Carney's decision, the death penalty continued to exist in California, although a state-enacted moratorium was in place and no one had been executed in nearly a decade. Funk, who routinely declined to discuss the Rhoades case publicly in any detail, did say the appellate court's decision, whether it upheld or overruled Carney, had no effect on his seeking the death penalty for Cherie. It was "case specific," referring to the constitutional challenge of undue delay. He predicted that Carney's decision would be overturned by the appellate court.

Funk was right. On November 12, 2015, the appellate court disagreed with Carney's "no rational person" logic. It reversed Carney's lower court ruling and agreed, as an integral part of its decision, with California Attorney General Harris that Jones had not pursued his claim to the state Supreme Court level. Reversing Carney's decision removed a legal barrier to potentially resuming executions in California. Confident in his opinion that an appellate court decision would have no influence on California's death penalty law as it stood, Funk made his announcement two days before the appellate court's decision went public. The expense to Modoc County taxpayers was not a factor in Funk's decision, nor were there any preliminary estimates.

28

ALVAREZ RETAINED CHANGE OF venue expert Dr. Edward J. Bronson immediately after Funk said he was going to seek the death penalty. A lawyer and professor emeritus of political science at California State University, Chico, Bronson testified in the Timothy McVeigh Oklahoma City and the Dzhokhar A. Tsarnaev Boston Marathon bombings. Both cases were granted changes of venue. He had qualified over two hundred times as an expert witness on change-of-venue motions in state and federal cases. For a number of years he wrote chapters on both venue and pre-trial publicity in *California Criminal Law Procedure and Practice*. He was also qualified to provide expert testimony on content analysis of pre-trial publicity. Bronson did not conduct a detailed survey of Modoc County's residents to determine their disposition toward Cherie as a Native or toward the death penalty—as he had in the McVeigh and Tsarnaev cases. Instead, on December 20, 2014, he wrote a short report to Alvarez citing that death penalty trials were "somewhat uncommon" and that to ensure a fair trial for her a change of venue was necessary—a recommendation Bronson said he rarely made, but he had a qualifier.

"It is important to observe that the defendant is an American Indian," he wrote in a letter to Alvarez. "In 2007, there were just 362 Indians residing in Modoc County, only 3.75 percent of the population, a fact that was somewhat surprising to me, and it is somewhat problematic for the defendant. I have dealt with the venue issue in several cases involving American Indian defendants in rural counties, and the prejudice and stereotyping have always been serious problems. But perhaps that will not be so in Modoc County."

He may have been holding out some hope that rural Modoc County, with a racist past, might be different. But he wasn't suggesting Alvarez take his chances on getting an unbiased jury. Bronson's letter conveyed the need for a change of venue and at the same time an open-minded chance that Modoc County might be different from other rural areas of the country. In fact, the letter was innuendo and not much substance. It was as if everyone, or at least he, Alvarez, and Judge Ball (Funk was not privy to the letter), knew what no one would say: people in rural areas are prejudiced against Natives, and Modoc County was likely to be the same. Racism in rural areas such as Modoc County can be implied, amorphous, or vague. Of the twelve state historical landmarks in Modoc County five are remembrances of great "Indian battles" such as "Bloody Point" and "Battle of Land's Ranch."

This was a tragedy of mass murder in Indian Country. It enveloped not only the Natives of the Cedarville Rancheria but the white population of Modoc County. Granted, it was not sensational like trials of the 1995 Oklahoma City bomber or 2013 Boston Marathon bomber, or the Dylann Roof trial (which was going on in Charleston, South Carolina, at exactly the same time as the Rhoades trial was taking place in Roseville, California). Alvarez said the substance of the letter addressed the issue of pre-trial publicity, and because he had "general anecdotal knowledge of prejudice against Native Americans in Modoc, I never needed to develop more specific evidence because I got the change of venue granted without needing to."

An anti-Native mind-set in Modoc County may have been more apparent to Natives than to whites, who are reluctant to say what they think. Sonny Craig, of the Pit River tribe near Alturas, worried that Cherie's killings would worsen the underlying fractures between reservation Natives and the neighboring whites. He said shortly after the killings that he was frequently followed by local police when he was driving through Alturas. "Racial blood lines have been drawn out," he told the *Los Angeles Times*, "and in my experience, it's only getting worse."

In late July 2015 Alvarez's motion for a change of was granted. Placer County three hundred miles to the south of Modoc County was selected for the site of the trial, scheduled for November 14, 2016. California voters were preparing to decide on two death penalty propositions on the ballot for November 8, 2016—just one week before

Cherie's trial was scheduled to begin. One ballot measure, Proposition 62, sought to abolish the death penalty in the belief that the concept of capital punishment as an ideology—at least in California—was past its prime. The other, Proposition 66, touting "mend not end," proposed keeping capital punishment by speeding up the time-consuming and expensive appellate process exercised by death row inmates. Prop. 62, the abolition measure, was defeated on a statewide margin of 54 percent to 46 percent. Prop. 66, mend not end, narrowly passed with 51 percent of statewide voters favoring the death penalty. In Modoc County Prop. 62, the anti–death penalty measure, was defeated by the second highest margin of any of California's fifty-eight counties: in Modoc County 77 percent of the voters were opposed to abolishing the death penalty. With the voters' rejection of Prop. 62 and their approval of Prop. 66, Funk now had not just county-level but statewide public sentiment supporting his decision to seek Cherie's execution. Funk was not obligated by law to pursue her death. Had he accepted her offer of pleading guilty in exchange for life without any chance of parole, he would have saved the financially marginal county an estimated $118,573 in expenses incurred by his office and the defense. By the end of 2017, nearly three years after the killings, the county had yet to receive an accounting from Sheriff Poindexter on what it cost to house Rhoades. And Funk would have spared the surviving victims and their families the ordeal of reliving the killings when they were called to testify. As Funk moved toward a decision, a slight prospect of Cherie's avoiding the death penalty rested with Judge Ball.

Judge Ball was an old school jurist. An amiable man, he gave the impression he'd enjoy sitting at a poker table and sharing stories with journalists outside the courtroom. He had a reputation as an avid duck hunter, but as he grew older he lost interest in killing ducks. One morning as he was leaving the courthouse Ball stopped to answer a few questions I had. I could see he wasn't feeling well. Yet, as he leaned against his car, he casually took time to talk about the prospect of the death penalty ballot later in the year and Attorney General Harris's waffling as she campaigned for the U.S. Senate. He said she could persuade voters in one direction or the other—if she went public with a firm position. Was Harris or wasn't she an opponent of the death penalty? Judge Ball smiled and surmised it was going to be an interesting debate. It was unclear what his hole cards were. Later I learned that the judge told Funk and Alvarez in a backroom discussion that he thought Alvarez's offer to settle for life without possibility of parole was reasonable and something he would approve.

"Judge Ball made it clear that he thought this case could and should resolve for life without possibility of parole," Alvarez confirmed for me later. "He possibly could have eventually exerted enough subtle pressure on Jordan to have him reconsider his position. At the time it was based on the fact that even if she was convicted of death, the execution would likely never be carried out in California."

Judge Ball had presided over two dozen death penalty trials, but he was in failing health. He never had a chance to follow through on his belief that the case could be decided without imposing death on Cherie. The eighty-two-year-old died on November 10, 2015, at a hospital in Reno, Nevada.

29

IN PRISON SLANG THERE'S hard time and soft time. Hard time is long-term incarceration spent in state prisons. Soft time is short-term county jail sentences. Cherie's nearly three years in the Modoc County jail waiting to go to trial was soft time. Her daily routine was the same as for all county jail inmates, regardless of the severity of their crimes or the charges pending against them.

Breakfast and the distribution of medications and cleaning supplies between 5:00 a.m. and 5:30 a.m., lunch and medications between 11:30 a.m. and 12:00 noon, dinner and medications between 5:30 and 6:00 p.m. Cherie took several prescribed medications daily and some over the counter medications for diabetes, high blood pressure, a heart murmur, and a persistent shoulder injury. Visiting hours were two days a week, Wednesdays and Thursdays from 11:00 a.m. to 12:00 noon. The only visitors she apparently saw, other than Alvarez, were her son Jack Stockton and her daughter-in-law Erin. She had access to the recreation yard, but she never used it. Nor did she use the jail's law library. Because of the multiple murder charges against her, she was not assigned to a work detail. The telephone in her cell was turned on at 7:00 in the morning and disconnected at 9:00 at night. Phone cards bearing values of five, ten, and twenty dollars were sold at the jail's commissary. Visitors or family could deposit money in her jail account, which she could then use to purchase a phone card with a money order. She was allowed only outgoing calls.

My wife, Barbara, and I had to follow an established procedure in arranging to interview Cherie in the Modoc County jail before her trial. First, so that there were no misunderstandings about the interview's purpose, I notified Alvarez. Did he have any questions or objections? No. Next was Sheriff Poindexter. He set policy for our visiting hours, length of the interview, and use of recorders. Notes could be taken, but no recorders were allowed. And then there was Cherie. It was her choice. I wrote her a letter and she readily agreed. To use our interview time efficiently Barbara and I went over our questions in advance. We also agreed on a system for simultaneously taking notes, which basically was to write as fast as we could when the other was asking Cherie questions and not to skip anything, including color.

March 19, 2016. The visitors' room at Modoc County jail felt like an abandoned walk-in cold box. Behind us a row of windows about two feet off the floor could have been one-way glass. Jailers wordlessly visited a soft drink dispenser in the corner during our interview. We sat on metal stools bolted to the floor. As we waited for Cherie to appear, we tried to look through a double-thick soundproof glass partition smeared with fingerprints on both sides. Cherie came in, sat down. She cradled two black telephone receivers, one on each side of her chin, so that she could hear and talk to both of us at the same time. Before we spoke she smiled knowingly and wiped the mouth and ear pieces of the phones on the cloth of her black and gray–striped prison blouse. Holding the receivers, one to each ear, she grinned. We said they should provide handiwipes. She laughed. Only once during the hour-long interview did she hold the receivers in one hand, and that was to look at a tattoo on her right shoulder. It was the date her mother died.

She was softer than when we had last seen her in court two years earlier. The lines in her face were gone and her dark, very dark, eyes were clear. Her salt-and-pepper hair was no longer braided down the back of her neck. Now she wore bangs. Gone was the purple dye of two years ago. On first impression, she looked completely comfortable with herself. Yet she was like someone who had taken a deep breath and held it in. There was a passing look of gloom and then suddenly a release and she was off, gleefully describing in great detail drawings she made of sheriff deputies' penises, sketches she used to paper the walls of her cell.

"It's totally crazy around here," she laughed, and her face lit up. She was like a child anxiously reporting on the day's activities at summer camp, a protective bragging.

She said she was in the old part of the jail, in her own cell which she called her room. There were six cells, two beds to a cell, and a dormitory. She spoke with tight nervous energy as she launched into how her walls were papered with penis drawings of the jailers, whom she called her COS, or correctional officers. In rapid succession she said "banana hammock" and "anatomical." She said she was a crotch watcher, that she had figured out each jailer's size.

"It took me a while to figure them out, but when they see the picture on the wall I can tell by the look on their faces, I got it right. And when guys see the other guys' pictures on the wall, I love the look on their face, they stop and look at it. Because of their shoes. One jailer, I asked him, what size shoe do you wear, he said thirteen. Another guy is an eight." She laughed at suggesting shoe size and penis size were related, and she quickly rattled off her opinion of each jailer. "Joe, the jailer, is a gossip-whore." For a moment she turned serious and said one of the jailers had been a cop with the city. "He messed with my son, gave him a ticket for parking too far from the dirt." She said she got even with the jailer with her penis art. She kept talking. Nothing strung together.

"Christmas Eve my roommate asked that I be allowed to attend the counseling session with AB109 inmates. They call them that because they're sentenced to county jail instead of state prison. Lisa, the counselor, who had previously taught preschool, came to the session in jeans full of holes, maybe a fashion statement. I told her she should dress more professionally. She was scared of me so Julie, the jailer, had to be in there with us."

She told about a woman doing four years for marijuana possession and then was caught concealing drugs in her body crevices when she was jailed. The woman told Cherie she didn't like murderers. "How stupid these people are, they get sentenced, are allowed to go home and get their affairs in order and on the day they're supposed to report to jail they stick some marijuana in a body crevice and think they're not going to get caught," Cherie said.

Cherie said everybody has their opinion and she didn't care if they didn't like murderers. She paused and added, "I don't like oxygen thieves either, someone in my cell using my airspace and telling me they don't like murderers. If I can't be nice to them, I'll tell them and they'll move. The jailers use me as blackmail against the inmates in the dorm. They say if you don't straighten up you'll get put in with Cherie."

There was a creeping unsaid panic between Barbara and me that our allotted hour for the interview was being totally controlled by Cherie. Skillfully she gave us a quick glimpse of jail life, in the telling about her drawings, her cell mates, and the male jailers. Her intent was to dominate from beginning to finish—as if her self-assignment was to entertain, keep the one-sided conversation going, and regale us with shock tactics. She sidestepped the reason we were there. We had to get our questions out before the time was up. We managed to change subjects and the mesmerizing answers flowed out with no sense of order.

"There's no glory in being chairperson," she said about her tenure as leader of the Cedarville Rancheria. "Shit rolls uphill, not down." She made a sweeping, rolling wave with her hand that went up in front of her face. Rurik was chairperson for seven months; he tried to disenroll her and her mother and brother Eugene. The tribe threw him out after seven months. He wanted to be paid to be chairperson, to be paid out of grant money. Some tribes pay their chairperson, but out of their own money, not development funds. In 2009 she was voted in as tribal chair the first time, for a three-year term. She was re-elected for three years. Rurik was pissed. Rancheria residents get warnings about upkeep on their places, but Rurik wouldn't give her warnings. He gave her violations, one for not cutting her lawn when she was away for two weeks. She said no one told her she was being recalled.

How did the feud with Rurik start?

"It started with the steaks, the meat, I was gone. I told Rurik he could stay at my place while I was out of town. I had some meat on the freezer shelf in the refrigerator and when I came back it had gone down (she makes a downward motion with her hand). I knew Rurik had eaten my meat. He was getting fat. Next was the housing and the extra fifty square feet. I was next in line to get a house. Rurik had a house and wanted a garage. Duanna said, 'No, Cherie needs a house.' My house ended up being fifty square feet bigger than Rurik's and he didn't get his garage. He was incensed. One time Rurik grabbed me by the hair and pulled me over the counter, you know, one of those wide ones that you put food out on, and threw me to the floor. He pinned me and twisted my fingers back hard. I had rings on and the shanks on the rings snapped. The tribe asked me, of all people, to write the incident up, and Rurik was voted out as chair. He is a piece of shit. I was a slave for my dad," she went on non-stop. "Rurik stole cars and gas when we were young. My mom, Rurik and I were tight, like the three stooges. Rurik had the look but not the heart of a Native. He never did the sweat lodge, my son has more Native in him than anybody in the tribe right now. In his heart he is more Native. Rurik had the 'look.' He is a male chauvinist pig."

Embezzlement charges?

"It's been two years, where are the charges? Someone found a receipt with my name on it, thought it was the tribal credit card. My son Jack and his wife Erin went to Susanville and I gave them my card for movies, ice cream. They used my debit card, not the tribal credit card. But the rest of them didn't know the difference between a credit and debit card. There have been eight forensic audits in two years, they're auditing the gas station. The manager and I were accused of stealing $80,000 from Rabbit Traxx. Duanna made sure all the ducks were in a row. We always had clean audits and at a meeting of all tribes we were referred to as a 'model tribe.' Not anymore. Sheila Russo? She was on probation."

Do you see yourself as a Native?

"No," she quickly answered. "Neither did Rurik. He took on the looks of a Native. My mother was a half-breed. No, he wasn't an Indian. I'm not a Native."

Have you been disenrolled?

The question caught her by surprise. No. She said she had not been disenrolled, as if the idea was unthinkable. The hour was up. She stood and backed away from the window. Then she stopped and looked past us at a young deputy who held the visitors' room door open.

30

FACING A RACIST MENTALITY in Modoc County, fortified by the views of a modern U.S. president, Alvarez asked for a change of venue.

Roseville was chosen, nearly three hundred miles to the south, the largest city in Placer County. Placer in place of Modoc because a Modoc jury would be prejudiced against Cherie. Anti-Indian bias was implied by change-of-venue expert Bronson and pre-trial publicity in the county's weekly newspaper. There was speculation on the Alturas Main Street that moving the trial out of Modoc County might mean Cherie would escape the death penalty.

Placer County went through decades of sea change because of suburban outward growth. Sacramento, the state's capital, is less than twenty miles away from Placer County's population centers. The county is a mix of urban, suburban, and recreation. Tahoe National Forest is within the county's northern boundary and includes much of the west shore of Lake Tahoe. It may appear that this blend would result in diverse demographics. Ironically, Placer County is similar to Modoc County. Like Modoc in 2016, Placer County voters favored the death penalty by a ratio of two to one. More than 80 percent of Placer's population is white, as is Modoc's. Both counties have low Native population numbers. Placer's poverty level is below 8 percent; Modoc's is almost 20 percent. Both are Republican strongholds and both are within the same state and congressional district boundaries. Coincidentally, Cherie and much of her immediate family—alive or killed—had previously lived in the Roseville area.

Funk and Alvarez both began practicing law in California in 1991, and this was their first death penalty case. Visiting Judge Candace Beason replaced Judge Ball. Beason retired from the Los Angeles

Superior Court in 2014. She had a personal style. Her blonde to gray hair was cut shoulder length, framing a roundish face that was neither stern nor judicial. Most striking was her voice. She spoke with compassion; a caring voice when she was conducting routine court business or admonishing a recalcitrant witness. Beason was an experienced capital case judge. She had presided over a number of death penalty trials, including cases in Riverside County, where in 2015 eight people were sentenced to death—more than any other county in the United States.

The trial to decide Cherie's guilt began on December 12, 2015. Funk opened with a travelogue description of Surprise Valley to orient the Roseville jury to Modoc County. He described where the Cedarville Rancheria is located and how the Warner Mountains—with peaks as high as 9,800 feet—separate Surprise Valley from Alturas, the county seat. He then brought the Paiute tribe into focus, explaining its federal status and the revenue-sharing trust funds known as "casino payments" that adult members receive each quarter. Narrowing in, he described the tribe's surveillance system at its Alturas offices. Then he brought the scene down to the conference table where the victims were sitting when they were murdered. He outlined the sequence of events leading up to the killings, the allegations of embezzlement, the suspension of Cherie and her son, and their eviction. Then came the critical evidence, Cherie carrying a backpack as she entered the conference room—and the fatal seesaw debate between Cherie and the tribal judge.

"Would you agree that there's no other method to appeal?" Funk said, rephrasing the judge's question to Rhoades. "And the defendant said, 'No, I don't agree.'" Funk again repeated the tribal judge's critical question. "Well, where in tribal law is there authority to do something different?" "And at that point," he said, "all hell broke loose." He then went into graphic detail of the killings—one by one.

Members of the jury may have wondered why they were there as they listened to Alvarez's opening remarks. After all, Cherie was caught on video surveillance cameras killing four people.

"She snapped and essentially lashed out against those she believed were trying to destroy her life," he told the jury. "This is a tragic, tragic incident. It's murder. I am not going to go around that. I am not going to sugarcoat it. It's four counts of murder. It's two counts of attempted murder." He said she was goaded into committing the murders, and provocation by law reduces the first degree charges to second degree. He said Cherie was diagnosed with a mental illness known as paranoid personality disorder. When pressured by her half-brother, she felt provoked into killing him and the others. To give purpose to why the jury was there, Alvarez argued that they were to decide the degree of the murders—not first but second. Although the death penalty went unmentioned at this stage of the trial, it was implied that a verdict of second degree murder would save her from execution.

The first witness for the prosecution was Cherie's son, twenty-seven-year-old Jack Stockton.

"How are you this morning, sir?" Funk asked.

"Obviously could be better, but . . ." Stockton answered.

"Am I fair in assuming you would prefer not to be here if it could be avoided?"

"Of course."

"Is Cherie Rhoades your mother?"

Judge Beason offered Stockton a Kleenex. Funk continued his questioning.

"Now, at some point were you on the Cedarville Rancheria governing council?"

"Yeah. Yeah."

"And at some point, possibly in December of 2013, did you get removed from your position?"

"Yeah."

"Can you describe what that was about?"

Stockton pieced out the story that led to his mother walking into the tribe's offices in Alturas and shooting at close range. He said tribal leaders suspected him, his wife Erin, and his mother of embezzlement. He and his mother were removed from the tribe's executive committee. Erin, the tribe's non-Native chief financial officer, was fired by Sheila Russo, the tribe's recently hired director.

"They, I guess you could say, banished me from all the tribal facilities, meetings. And they were taking action of removing me and my family from our home, as well as my mother from her home," he told the court.

He said his mother owned several handguns, that she purchased the Taurus 9mm she used in committing the murders from someone at Strong Family Health. He did not attend the fatal meeting on the advice of an unidentified attorney—even though eviction enforcement was a critical step in losing his home. Funk did not ask Stockton who the attorney was. Stockton did say he and his mother went to the meeting the day before the killings when they appealed the tribe's eviction decision. Why he attended one meeting and not the other was never explored.

Because the tribe did not have its own police force it sometimes relied on security from the Alturas police department. For unexplained reasons there was no security either the day of the eviction or the day of the murders, though on the day of the eviction proceedings Rurik Davis asked if Stockton was carrying a weapon.

"At some point did he search you?" Funk asked, referring to Davis.

"He—he may have tried. This is over two years ago. I'm trying to remember, but he may have tried. I just blocked him out, because I was just there to do what I had to do and get out," Stockton said. "I just walked right by him and just continued on with my agenda which was the meeting that day."

"Was your mother in your immediate presence when you and Rurik had this discussion about weapons, he may have patted you down?"

"Yes. She was to my left and just a few feet behind me."

"Do you have an opinion as to whether she saw and heard what was going on between you and Rurik?"

"I would say she did, yeah."

"Do you have an opinion as to whether or not there was hostility between Rurik and your mother?" Funk went on to ask.

"Since as long as I can remember, there was."

"As long as you can remember?"

"Yeah."

"Do you remember being present when you were younger, having to pick your mother up at a hospital in connection with injuries she may have received in an assault by Mr. Davis?"

"Yeah. And, unfortunately, and, unfortunately, that's one of the—one of the only few memories I do have as a child."

"All right. Now, you weren't actually present, were you, for any physical confrontation?"

"No."

"But is it your belief that Rurik assaulted your mom?"

"That is correct."

Under Alvarez's cross-examination Stockton described the sequence of events that led to the killings, occasionally repeating testimony he gave in answering Funk's questions. That he was removed from his vice-chair position on the executive committee about four months before his mother "snapped," using Alvarez's words. At times during cross-examination Stockton's memory seemed clouded, other times clear. He was vague on the roles and membership of the executive council and community council, the tribe's two distinctly different bodies. He was uncertain who actually succeeded his mother as tribal chair after she was deposed—that it was his uncle. He repeated that the relationship between Rhoades and her half-brother was "great when they agreed on things, but the majority of the time, not good."

"What do you mean by not good?" Alvarez asked.

"You could just sense the tension and just . . . it wasn't great at all. I mean, just from my perspective, my uncle was always trying to sit there and get penalties and punishments put against my mother when he was in authority, power, and for no reason at all, I would think, but it was like that all the time." And he denied knowing his mother intended to commit murder just after they left the Alturas Subway. There was no indication of what she going to do.

Funk followed up during redirect. "She didn't tell you anything?" Funk asked in a tone bordering on incredulous.

"No," Stockton answered. "And . . . I gave her a hug. I said, 'I'll see you after the meeting. Let me know how it goes.'"

Funk's next witness was the tribe's attorney Hedi Bogda. She said she narrowly escaped being killed because she had fallen underneath Sheila Russo during the chaotic scene. She and Sheila were best friends; they had once roomed together in Palm Springs. It was Sheila who arranged a meeting with Rhoades and Davis that led to Bogda becoming the tribe's attorney. Then Bogda gave an unnerving account of the killings in progress. She described Cherie entering the conference room, asking that the windows opening onto the street and the empty lot be closed because she was cold, and then walking over to where Rurik sat, taking out a handgun and shooting him in the head.

"Did you see that happen?" Funk asked.

"Yes."

"What happened next?"

"She walked over to the center of the table and shot Glenn Calonico."

"What happened next, if you remember?"

"She turned towards Sheila and I, and Sheila—I believe she grabbed me and threw me on the ground, and everybody started scrambling because she kept on shooting at us."

"She kept on what?"

"Shooting the gun."

"Were you shot?"

"No."

"Where—where did you end up, your body, in relation to Sheila Russo?"

"We crawled—everybody was trying to crawl around to escape. There was no place for us to go because of the setup of the room. We were trapped, and I ended up underneath Sheila."

"How did you end up under Sheila?"

"Sheila was shot and landed on me. Next to me, I believe."

"Were you under her body?"

"I believe part—part ways. Partially."

"Were you able to hear the rest of what was going on inside the room?"

"Yes."

"Can you describe it?"

"It was a lot of commotion and screaming."

"Who was screaming? Do you recall?"

"I believe I was at some point, but I don't know exactly who screamed, but there was a lot of screaming going on."

"Did you hear the defendant say anything?"

"Yes."

"What?"

"She said that 'I'm not going to stop until everybody in this room is dead.'"

"What happened next? Let me ask it this way: At some point did the shooting stop?"

"Yes."

"Do you know for how long the shooting went on?"

"A few minutes, I guess."

"From your vantage point being, I think, underneath Ms. Russo, could you see what the defendant was doing?"

"Yes."

"How is it that you were able to see anything she was doing? Were you able to look under the table?"

"Yeah."

"All right. What did you see?"

"Well, previously I saw her shooting the gun at people."

"That's before you went down under the table?"

"Yeah. Well, we were—Jenica, Sheila, and myself—well, we were trying to escape and crawl, and that's when we could—I could see her aiming the gun at people in the far side of the room and shooting them."

"Did you ever see her get down under the table?"

"I believe so, yes."

"What do you remember in that regard?"

"That she was trying to aim the gun at people that were trying to hide."

"Do you know who she was aiming at?"

"I don't."

"Did you have a perception that at some point the defendant had left the room?"

"Yes."

"What did you do?"

"I was breathing quite heavily at that time and told myself that I needed to shut down, and so I just pretended I was dead."

"At some point did you form an opinion that maybe it was safe for you to get up?"

"At that time I heard her coming back in, and that's when I heard Glenn Calonico say something."

"What did you hear? What did he say? Do you recall?"

"He said, 'Stop, Cherie. Stop.'"

"Did she say anything in response?" Funk asked for the second time.

"That's when she said, 'I'm not going to stop until everyone in this room is dead.'"

"So how is it you were able to ultimately get out of the room?"

"I heard the sirens coming, and I heard the police walk into the building. I heard them break down a door. And I heard them in the room talking and finding bodies, and at that point I stuck my head up."

"And did they seem to locate you and find that you were there and alive?"

"Yes."

"Did you have any blood on you?"

"Yes."

"Describe it, please."

"Sheila's face was directly next to mine, and she had been shot in the back of her head. And as a result the blood was pouring all over my face, and I had to basically swallow and breathe it in, and it just kept on dripping onto me."

After establishing that Bogda had been hired by the Cedarville Rancheria as their attorney in the summer of 2013, Funk began a step-by-step questioning of the tribe's series of actions against Cherie and her son.

"The tribe, as well as myself, started a fraud investigation due to alleged theft from the tribe. Ms. Russo had terminated Erin Christensen's employment. That happened around mid-December," Bogda said, referring to Stockton's wife by her maiden name.

"The embezzlement matter that the tribe was suspicious about, was that under investigation at this time?" Funk asked.

"Yes. I contacted the FBI and the U.S. Attorney's office in December of 2013, and I, again, contacted them in January as well, and I also contacted the Modoc County Sheriff," Bogda answered.

"And do you know what the tribe intended to do if the investigation had shown no embezzlement?"

Bogda admitted she did not know what the tribe would have done. She started to say that the tribe had an auditor's report showing how much money was taken. Alvarez interrupted with an objection that Beason sustained. There was never any evidence presented at the trial that the embezzlement had taken place—or, if it had, how much money was stolen.

Funk returned to the sequence of the tribe preparing to cast out Rhoades and her son. Bogda explained that the tribe formed its own court about two months before the murders. This led to the hiring of Judge Patricia Lenzi. The intent—if Judge Lenzi were to rule in the tribe's favor—was to gain legal status under state law that allowed the sheriff physically to carry out the eviction order.

Spencer Bobrow, forty-one, the tribe's environmental coordinator at the time, was called by Funk the first day of the trial. Bobrow was the only person to follow Cherie from the time she was waiting in the parking lot to when she entered the conference room. He could see her from his office window and at the same time watch a live surveillance video from the conference room on a monitor screen in front of him. Bobrow was standing on the handicap ramp leading to the office's entrance when he saw the injured Melissa Davis come out of the building.

"She was coming down the ramp, very unstable, wobbling, I kind of met her half way up the ramp and braced her with my arms and kind of backed down the ramp with her towards her car and was going to be setting her against her car," Bobrow began his description of the scene. "And I turned to my—I looked over my shoulder and Cherie was coming down the ramp with a knife in her hand, and came straight at me and Melissa, and started trying to stab her over the top of my shoulder. It was a butcher knife from the kitchen. We were standing next to her car and I set her down, set her against her car, and turned to ward off the knife, grabbed Cherie, spun her away from Melissa, and put her on the ground, sat her on the ground."

"Do you know how many stabbing motions she made?" Funk asked.

"I'd say six. I warded off four, maybe five with my elbow before I said, 'That's enough' and spun around and grabbed her."

"And did you and her have any conversation besides you telling her, 'That's enough'?"

"After she was sitting on the ground I asked her why she did this, and I said, 'Over a house?'"

"And she said, 'No.' She said, 'It's the principle.'"

"And I said, 'What principle?'"

"And she said she had to take the head of the snake off, take the snake's head off."

After Bogda and Bobrow testified, twenty-six-year-old Monica Davis, one of Rurik Davis's three daughters, told how Rhoades killed her father.

"I remember it really startled me. So I looked up, and that's when I seen her have a gun, and she aimed it at my father and she shot him."

"Did you see that happen?" Funk asked.

"Yes, I did."

"Can you describe in any more detail than what you have?"

"I remember when she pointed the gun at him, he looked her—they were locked—kind of, like, locked eyes, and she pulled the trigger. And it took me, like, just a second to think that maybe this was some kind of joke. But then when I seen, like, the blood pour out and he dropped his head, I realized it wasn't. So I ducked underneath the table and I hid."

"Can you describe what you remember next?"

"She—I honestly thought that maybe she was—just that, and she was going to run off because she killed somebody. So I was hoping that maybe, you know, the rest of us are safe. But then she just started opening fire. And I was ducked underneath the table. I couldn't see what was going on. And I kept weaving in and out between the pillars because it was a really nice, thick pillar. So she would be one side, so I whipped over to the other side hoping that would protect me. I remember actually locking eyes with her before she shot me. And I ducked underneath the table and I tried going back over, and that's when I—I felt something hit me, but I lost all feeling, so I just laid down and I tried to pretend I was dead, which I was hoping would work for a little while."

"And so when you lost all feeling, what part of your body did you lose feeling in?"

"My lower back."

"Did you have any kind of an injury?"

"I was shot through the leg and it went out underneath my tailbone."

She told the court what led to her wounding, her father's death and the three others, was an "always ongoing battle between the two, the power." Battles over who was going to be the chair of the tribe's executive committee. Screaming and yelling at each other "just like squaring off at each other." Battles over what she called "blood quorum," meaning "blood quantum," or the specific minimum percentage of Native heritage a person must have to qualify for tribal membership. Most tribes require their members to have at least one-sixteenth Native heritage. She thought her father was against the blood quantum requirement, but she wasn't certain. She wasn't asked what Rhoades's side of the argument was. "It's been a while," she said. Monica Davis said she kept her distance from Rhoades because she "gave off this feeling—I know it sounds weird, but she—I didn't like the vibe that she would put off. I just never felt comfortable around her." As her father's methodical plan to get rid of Rhoades gained momentum, Monica drew a line between herself and her aunt. She sided with her father, and she cast a vote in committee to eliminate Rhoades from the tribe.

Melissa Davis, twenty-eight, was the next witness. She described seeing her father after he was shot, seeing Rhoades turning on the others at the conference table before she, like her sister, ducked under the table. Melissa Davis was shot at least four times, including a wound to her right forearm.

"That's when I realized she was actually shooting at us, because it sounded like pops, and at first, I thought maybe a BB gun or something, and it wasn't bleeding. It was real. And, when I got on my hands and knees, and I seen a shell . . . that's when I realized she actually was shooting us . . . and I—I recall I screamed, realizing what was actually happening."

Melissa said when Rhoades saw that they were diving under the table for protection, Rhoades also leaned down.

"I remember she looked right at me and she was shooting. She was pulling the trigger. She leaned down towards us and I remember trying to get behind the thick table legs to the other side where she couldn't get to be on that side."

"Were you able to get behind that?" Funk asked.

"Partially, like, my upper part of my body. The rest of me was still kind of exposed."

"Do you recall the defendant saying anything while she was shooting in the room?"

"Yeah."

"What did she say?"

"That none of us were going to leave that room alive, that she's going to kill us all."

Funk asked how she managed to escape. Melissa described kicking herself free of Rhoades, running down a hall, hearing a phone ringing, and answering it with the desperate hope that someone was on the other end and she could cry for help. "Someone please, send help," she screamed into the receiver, but no one was there. The caller had hung up. She dropped the phone and ran out of the office. Rhoades ran after her with a kitchen knife, yelling she was going to cut the head off the snake. Spencer Bobrow tackled her, knocked the knife out of her hand, and held Rhoades until sheriff deputies arrived.

Nikki Munholand, thirty-one, the tribe's non-Native financial and administrative assistant, described Cherie entering the office, heading for the restroom carrying a backpack. Munholand thought this was odd because Cherie never carried a backpack. In questioning Munholand about the backpack, Funk implied that it concealed the two 9mm handguns. That Cherie went to the restroom to transfer the guns to the pockets of her shorts. Munholand also thought it unusual for Cherie to tell someone to shut the windows because it was an unseasonably warm day for February. "When she entered the conference room it felt like she was trying to get everyone to look her in the eye, sort of commanding everybody's attention."

Jacob Penn, twenty, who was adopted by Cherie although he was a blood-related nephew, said she asked him and Richard Lash to clean her handguns the day before the murders. He identified one of the handguns as the same 9mm that she used the next day. "She seemed quiet. She wasn't really talkative like she usually was," Penn recalled.

Brandi Penn, twenty-four, Jacob's sister, said she escaped when she made a split-second decision and buy her uncle Rurik's truck. She left the meeting to go to the bank for the money. When she returned fifteen minutes later she saw blood-covered Jenica McGarva running in the direction of the police department one block away. Brandi's three-year-old son had walked through the carnage. Her eighteen-month-old daughter toddled out the front door of the tribe's offices. Brandi scooped her up and ran. Cousins Richard Lash and Monica Davis were outside near a dumpster. Monica was on the ground. Cherie was going after Melissa Davis with a knife. A sheriff deputy was handcuffing Cherie.

"I started pretty much screaming at Cherie," Brandi said, "asking her why she killed my family. And she told me that she was glad that she did it, and she would have did it—she would have killed me too if I was in that room."

Alvarez's line of defense, as he predicted in his opening remarks, was that Cherie was provoked into committing the murders. The provocation was not just the well-known bitterness between her and her half-brother. It was her own vulnerability to mental illness pressures brought on by that bitterness. His first witness was Dr. Alex Yufik, a forensic psychologist, consultant to the Los Angeles County District Attorney's Office and adjunct lecturer at the University of Southern California.

Yufik told the court that a year and half after the murders he met with Cherie "to determine if Ms. Rhoades has any psychiatric or psychological condition that could have impacted her behavior." He spent ten hours interviewing her over a two-day period. He gave her an IQ test, interviewed her son Jack, and reviewed a clinical social worker's report. Out of the jury's presence Judge Beason brought up the question of whether the jury should know Cherie's IQ. "People have misconceptions as to what those numbers mean," she advised. The attorneys mutually agreed that Yufik could only refer to Cherie's IQ as average.

"Now, after your evaluation of Ms. Rhoades, what conclusion, if any, did you reach?" Alvarez asked.

"I reached the conclusion that Ms. Rhoades has a paranoid personality disorder."

"What is paranoid personality disorder?"

Yufik embarked on a detailed explanation of Cherie's mental state. Paranoid personality disorder is a psychopathological way of relating to other people and to yourself. Psychopathological, meaning that it's a dysfunctional way of relating to other people, characterized by pervasive and chronic suspicion. Such individuals believe they are at the mercy of hostile forces. They are hyper vigilant, meaning they're scanning the environment in the belief that other people are going to take advantage of them. They hold grudges. They're often described as belligerent, antagonistic. It's a painful way to exist.

"The person starts to have problems in their relationships with coworkers, their family. Their emotions are no longer regulated normally. Their impulsivity is severely affected. They tend to act out because they misunderstand social cues." Impulsivity, he said, "is when you act on impulse without really thinking about the consequences of your behavior."

During cross examination Funk sought Yufik's opinion on Cherie's capability of planning the murders in advance. Would a paranoid personality disorder prevent a person from premeditation or deliberation as opposed to insanity where a person does not know what she's doing?

"A person who has paranoid personality disorder clearly understands the nature of their actions," Funk stated. Yufik said they also understand the consequences of their actions. The disorder does not prevent a person from thinking rationally or inhibit deliberating.

Funk moved on to establish that the ongoing hostility between Cherie and her half-brother was not an isolated example of her mental disorder. He asked Yufik if she had difficult relationships with anyone besides Davis. Yufik said she had problematic relationships with virtually everyone with whom she came in contact. "She told me that she was actually dismissed from school because she had struck a teacher, an example of acting out impulsively at a very young age," Yufik answered. "I believe she told me that she acted that way because she believed the teacher was unfair towards her. So you see the developmental trajectory starting fairly early on."

Funk asked how well she got along with members of her tribe. Yufik said she felt persecuted by the tribe. That they suspected her of embezzlement. Their attempt to take away all her privileges and severely restrict her from tribal meetings affected every area of her life. She told Yufik that when she was chair of the tribe's executive committee there was constant friction and difficulty. That she had continuous problems dealing with committee members.

"That is typical of having PPD?" Funk asked, referring to paranoid personality disorder by its acronym.

"In some sense, yes," Yufik said.

"That doesn't mean she couldn't act rationally in her functions as a tribal chairman, does it?"

"It does not."

"It doesn't mean she couldn't make logically consistent rational decisions."

Yufik explained that Rhoades was not having a psychotic break from reality. People with PPD could distinguish right from wrong, think rationally, and reason their way to what they thought was the best course for them. He said PPD presents a problem for persons suffering from it and also for anyone in contact with them. "It presents a very significant problem for the individual, and it presents a very significant problem for the people that are around the individual and have to work with them or are a part of their family," Yufik explained. "The problem is that the person often doesn't recognize that they have a serious problem. It's oftentimes the people around them who will typically bring that person in. It's very rare for an individual to come on their own."

While this is admittedly speculative, it appears Yufik may have under-diagnosed Cherie in his assessment that her mental health issues were limited to a paranoid personality disorder. Yufik said he spent ten hours over two days interviewing her. He gave her an IQ test that revealed an average score. He interviewed her son and read the clinical social worker's report. Had he interviewed those who worked closely with her over a period of years, Yufik might have uncovered another version of her mental health—a blatant and embarrassing sexual fixation that she openly bragged about. This from four people—all women:

At Strong Family Health:

Her moral and ethical standards were very skewed. When we were at a youth campout at Blue Lake she had weird and disgusting photos that she would bring out and show me as if I thought they would be funny. They were not funny and were totally inappropriate to have at a youth activity. I was not amused, but she thought they were funny.

A RISE volunteer:

I know that Cherie bought her son, Jack, a fur jock strap and she was accused of grabbing the security guard at Strong Family by the balls and then flashed him her boobs by lifting up her shirt. At a meeting, she complained that she didn't eat fish because it smelled like a woman's vagina. Basically, she was constantly involved in sexual harassment.

Another:

When Cherie hooked back up with Jack's father, Jack Stockton Sr., he had erectile dysfunction. Or, at least he could not meet Cherie's pretty vocal demands about her sexual wants. About the time she was getting more tattoos, she drove Jack Sr. around to finally have him get the implant. She was quite proud of the fact she could have sex on demand.

Yes, she would dye her hair for a statement or team support. Purple was Modoc High's team color. I have not ever heard any suggestion of lesbian. She liked to shock.

When Cherie talked about "men are only good for sex" or Jack Sr.'s implant and sex on demand, I was not listening for any recall. With that talk her attire became more revealing, as she is busty, but it seemed her intent was more to reveal her tattoos. The last few social interactions around Cherie were conscientiously shortened on my part, not for the actual language and content of her conversation or for how loud she was but her energy drained the space. Her eyes were the most piercing and darting when she laughed, which was quite often without humor but as though nothing was serious to her. She would hone in to control the conversations around her. A few times Cherie was despondent and the dramatic change created a sense of sadness for me. Sadness of concern for her, but not enough to venture close to inquire how things were.

Sadly, her behaviors were not so unfamiliar to my experiences growing up. I am pretty good at "deadpan" without contributing or judging. A few people asked me what I would do if she hit me and I just said, "I know a mean crotch kick" and that ended it.

A former Rancheria administrator:

Those are good examples of her behavior.

My intent is not to propose a formal diagnosis or arrive at a clinical conclusion about Cherie's mental health. However, the observations about behavior patterns speak to her need to dominate. It can also be argued that her behavior patterns reflect a form of disconnect from reality. This raises the question, Is this evidence of compulsive social behavior and hypersexual addiction? Was she actually displaying what are called "comorbid traits"? Examples of comorbid traits are multiple conditions such as severe anxiety, aggression, suspicion and paranoia, eccentricity, or obsessive behavior. When these traits overlap in a psychological disorder, it is possible that the clinician might be misrecognizing a primary psychiatric disorder and under-diagnosing the patient.

"Poor recognition of comorbid conditions may be related to the way in which clinicians diagnose their patients," according to a psychiatric study. "Psychiatric evaluation is often directed toward identifying a single diagnosis that will account for all or most of a patient's symptoms, rather than identifying multiple conditions."

Cherie's aggressiveness and volatility could possibly peg her for Bipolar 1 or Schizoaffective disorder, slightly below schizophrenia in severity. Both conditions involve recurring bouts of mania. The question remains: was Cherie having a psychotic episode driven by anxiety, paranoia, and thought disorder leading up to the murders?

Such personality disorders have their beginnings in genetics—from mother to daughter, for example. Had there been in-depth diagnoses, anti-psychotic medications could have kept her from having manic-psychotic episodes. However, there was no evidence she was taking anti-psychotic medications

On the morning of the fourth day of the trial Cherie took the stand in her own defense. Before she was questioned by Alvarez, Judge Beason spoke to a gallery of witnesses, friends, and relatives of victims.

"I know that this may be difficult for some of you, perhaps all of you, but I'm going to ask each of you to do your very best to not visually react. Unfortunately, I've had the situation where members of the public have shouted out during a court proceeding. I don't expect that from you. If you feel like you're not able to do that, then quietly get up and leave the courtroom. Everybody clear on that one?" Once, in the absence of the audience and jury, Judge Beason told Funk she was concerned with Russo's behavior—he was consistently staring at Rhoades. Funk admonished Russo outside the courtroom and there were no problems after that.

Alvarez led Cherie through her background: she turned forty-seven the day after the trial began. She was a high school dropout, the youngest of five brothers and sisters. She had a child out of wedlock, married when she was thirty to a man forty-one years her senior. Moved to the Cedarville Rancheria in 1993 and registered as a member of the Northern Paiutes. Her half-brother Rurik moved to the Rancheria the following year. Their relationship soured when he tried to disenroll their mother.

"He became chairperson, and my mother and my brother Eugene and I are the only three that didn't vote for him so he was mad. At that time he tried disenrolling my mother from the tribe," she told the court.

"And what happened with that?" Alvarez asked.

"Duanna Knighton was our administrator at the time, and I asked her, I says, 'Does he realize if he disenrolls his mother, he disenrolls himself?' Because he was under the impression if he disenrolls her, he would get rid of my brother Eugene and I. And so she explained that to him and he goes, 'Oh, well, we can't do that then, can we?' It kind of hurt my mom's feelings, you know."

"What about your feelings?" Alvarez asked.

"When my mother's feelings get hurt, it doesn't make me very happy," she answered matter-of-factly.

"Anything happen, any confrontations, or ugliness occur?"

"We would argue over tribal stuff. We have rules, regulations, and we also have a Constitution that we have to follow. And everybody— him and I interpreted them in a different way."

"Now, these arguments, just describe them for us."

"It got to the point where we needed to have a person like the officer over here sitting off to the side to get us to shut up and sit down," she answered pointing to a uniformed court bailiff.

"Any of your confrontations become physical?"

"The year that he was going for chairperson, we had a housing meeting, and we were at a house that was empty. And we were discussing the application of the person that wanted to go in, and because of the housing rules I was saying that she couldn't have her adult son in there with her. He was arguing with me until he reached over the counter, grabbed me by my ponytail, and drug me over the eating counter to the floor. He sat on my chest, and was bending my fingers backwards to where I had rings on and my shanks actually broke on my rings."

"Is that the incident that Jack Stockton said you ended up in the hospital?"

"Yes."

She related the sequence of events that led to her killing the four: embezzlement charges, suspension as the tribe's chair of the executive committee, loss of quarterly "casino" payments, being banned from the tribe's offices in Alturas. It became apparent that most of the tribe's thirty-five members lived in Oregon and were not residents of the Rancheria. Those living off the Rancheria received only medical benefits and did not share in the quarterly casino payments. At the time of the murders an estimated fourteen adult members of the tribe were eligible for casino money. Nearly all of them were from the Lash family.

"Now, I guess with a small number, if that number decreases, does that mean the money received by the other remaining parties increases?" Alvarez asked.

"Yes."

She said it was not unusual for her to have loaded guns in her possession. She routinely carried loaded guns in her car whenever she drove her mother along the desolate Highway 447 route to Reno. She was afraid her truck might break down and somebody would try to attack her. "I'm not going to sit down there and tell them to wait until I load my gun." She asked Richard Lash and Jacob Penn to clean her handguns before the killings because she planned to test-fire them the day her eviction appeal was heard. Contrary to Jacob Penn's identifying one of the 9mm handguns as the same one she used in the murders, she said she couldn't remember. She didn't know which guns she had asked be cleaned. As it turned out, she didn't test-fire the handguns. One of them jammed as she pulled the trigger at the murder scene. Navigating her closer to the afternoon she "snapped," Alvarez asked if she knew who was trying to get her evicted and thrown out of the tribe.

"Do you have any thoughts or suspicions as to who was trying to get you evicted?"

"Oh, I did."

"And how did you come to whatever it is you believed?"

"Oh, he was happy to let me know it was him."

"Him?"

"Rurik. That it was him that started it."

"Started what? The eviction or the suspension or both?"

"When I asked about the eviction, it was him."

She went back to the scene during the telephonic hearing. The scene when she told Judge Lenzi, "You're supposed to be able to appeal to the community council 'cause three people shouldn't have the right to tell people they need to move." And the judge asked, "Where is that in tribal law?"

Alvarez plunged into the debate over tribal law. "Now, you had an appeal at some point. Did you get notice of another hearing the following day?"

"You have to understand our appeal process," she began. "I asked for the next appeal because there's actually three appeals. And I was told by Melissa Davis that that was our one and only appeal that we already, you know, gave up the other appeals, and we didn't."

How Cherie believed she was entitled to three appeals was not explained. The tribe's enrollment ordinance stated in its disenrollment clause that there is only one opportunity for appealing a decision by the executive committee. There was no provision in the enrollment ordinance for evictions. The constitution, separate from the enrollment ordinance, makes no mention of rules governing eviction of members.

"Did you get notice of another hearing at the Rancheria offices in Alturas?"

"They already had that set up a week before, and that was to do the actual eviction."

"How did you know that?"

"Because they let us—well, I'm not sure if they let us know or if it was Richard because Richard is still at the office. He's my other nephew."

"Richard Lash?"

"Yes."

"Now, did—at what point were you notified that there was a hearing on the twentieth and that your presence, I guess, was required?"

"I think it was the following Friday or something. I mean, the previous Friday."

"So you knew you had a hearing on the nineteenth and the twentieth?"

"Well, no. The nineteenth, they called us and said you want— because we told them, you know, we haven't had our appeal yet, and they already sent us out this—you know, that we're going to have this other thing going on the twentieth. And I said, 'We haven't had our appeal yet.' And they said, 'Fine. Come the day before.' So that's why we went on the nineteenth."

"For the appeal?"

"Uh-huh."

"And then you came back on the twentieth ?" Alvarez asked.

"Yes, I did."

"And for what purpose?"

"No purpose at all."

No purpose at all, she told the court. Like her son who saw no need in attending the eviction enforcement hearing on the unexplained advice of an unknown attorney, she saw no need to go to a meeting that would determine whether or not she kept her home.

"So I was debating on going or not, and actually I didn't decide to actually go until Richard called."

"This is Richard Lash?"

"He called us, and we were at Subway. Richard called and he says that they hired a judge. I didn't see any point in going back over there if they already have it planned, you know. They're going to give us our decision from the housing committee that day too." When she learned the tribe had hired a judge she said she changed her mind and decided to go to the hearing. "My way of thinking is if they hired a judge, maybe the judge will understand that they're not going by the policies, that they're doing wrong."

"So what were your actual plans then for the twentieth of February, 2014?" Alvarez asked.

"My actual plan was I was going to hop, skip, and alou over to Reno to pick up my money from Donny, and plus I had this—I had an idea that if I won the case and got to stay in my house, it was only going to be temporary before they decided to do it again," she said. Donny, Angel's brother, was a nephew with a prison record who owed her money and she was afraid he might spend it before she could get it back.

"Decided to try to evict you?"

"Try to evict me again. So, you know, I was just fed up with it."

Alvarez asked if she had any plans for the 9mm handguns she owned. She said she intended to sell two of them and keep a third that was a Mother's Day gift. "That's why I was going to test-fire them the day before because I never fired either of them."

"But you never did test-fire them on the nineteenth?"

"No. I had them all ready to go. I loaded them, stuck them in the safe. I was going to come back after the meeting on the nineteenth, go up on the hill with Richard and Jacob, go test-fire them. And after the meeting went the way it did, I already knew what was going to happen. You know, I was irritated. It was late. By the time I got back home, I just never went up there."

"But on the twentieth did you get the guns?"

"Yeah. I grabbed the guns because I was going to take them over to Reno."

"And how did you transport them or what did you do with those guns?"

"Stuck them in my pockets."

"What were you wearing?"

"Shorts."

"So, just in your pants pockets?"

"Yeah. I had real deep pockets."

"One gun in each side . . ."

"Uh-huh."

"Left and right?"

"Uh-huh." Her reply was so soft and difficult to hear that the judge asked if she had answered yes. Then Alvarez also asked if her answer was yes.

"Yes. Sorry. Yes," Rhoades said.

Then she described waiting in the vacant lot across the street from the tribe's offices. She was carrying a black backpack. Inside the backpack was a notepad with "eviction meeting 2/20/14 bunch of bull shit!!!" written on it. There was also a notarized letter giving her home at 101 Rancheria Way to Donny Torres, as of February 18. Questioned by Alvarez, she testified that her home was to be given to Donny if she lost it and was evicted. Her plan was if she lost the home and Donny now owned it, she could always come back and stay with him. Hang out, she said. She couldn't be evicted from a home she no longer owned. Now, she had been waiting outside the tribe's offices and was finally told by Richard Lash that the executive committee was ready for her.

"What was the first thing you did when you walked into the meeting room?" Alvarez asked.

"Well, while I was sitting out waiting all that time, they had the windows open over there, and you can hear them talking and laughing, you know. And I was thinking, 'If this here is supposed to be a court hearing and not open to the public because our meetings aren't for public that, you know, you might want to shut those windows.'"

"It wasn't because you were cold or anything like that?"

"Oh, no. It wasn't cold that day, not really. That's why I was in shorts."

"And while you were waiting outside in the parking lot you could hear what was going on inside the meeting room?"

"Yeah. And I was already all the way across the street, and I have a hard time hearing anyways. I could hear talking. I couldn't understand it from that far away, but I could hear them when they were laughing, you know, really loud."

"Was there a lot of laughing that you heard?"

"Well, yeah."

She remembered talking with Lenzi, trying to explain the tribe's policies. She couldn't remember the phrase *unlawful detainer*. She didn't know what that was and said she still didn't know. And she said she and Jack were denied their appeal process.

"Were you getting frustrated at that meeting?" Alvarez asked.

"Yes, she [the judge] didn't know what she was talking about because they just hired her, and she was getting dates wrong, and what happened on that date wrong. I was trying to tell her, 'You're wrong. It happened on this day.' That she was saying, 'You know, it happened this day.' Well, no it happened this date."

"And so as the meeting was going on, how were you starting to feel?"

"I was flustrated," she told the court, elegantly conflating *flustered* and *frustrated*.

"Then what happened?"

"After the second time of trying to explain to her that we have appeals processes that we were denied, I looked over at Rurik, and there he was, arms crossed with a smug on his face."

"Arms crossed across his chest?"

"Yep. Smug on his face, doing this again to me," and she demonstrated that he was nodding his head up and down.

"So nodding his head up and down?"

"And I went over to him, and he just smiled at me, and like this, you know," and she again demonstrated Rurik's smiling at her.

"I'm sorry, when you said 'like this'?"

"Well, like he was going to get up, you know, confront me, I guess."

"So he put his hands on the table?"

"Yes."

"And was it a motion of pushing up?"

"Yes."

"Pushing up?"

"Yes."

"Then what happened?"

"I talk with my hands a lot. Whenever he wants to try to get me in trouble and I'm talking with my hands, he always sits there and goes, 'You're being aggressive.' So I stuck my hands in my pockets because if I don't, he's going to sit there and say I'm being aggressive. And when I stuffed my hands in my pockets, that's when I felt the guns. I forgot they were even in there. They—it wasn't—they weren't there for any reason. I forgot they were there in the process of arguing with the judge, and I felt them."

"Then what happened?"

"I just wanted him to stop smiling, you know, get the smug smile off his face. So I pulled one out, and I stuck it at him."

"With your right hand you pulled one of the guns out?"

"Yes."

"Do you remember which gun you pulled out first, if you remember?"

"I don't know which one it was for sure."

"So you pulled out a gun and extended it towards Rurik?"

"Yes."

"So what part of his body did you point the gun to?"

"At his face."

"And why did you do that?"

"To get the smile off of it."

"What were you planning to do?"

"Nothing really. I wasn't planning nothing. I just wanted him to stop smiling, and when I pointed at him, he stopped smiling."

"Then what happened?"

"After that I couldn't even tell you really."

"What do you mean?"

"I don't—I don't remember any gunshots. I don't—I don't remember anything after that really."

"You don't?"

"Not really. I remember pointing at him. I don't know if somebody might have said something because I think I, like, turned this way, and I don't know if somebody said something or somebody—I don't know, but that's all I know."

"Well, you've—you heard the audio of what happened. You've seen the video of what happened. Doesn't that jog your memory at all?"

"I heard that there was a baby in there. I didn't know there was a baby in there so it freaked me out because I would never hurt a baby, any children, and . . ."

"Did you go into that conference room with the intention of shooting people?"

"No."

"Did you bring guns to the Cedarville Rancheria office with intent of using them?"

"No."

"How—what do you feel about, you know, what occurred, what you did?"

"I—I wish we could turn back time, but we can't."

"Did you intend to shoot and kill Rurik Davis, Glenn Calonico, Sheila Russo, and Angel Penn?"

"I didn't intend to shoot anybody."

"But you know that you did?"

"It was on the video so, yeah."

"Thank you. Nothing further."

There was a fifteen-minute recess and then Funk began his cross examination. Cherie's demeanor instantly changed. She was evasive, cagey, wily, and argumentative. She deflected questions, protested a poor memory, threw words back at Funk rather than answering his questions, and sidestepped him whenever she could.

Funk began with the hiring of Sheila Russo, the firing of Erin Stockton, the allegations of embezzlement and the tribal roles of Cherie's nephew Glenn Calonico and nieces Monica and Melissa. She denied knowing that Calonico was on the housing committee. She said she was not close to Monica and Melissa. She repeated her motive for signing over her home to her nephew Donny. Said she was moving her firearms, including the 9mm handguns, from her home in case he came to stay there. Rather than having a recall of the killings, she deferred to the incriminating audio-video of the killings. Edging closer to the prelude to the mass murders, Funk asked if she remembered her disagreement with Judge Lenzi.

"Do you remember in the meeting when you told Judge Lenzi . . ."

"That we didn't have time to hire a lawyer."

"Do you remember that?"

"I heard it on the audio, yes."

"Do you remember what she said?"

"No."

"This is a complaint, an unlawful detainer, so this is just a first hearing, if you need more time, then we can talk about that," Funk said, quoting Judge Lenzi before the shooting started.

"Yes."

"So she offered you more time potentially. That was still an open possibility; correct?"

"Yes."

"And . . ."

"I guess."

"And you never got to the resolution of whether you were going to get more time because you shot up the place?"

"No. I think it was after that that I told her that there was other avenues that they didn't let us go to. She asked if I agreed with the fact that I had all of my, um . . ."

"Appeals," Alvarez interjected.

"Appeals, yes, if I received all my appeals."

Cherie brushed off Funk's questions about who in the tribe might have sided with Rurik in favor of her eviction, saying "it didn't really matter." She was indifferent about how she got along with her nieces. She was vague when she answered questions on owning guns or selling them. Had she previously carried firearms into the tribal office? At times she tried to throw questions back at Funk. That was when he abruptly and bluntly shifted his indirect approach. Did she think anyone suspected she would kill her own family? Would anyone suspect she would kill Angel Penn who was holding her newborn baby? Was she glad she killed her half-brother? Was she sorry?

"You're glad you killed him, aren't you? Come on. Let's be honest," Funk challenged her. It was a calculated attempt. Was she remorseful?

"You want to be honest?"

"Yes."

"About Rurik?"

"Yes."

"After years and years of constantly, constantly having to watch myself with him, you know, I used to be stressed out a lot. And, honestly, this stress is gone."

"After killing him the stress is gone?"

"After knowing that he can't come after me no more for whatever, yeah, I guess the stress is gone."

"He can't mess with you in the tribe. There's no more drama between you and him. The stress is gone?"

"Yes."

"You're glad you killed him?"

"Not really."

"Well, the stress—"

"I wished that it was totally different with us like it was when we were younger."

"That's a different question. You're wishing that things could go back the way they were when you were kids."

"I wish everything could have been totally different and changed, yeah."

Remorse. Both Alvarez and Funk pressed her to tell the jury what her innermost feelings were in looking back at the murders. "What do you feel about, you know, what occurred, what you did?" Alvarez delicately asked her. "You're glad you killed him, weren't you? Come on. Let's be honest," Funk pushed less delicately. She wasn't remorseful, she was relieved. Her closest expression of remorse was when she said she wished she could turn back time, but she couldn't. She said the stress in her life was gone. That was not what the jury wanted to hear.

Juries want to hear the convicted say they are sorry. And Cherie was as good as convicted. At judgment time—when the punishment to be decided is the death penalty—the expression of remorse or its absence is complex. Once the jury begins their deliberations under the standard of "justice served" they may ask: does remorse lessen the degree of the crime?

The expression of remorse and its role in court proceedings has been dissected and examined. There is general agreement in the U.S. court system that remorse, or its absence, is allowable evidence. "Yet, there is currently no evidence that remorse can be accurately evaluated in a courtroom," according to a DePaul University College of Law study. For the accused to be remorseful before the court is to ask the court to show mercy. At what phase of a trial is the expression of remorse appropriate—the guilt, penalty, or sentencing phase? Timing is critical. The sentencing phase may be too late. Remorse is allowable but undefined.

There are widely held views by both the courts and juries on remorse and its relevance to guilt and sentencing. Even so, jury and court systems are pre-conditioned by the repetitive and public exposure demanding remorse in all forms. Admitting to a crime or being found guilty of a crime is not enough. Self-condemnation is the kind of remorse or self-humiliation that jurors want to hear. Cherie failed to express remorse or to beg the mercy of the court.

Mental illness is the exception. How is remorse measured in someone with a mental disorder? The role of forensic psychiatrists, such as Dr. Yufik, is gaining greater relevance in the courts but raises questions. Could a diagnosed paranoid personality disorder cause a lack of remorse? Can a mentally ill person express sincere remorse? If she was sorry when all she wanted was to escape punishment, was she truthful? To ask if a person is remorseful is a turning point in a criminal trial. For Cherie to say the stress was gone was as far as she could go toward being remorseful.

"So was it just a coincidence that the only time—the only time you brought loaded handguns into the tribal office you ended up shooting a bunch of people including the brother you hated? Is that just a coincidence?" Funk went on.

"Is it a coincidence that I shot him?"

"No. Was it a coincidence that all of those factors came together at that one moment, because you said you didn't plan it?"

"I didn't plan it. And if you remember the day before their attorney says that Rurik was patting us down and checking us."

"Do you remember that?"

"Do you think that I thought that I was going to get away with having a gun in my pocket?" she countered.

"Yes, I do."

"Why would they not pat me down on the twentieth?"

"Because you had the guns in the backpack."

"They were in my pocket. Even if they were—even if they were—let's assume they were in the backpack, but they weren't, okay, when you pat somebody down, do you not search their bag?"

"They didn't search anything other—the day before."

"I didn't have a bag the day before."

"That's right. And you didn't commonly bring a backpack, why would they search it?"

"Isn't that like protocol usually when you're searching people for weapons, you would search what they're carrying too?"

"Probably, yeah. Do you think anyone suspected you would murder your own family?" and Funk changed the subject.

"Why did they suspect it the day before?" she answered back.

"Do you think anyone suspected you would shoot Angel Penn with a small baby in her arms?"

"I didn't even know Angel was there."

"You knew she had a small baby?"

"Like two days before my dad told me she did have a baby, yes."

"You put a bullet right through her chest."

"I didn't see Angel in the room."

"Ma'am, you're skilled with a firearm. You can hit a target?"

"I didn't say how far away."

"You put two bullets behind the ear of Sheila Russo. You heard the testimony?"

"Okay."

"You put another bullet right between Rurik Davis's eyes. You heard that testimony?"

"Okay."

"You put eight or nine rounds—eight rounds in Glenn Calonico."

"Okay."

"Just a coincidence that you shot Angel when you didn't know she was there?"

"I didn't know she was there. When I seen that video, which honestly is kind of blurry because I don't have glasses on, I seen people on that video I didn't even know that was in the room. I wasn't focusing on who was over here. I was focusing on that telephone. I was focusing on the attorney. I was focusing on Rurik. I was focusing on the telephone where the judge was."

While Funk was setting up a re-run of the video tape he asked a series of questions about events leading up to the shootings. Why didn't she sit down on the chair? Was she at the meeting to defend herself against eviction? She stood over the table and made eye contact with everyone. She put her hands in her pockets and realized for the first time the guns were there.

"How is it that you remember everything before the shooting and nothing else? How is that?" Funk asked her.

"I don't know what to tell you," she answered. "I don't remember anything."

It was an interesting lull in cross examination. Now Funk's motive was not to elicit incriminating testimony but to impact the jury with the repetitive playing of the video that graphically captured the murders. The rhythmic cries of Angel's frightened five-day-old baby were mesmerizing. Funk frequently stopped the video during the trial to ask questions before starting again—at times enlarging the image on the screen. Judge Beason advised spectators that if they wanted to leave the courtroom they should do so before the video started.

"I want to ask you one more question before we start the video. Do you remember stating several times when you were being taken into custody that you had cut the head off the snake, and you had told them if they messed with you . . ."

"No."

". . . you don't remember that?"

"No. I do not remember anything about snakes. I don't remember a lot of it."

"Well, Rurik kind of was a snake as far as you were concerned, wasn't he?"

"I guess so, yeah."

"And he was the head of the tribe, wasn't he?"

"If you want to put it metaphorically, yes, at the time."

When it came to the critical moment in the telephone exchange between Cherie and Lenzi, the tribal judge, Cherie said she believed if the judge would hear her out it would be clear the tribe was going against housing policy. To discredit Lenzi, she said she had doubts because the judge had just been hired that morning. She said she didn't bring the supporting housing policies with her because she didn't need to—she knew them.

"You didn't think that maybe you could cite those housing policies and read them to the court?" Funk asked.

"She was just hired—"

"That's not what—"

"—that day. I didn't know she had the housing policies, and the way that she talked, she didn't know a lot about the policies."

"But you didn't know that when you came to court?"

"I knew that she was just hired because Richard told me she was just hired."

"But you didn't know how much she knew about the case?"

"Well . . ."

"For example . . ."

"If she was just hired that afternoon, I didn't know, you're right, but the housing policies, they have their own policies. You can just sit there and go through them. It's not that big of a policy. And there are separate policies. One for non-ownership and one for ownership."

"But you didn't bring those to your court hearing?"

"No."

With the video image on the screen showing Cherie at the conference table moving ever closer to her half-brother, Funk shifted from the housing policy to questioning her about the handguns. He repeatedly questioned her about the placement of her hands. She denied she was already holding a gun in each hand deep in the pockets of her shorts, countering that she had her hands on her hips. Funk replayed the scene four times, said he would show the scene again during closing arguments.

To expand the visual impact of the video, Funk continued: "You shot him right between the eyes, didn't you? And then you see yourself immediately going to the left and shooting Glenn Calonico? You shot Glenn Calonico eight times. Let's just watch a little more. It won't take long. Was it just a coincidence that you put two rounds to the back of the skull of Sheila Russo? When does the silver Lorcin end up jamming on you? You don't remember Glenn putting his foot up to try to protect himself? You would agree with me from the video this is a very traumatic event, isn't it? I'm going to start the video again. That's when your handgun jammed, isn't it, the Lorcin? Do you agree that's the silver handgun in your hand right there? I want to start the video again. I'm going to start it. Can you see it clearly? Now, do you agree that right there the video appears to show your right hand raised with something in it? Do you see the flash of something silver? I'm going to start that again. Let me try and stop it. You see the flash of something silver just then in your right hand?" And for the jury's benefit Funk said the flash of silver was a butcher knife. Judge Beason called for a lunch break.

Funk reopened his cross examination by first playing the audio segment of the murder tape. The dominant sound the jury heard was not the firing of the handguns but the unremitting crying of Angel's frightened baby—cries as regular as a heartbeat. During the trial Funk frequently played the audio without the video. The two systems had recorded the murders separately. Synchronizing the audio and the video must have been challenging for Funk. At times he came across like the fumbling television detective Columbo. Professing a lack of technical skills, Funk frequently asked the judge to bear with him for just a moment while he made various adjustments. Cherie asked him to turn up the sound. Funk said the volume was as high as it could go. When he stopped the video he paused before turning off the audio, letting it run a moment or two in dramatic conclusion. The entire episode was a staged return to the question of remorse.

"Do you remember telling Dr. Yufik that you felt little remorse at the thought of your brother's death?" Funk asked. It was the last question he asked her.

"I remember telling him much of nothing," she replied.

On redirect Alvarez asked essentially one question: Did she ever walk into the tribal office carrying a gun? She said it was possible. Did she ever carry guns to tribal council meetings. She said no, because the meetings went on for hours. This was the last time Cherie testified.

The first case of a woman ever tried for mass murder in the United States was on its way to being decided by a jury of eight women and four men. The trial ended on a Thursday afternoon. Winter weather was closing in on Interstate Highway 80, the fast track freeway to Lake Tahoe skiing and the gaming tables of Reno. Judge Beason lived in Reno. She held off reading the jury instructions until Monday, December 19. She told the jurors to drive safely.

Back in court after the weekend break, Judge Beason gave instructions to the jury, including how they should weigh Cherie's paranoid personality disorder.

"You have heard evidence that the defendant may have suffered from a mental disorder. You may consider this evidence only for the limited purpose of deciding whether at the time of the charged crime the defendant acted with the intent or mental state required for that crime. The People have the burden of proving beyond a reasonable doubt that the defendant acted with the required intent or mental state, specifically, malice, aforethought, premeditation, and deliberation. If the People have not met this burden, you must find the defendant not guilty of murder and attempted murder."

Funk in his summation held the Taurus in front of the jury. He told them not to worry—there was no ammunition in the semi-automatic's twenty-five-bullet magazine. "She wants us to believe that she didn't know the guns were in her pockets. Are you kidding?"

As a motive for killing, he reminded the jury that all Cherie's benefits except medical were taken away. Her tribal quarterly stipend estimated at between $60,000 and $80,000 annually was suspended. The tribe was moving to evict her. She was not allowed to attend any meetings. She was not allowed to participate in any tribal functions. He replayed the tape of the murders—the audio-video simultaneously for several minutes—stressing that everyone injured or killed wanted Cherie out of the tribe: Rurik Davis, Sheila Russo, Angel Penn, Glenn Calonico, Melissa Davis, and Monica Davis.

He dismissed Dr. Yufik's testimony, telling the jury: "She seemed to act like she has a paranoid personality disorder, but there's no question at all she was able to form the intent, and there's no issue that her disorder made her act rashly or impulsively. This had been building for a long time, and that's why she said, 'They brought it down on themselves.'"

As for the black backpack, Funk admitted, "I can't prove to you that she brought the firearms in her backpack. Although it is odd she would bring the backpack in to carry a piece of paper and a notepad."

In his final statements to the jury Funk argued the murders were clearly premeditated, proven by the fact she had no remorse.

"I want you to think about that for a moment, ladies and gentlemen," Funk began. "If this had been some situation of spontaneous combustion where she happened to have side arms in her pockets and she overreacted, don't you think you would see a scintilla of remorse from her in this courtroom?

"She got a little bit emotional when she cried about harming a baby. No baby was harmed in this case. The baby's mother was. She exhibited no remorse or compunction about killing her sister's daughter, about wanting to kill Brandi Penn. No remorse. Why is that? She testified that with Rurik gone, her angst and her level of emotional upset was ratcheted way, way down. Doesn't that support the idea she planned this? She premeditated, she thought about it, she weighed the consequences. This is a classic mass shooting event. She armed herself. She had a captive victim audience who had nowhere to go, no place to run, no place to hide. Don't you think she knew the video was on? Don't you think she knew she was being taped? Of course she did. She didn't care. She said, 'You guys have gone too far, you've crossed the Rubicon.'" Funk hoped the jury knew the story of Julius Caesar's crossing the River Rubicon and inciting a war with the Roman Senate. Cherie thought her tribe had gone too far. It had passed the point of no return.

Alvarez countered point by point. He argued that Cherie was provoked, that there was an "explosion of pent-up provocation, hostility, having to fight for everything, having her own family take everything away." As for the backpack? It also held a sanitary pad because she had a weak bladder. She was in the women's room for three minutes, "about the approximate time it will take to do your business."

He gave considerable effort to defending Dr. Yufik's testimony. "Mr. Funk did what he could to undermine Dr. Yufik, but what Dr. Yufik gave us was a scenario where it's possible that she acted rashly and impulsively based on science. It is very reasonable that the provocation was there over the years. The reasonable conclusion is due to her mental disorder, she did not carefully weigh the considerations for and against her actions."

In an attempt to turn Funk's dramatic use of the incriminating video of the murders to the benefit of the defense, Alvarez asked the jury to look at the video again. "One of the first human reactions you have is, 'That's just crazy. That's just . . . what is going on in that video?' You say that realizing these were not the actions of somebody who carefully deliberated, who carefully weighed the considerations for and against her actions. What I submit to you, ladies and gentlemen, is that based on the evidence, based on the law, it's a reasonable conclusion that Ms. Rhoades did not, because of her mental disorder, did not carefully weigh the considerations."

He concluded with a plea for second degree murder.

"There's just no getting around just how tragic the situation is. There's no getting around a lot of horribly, horribly bad decisions were made by Ms. Rhoades. Frankly, by a lot of the other people in this case. And she walked in there. Should she not have had the gun? Absolutely she shouldn't have had the guns. She had them. But she walked in there, you know, thinking, 'Maybe I've got a shot,' and again you know that based on what's in her backpack, based on the notarized document. You know that she was frankly getting railroaded. You heard it. You hear it from the video. And again, imagine facing a murder charge, four murder charges with the associated consequences, and yet you feel less stressed by that prospect than you were when you were dealing with the tribe, when you were dealing with getting booted out, when you were dealing with just the daily hostility and challenge. That's provocation, and provocation makes this a second degree case."

With that, and after a few additional jury instructions from Judge Beason, it was time for lunch.

At 1:47 p.m. the eight-woman, four-man jury sequestered. At 3:33 p.m., after appointing a foreman, going over the judge's instructions, reading and discussing the verdict forms, and finally deliberating, the jury was back in court with its decision. For a tense twenty minutes the court clerk read aloud each of the verdicts and findings: Cherie was guilty of all charges—four counts of first degree murder, two counts of attempted murder, lying in wait, premeditation, and special circumstances in the use of firearms causing great bodily injury or death.

The next decision facing the jury was did she deserve execution or life in prison without the chance of parole. That judgment would come after the penalty trial started on January 3, 2017.

31

TWO OF FUNK'S EYEWITNESSES, Hedi Bogda and Nikki Munholand, waged an aggressive campaign against him before and during the trial. Munholand wrote Funk a letter demanding he take himself off the case. The two staged a social media crusade against him, and he had calls from the tribal judge Patricia Lenzi.

"What Ms. Munholand did not understand was that the tribe and the persons present in the courtroom were not my clients," Funk said later. "My client was the People of the State of California in Modoc County. You don't just get to kiss off a case to the Attorney General's Office because a victim or witness demands it. Frankly, I couldn't have cared less personally about the criticism on social media. What I cared about was that it had the potential to bleed over into the attitudes of other victims and witnesses and the quality of their courtroom testimony and thus had the potential to undermine our attempt to obtain justice for my client—and ultimately, the victims themselves."

Funk confronted Munholand before the trial started, telling her: "Here's the deal. I don't take legal advice from non-lawyers, let alone in a capital case. I am through with you acting like a spoiled, petulant little child because you're not getting your way. You are not my client and I am done with you and your conduct potentially harming our case. Cease and desist." He said she stormed off before he could finish.

"I followed up the encounter with a very firm letter to Munholand, which I also sent to the tribe's lawyer, that I would not take legal advice from her and that her attitude and actions were harming our case and would no longer be tolerated." After receiving the letter Funk said Munholand and Bogda complained on social media that he didn't represent them. They, too, were victims of Cherie's murderous rampage.

"What kind of DA does that?" Funk asked rhetorically. The crime victim is not the client. The law says that a prosecutor who becomes too wedded to the legal position of his victims can be recused for placing the demands of the victims over the pursuit of justice for the actual client. As they got closer to trial the relationship between Funk and Bogda and Munholand got worse.

"Once I told Munholand that she was not in charge of this case, that she and Bogda weren't my clients and I didn't care what they thought, they sort of came around, in a grudging sort of way." Several months before the first trial started Funk was in contact with Patricia Lenzi, the tribal judge. "She said, 'You know, you're in danger of losing your witnesses.' I told her, 'Yeah, I know and it's a problem of their doing, not mine.'"

He said he more than met the standard of competency and humaneness and decency. "I wasn't unkind to anyone. What it came down to was Bogda's desire for control and dominance. I thought she had some sort of psychological need for me to grovel and for her to be able to exert control over the case. That was not going to happen because it wouldn't help us obtain justice."

Funk continued. "Living out of a motel while you try a murder case is not optimal, but I came to appreciate that the case had been venued to Placer County. Potential jurors there would be much less likely to learn what Munholand and Bogda were saying on social media. The potential negative impact upon our case by Bogda and Munholand was greatly reduced."

32

FUNK WAS IN A fender bender on his way to Roseville. The start of
the penalty trial was the next morning. He was nursing a scratchy
throat. He waved his opening statement, admitting, "Frankly, I don't
have anything earth shattering to say." Alvarez also waived his opening statement.

Judge Beason told the jury the penalty phase was not the time for
the mass murder survivors and affected family to express their opinions on what the penalty should be. That decision was reserved for
the jury. Life or death.

Funk called nine witnesses. Alvarez declined to cross-examine any
of them. One after the other, witnesses told of their nightmares, dis-
trust of strangers, anxiety, depression, loss of self-worth, paranoia,
PTSD, and need for psychiatric counseling. The loss of Rurik Davis
meant the loss of their tribal culture. Tribal Judge Patricia Lenzi said
every time she read or heard of a mass murder in the United States she
relived the Cedarville Rancheria killings—specifically, the Orlando
Pulse killings of forty-nine on June 12, 2016, and the wounding of
fifty-eight more. "There was a story about the cell phones ringing
and the police having trouble hearing that," she said, "that made me
relive my nightmare because I was on the phone and the phone was
live through most of it, if not all of the shooting. And when it went
dead I lost connection. I waited a couple of minutes and called back,
and I couldn't reach anyone. I got the voicemail for the tribe. I tried
to call Hedi's phone and I got her voicemail. I texted her and I got
no answer." Lenzi was on the phone for a total of nine minutes. She
could hear crashing sounds which she realized were pistol shots. A
woman cried out and the phone went dead."

Alvarez called four witnesses, and Funk cross-examined them all. Alvarez's first witness was Gina Davis, Cherie's fifty-two-year-old half-sister. Her testimony was via a live feed from the prison hospital. She appeared on a large flat screen that could be seen by everyone in the courtroom. She could only see the judge, who instructed her not to answer any questions if Funk objected to them. If there was an objection, the judge would raise her hand, signaling Gina to stop talking. Gina had been through California's juvenile court system, the California Youth Authority, and state prison. Now she was an inmate patient at Patton State Hospital, a forensic psychiatric hospital in Southern California. She was serving twenty-eight years to life for assault with a deadly weapon. She described herself as schizophrenia bipolar type. Gina told how Cherie was always there for moral support. When Gina wasn't in prison Rhoades was there, to get her off the street, making regular telephone calls to the hospital, writing letters, keeping their family together after the death of their mother, Virginia.

"I love Cherie," she said. "Cherie has always helped me out. She's helped me through the years. I haven't been such a great sister to her by all the trouble that I've been in . . . but she's always been there for me whenever I've called upon her to help me. I have been in trouble on the street. I've been in bad situations. And every time I've called upon her, she has been there to help me every time. I want her in my life."

Alvarez then called Cherie's son Jack. He said his mother's crimes were heinous and grizzly, but the person who did that was not his mother. "That's not who my mom is to me. I know my mother," he told the jury. "There's no other way to explain this unless . . . to where everybody can understand unless they were in my shoes, but I would . . . you know, I would like to see my mom's life spared." But in cross-examination Funk asked Stockton a question that was not asked at the guilt phase of the trial.

"Did you have any conversations with Philip Russo where you said to him, in the presence of your mother, or it was discussed by you and your mother that someone needed to kill Rurik Davis?" Funk asked Stockton.

"No."

"Are you sure about that?"

"I'm sure."

"You didn't notice anything about your mother's behavior in the period leading up to the killings that caused you to be concerned that she wasn't her normal self, did you?"

"As we discussed this before, no, I did not."

Curiously, Funk did not pursue this line of questioning with Stockton, but he asked the court to have Stockton subject to recall. Funk did not recall Stockton. If the jury caught the implied message in Funk's question there was no follow-up.

Dr. Alex Yufik took the stand a final time for the defense. He illustrated Cherie's emotional welfare and psychological development. He described how well integrated she was into her society, her impulse control, her ability to act out or restrain impulses and emotions.

Dr. Yufik said he thought Cherie's mental illness amounted to an extreme emotional disturbance. "This is going back to what occurred during the tribal council, and the idea that a person is directed by their feelings, not by their thoughts. In other words, they're not thinking in terms of what's the best kind of outcome? What can I do in order to alleviate this type of situation? They're driven by their emotions, which really takes over the intellectual, the thoughtful part of their brain." He said after reviewing the police and autopsy reports, seeing the video of the murders as they systematically took place, listening to the audio dominated by the cries of the baby, nothing changed his analysis that Cherie had a paranoid personality disorder—and that she was capable of impulsively reacting in anger.

Funk continuously referred Yufik to the *Diagnostic and Statistics Manual*, or DSM-5, and quoted from it at length. The DSM-5 classifies mental disorders and is considered an authoritative work by international experts in mental health. He tried to bait Dr. Yufik into agreeing that the DSM-5 was the "bible" for mental health professionals. But Yufik disagreed. He did not consider the DSM-5 a bible in any use of the word. "I have never used that word," Dr. Yufik answered. "The word 'bible' in Latin just means book, and it is a kind of a book, but that is all that it is."

"Would you agree with me," Funk began his question, and again cited the DSM-5, "there's no reference to impulsivity being either a diagnostic criteria or a behavior associated with PPD, paranoid personality disorder?"

The question was aimed directly at discrediting Dr. Yufik's testimony—a critical element in the defense strategy—that Cherie, with paranoid personally disorder, was capable of impulsive behavior and in anger could kill. If impulsivity wasn't in the DSM-5, Funk was arguing, then there was no merit to Dr. Yufik's findings.

"Even as a behavior that is associated with PPD, impulsivity just doesn't show up anywhere, does it?" Funk persisted.

Dr. Yufik stood by his testimony and told Funk, the DSM-5 "is used by people that have advanced professional education, training and experience in order to diagnose someone. The problem comes when people that don't have the requisite education, training and experience simply look at it as a checklist."

"But the fact remains that the DSM and other sources that catalogue the salient features of PPD do not use the word 'impulsivity.' Is that a fair statement?" Funk asked. Later in his questioning he said he couldn't find it on the internet.

"In the *Diagnostic and Statistical Manual*, the word itself, *impulsivity*, is not used, that's correct," Dr. Yufik conceded. But Funk's cross examination drifted away from the issue of impulsivity. It ended with Cherie's history as a victim of child sexual abuse, growing up in poverty, homeless, with an abusive father, marriage to a much older man, and her difficulty in finding a job.

Remorse surfaced in the absence of the jury when the judge and attorneys discussed if it should be in the instructions to the jury and how the attorneys could use it in their arguments. Judge Beason characterized it as "threading a needle delicately in terms of how it's handled. She said she did not intend to instruct the jury on the subject. Would Funk be allowed in his final argument to remind the jury that Cherie showed no remorse? Alvarez pointed out that in one penal code section on the death penalty an absence of remorse is only relevant if it is expressed at the time of the killings—rather than later. Judge Beason cited *People v. Bonilla*, a first degree murder conviction from 1987 and appealed in 2007 to the California Supreme Court. In review of the prosecutor's arguing the use of a lack of remorse in *People v. Bonilla*, the court stated, "The gist of the prosecutor's argument throughout . . . was that because (Steven Wayne) Bonilla had shown no remorse, the jury should take his mitigating evidence, which amounted to a plea for mercy from his family, with a grain of salt, and should be less inclined to grant him mercy. We have consistently approved similar arguments." However, for balance the court also ruled that the absence of remorse could not be used as aggravating evidence.

Judge Beason and Alvarez suggested that Cherie's lack of remorse could sway the jury and give her the death sentence. Except for Funk's final argument before the jury, remorse was never again uttered at the mass murder trial of Cherie Rhoades—not by Judge Beason in her instructions to the jury nor by Alvarez or his associate Serita Rios. But Funk used "remorse" or "lack of remorse" sixteen times in his final statement—an average of once every twenty-two seconds.

"There was a little bit of remorse for the baby. But there was no remorse or compunction whatsoever about killing the baby's mother. That was the striking thing about the defendant's demeanor on the witness stand and throughout the trial is the lack of remorse."

Alvarez closed with a quotation from Hamlet.

"'To be or not to be. That is the question.' When Hamlet gave that soliloquy, he was contemplating death. 'Do I live? Do I die? Do I choose to live and if I do so, whether it is nobler in the mind to suffer the slings and arrows of outrageous fortune, or do I choose death and in dying do I end the heartache and the thousand natural shocks that flesh is heir to.' He didn't know whether death would stop the grief. And he didn't know if death would bring back that loss. He eventually chooses life. And he chooses life partly because he concluded he didn't know if death would cure the heartache. He didn't know if death would stop the grief. I submit to you, ladies and gentlemen, that is the case. Death will not ease the suffering that we've all seen through these past weeks."

The jury went into seclusion on January 5, 2017, at 11:25 a.m. It did not take the customary hour and a half lunch break but returned to the jury room in an hour. At 2:25 p.m. the jury sent this question to the judge: "What happens if we cannot reach a consensus?" Judge Beason estimated that the jury deliberated about one hour and forty minutes. The judge asked that the jury return to the courtroom so that she could answer the question. The jury didn't want to return to the courtroom because they were still deliberating. The question, they said, was meant as a "what if." Beason insisted, saying she had additional instructions to read, so the jury returned to the courtroom.

Judge Beason informed them they should choose a foreperson and try to come to a verdict if possible. Each juror she told them, must decide for herself. A juror should not hesitate to change her mind if she realized she was wrong. "Don't change your mind just because other jurors are in disagreement, do not use the internet or social media or a dictionary. The verdict must be unanimous, not a flip of the coin."

The jury returned to their deliberations at 2:40 p.m. and less than two hours later, at 4:12 p.m., after deliberating less than four hours, they had their verdict. Read by the clerk of the court, the verdict was death. Under the 6th Amendment of the Constitution the jury's word was final. It could not be overturned by the judge even if she disagreed. The silent pause that followed was broken by Judge Beason. She thanked the panel for serving. "I have seen your tears throughout the guilt phase and through the penalty phase. I have felt your tears, and I know that this has been a singular experience for each of you, and so my thoughts and my prayers go with you."

Cherie was the first person sentenced to death under the new provisions of California's "mend not end" Proposition 66, the statewide measure that kept the death penalty alive. But opponents of Prop. 66 filed suit in California's Supreme Court, arguing that the voter-approved proposition unconstitutionally restricted the role of the Supreme Court. Also, a five-year mandatory time limit provision on death penalty cases violated the constitutional rights of death row inmates. In August 2017—about eight months after Rhoades was convicted—the court split five to two upholding the proposition in general but rejecting arguments that the time limit provision could be imposed. The "mend not end" answer to the prolonged appeal system went unresolved, but the death penalty law held—for the time.

The day after the death penalty verdict was announced the local weekly in Alturas published a letter written by Philip Russo. The letter appeared under the head "Justice Is Served."

He did not refer to Cherie by her name. Instead he said he would not use her name. And he reminded readers that his wife, Sheila Russo, was one of the victims in the mass murder of February 2014. Now, he said he was at peace. Still, the death sentence did not bring a final closure. He thanked the people of Alturas and Modoc County for their support and friendship.

33

"I've never encountered the palpable animus against the prosecution from victims and witnesses in a murder case that I experienced in this case—when all we were trying to do is what we were supposed to do—obtain justice," Funk said as he unwound after the two trials.

"I've encountered hostility from Native Americans toward whites before and at a certain level it's completely understandable. The history of the colonization of the new world is the vanquishment of indigenous populations by Europeans and their descendants." Funk believes vanquishing of one people by another is also the history of colonization throughout the world, not unique to America and white settlers. In his opinion, it is contrary to our conception of "justice" to hold a person responsible for the wrongdoings—perhaps—of past generations who happen to have the same skin color and ethnicity of those who went before him.

"After the trial, I wasn't thanked by any of them. I did get criticized. I had one of the Davis girls on the witness stand. At some point, she began having difficulty testifying and paused repeatedly, for a substantial time in her testimony. I said, 'Let's come back to that part of your testimony in a few minutes.' I came back to it, but even then there were long pauses in her testimony where she couldn't find the words she was looking for, where she couldn't express very well what she wanted to say. It was perfectly understandable in the circumstance. I gave her what I thought was a fair and thorough opportunity to explicate the facts that I wanted to bring out through her as a witness. After she testified, she was upset because she said I went too quickly; I moved through her testimony too rapidly and didn't give her a chance to say everything.

"Shelia Russo's husband was always very supportive. He never got involved in any of Bogda's and Munholand's drama and didn't seem to like what they were doing. After the verdict he was very appreciative. He thanked me and Ken Barnes. He's the only one who did.

"My belief is that most if not all of the anti-prosecution animus emanated originally from Bogda, that she negatively influenced Munholand and, to a lesser extent, Monica and Melissa Davis. Absent Bogda, I don't believe Monica or Melissa Davis or Nikki Munholand would have been problematic in the least.

"In my opinion there is a tendency in some, not all, Native Americans to harbor some antipathy toward whites, especially white men in light of American frontier history. It's entirely understandable, though not necessarily excusable. But when you are on the receiving end of that, you find yourself asking, 'Why the hostility toward me personally? What did I do?'"

34

"THE STRONGEST ARGUMENT FOR not seeking death in this case was that the death penalty was arguably dead in California," Funk said. "No pun intended. What's the point of seeking death when she'll never be executed?" Months after the trial and sentencing were over Funk revealed there was another consideration beyond the pros and cons of capital punishment and the expenditure of taxpayers' money.

If Cherie was on death row awaiting execution there were years of appeals ahead of her. Her confinement on death row would be easier than if she was a lifer in the general prison population.

"We had not ruled out the possibility of a plea agreement that avoids death. But one of our struggles was that the Native American victims were very hostile and distrusting of us, as they were of the attorney general and the FBI. Nothing we said or did was ever good enough to satisfy them. This could have some very adverse consequences as to how a jury reacted to the victims."

35

NINE DAYS AFTER CHERIE was convicted and a week before the jury would return to the Roseville court to decide her sentencing, Nikki Munholand stopped to talk with William "Tex" Dowdy. It was that edgy lull between trials. They were leaving a board meeting at Strong Family Health Center. She was the board's chair. Dowdy, a Southern California La Jolla Tribe member, was an ex-officio board member. He was also the Alturas police officer who logged Cherie's black backpack as evidence. Like Munholand he testified for the prosecution at the trial. His boss at the time was Alturas Chief of Police Ken Barnes, who also testified about the backpack.

It's not clear who initiated the conversation, but Munholand and Dowdy spoke privately. Dowdy asked Munholand how the trial went and she told him it had gone well. But she had something else she wanted to tell him. She told Dowdy she suspected Barnes had perjured himself. She believed he had given false testimony about when and where the backpack was discovered. Dowdy's police report documented his personal collection of the backpack exactly five days after Barnes said he first saw it in the conference room. Cherie is seen on the video carrying a black backpack as she enters the conference room. The need to collect the backpack became obvious after Barnes viewed the shooting video. According to Dowdy, Barnes wasn't in town when the backpack was entered into evidence. Munholand and Dowdy concluded that because Barnes was out of town when Dowdy placed the backpack in evidence, there was a contradiction in Barnes's testimony. The conflict, they believed, was over where the backpack was discovered and when. Barnes, they thought, lied under oath.

Intentional or not, Munholand set in motion a bizarre turnabout. She was going on memory alone. She did not inform the district attorney of her suspicion that Barnes lied under oath, nor did she tell the tribe's lawyer. Perhaps she thought Dowdy would report what she told him to his new boss, Sheriff Poindexter. But the sheriff wasn't in charge of the investigation. The lead investigative agency was the Alturas city police department, and Barnes was the chief. Whether Munholand knew it or not, Dowdy and Poindexter's interests differed from hers. It was publicly known that Funk and Poindexter were frequently at odds. "Make no mistake about it, we have a terrible relationship," Poindexter once said. Dowdy took Munholand's speculation of perjury straight to his boss. The sheriff's internal discovery policy required him—especially if he believed he had uncovered the existence of "Brady" evidence—to tell the district attorney. Under the Brady doctrine Poindexter was legally obligated to reveal information or evidence that could upend Barnes's testimony and potentially exonerate Cherie. Poindexter didn't tell Funk, who should have been his normal ally, that he might have discovered new evidence material to Cherie's innocence. Nor did Poindexter tell the civil attorney contracted by the county, or the California attorney general. Instead, Poindexter contacted an attorney he occasionally consulted on personnel and related matters. That attorney then passed the information on to the California attorney general. The deputy attorney general who reviewed Poindexter and Dowdy's allegation knew of the friction between Funk and Poindexter. She decided the accusation that Barnes had perjured himself at the trial was political and without merit. She declined Poindexter's request for intervention.

Instead, Poindexter told Antonio Alvarez, Cherie's defense attorney.

Cherie's date for formal sentencing was April 10, 2017. All that remained for Funk to wrap up a successful prosecution was for Judge Beason to confirm the jury's death verdict. Two weeks before Cherie was formally to hear her death sentence, Poindexter sent the first of a series of letters and emails to Alvarez. Poindexter built an argument against Barnes and by inference Funk. He based his argument on Barnes's testimony establishing the black backpack's chain of custody. The sheriff told Alvarez he didn't know the proper protocol for handling the allegations against Barnes. But the sheriff maintained there was a flaw in Barnes's testimony. He left unanswered why he insisted

Dowdy and Munholand's—and now his own—interpretation of the trial testimony was the opposite of what the jury had heard. Why did the sheriff persist in his counter-interpretation when it could be used to overturn a mass murderer's conviction? The sheriff's answer was, "We're saying this may have occurred, that it appears to us it may have occurred, judging by what we have looked into."

In the interim, Dowdy followed up on February 24, 2017, with his own letter to Alvarez, doubling down on Munholand's belief that Barnes had perjured himself at the trial. Dowdy said his recollection was supported by events following the murders. He said he didn't know what to do with his alleged new information, and he asked the sheriff for advice. The sheriff suggested Dowdy get a copy of the trial transcript. In his letter to Alvarez, Dowdy went on to say, "Upon reviewing the transcripts, Ken Barnes testified that he was present for the location of a black backpack. He testified that I located the backpack in the conference room and that he was present when I found it. Ken Barnes did admit in his testimony that he didn't recall where I found the backpack in the conference room but it . . . was in the conference room. That is simply not true."

On March 16, 2017, less than a month before Cherie's' sentencing, Alvarez filed a motion for a new trial in Modoc County Superior Court. The motion was based on the "grounds that during the guilt phase of the trial Barnes lied, the district attorney committed prejudicial misconduct, new material evidence was recently discovered, and Ms. Rhoades was denied her right to a fair and impartial trial." Barnes may have been the original target, but Funk was now front stage. Alvarez went on to argue: "The defense would not have known that Chief Barnes's testimony was false but for the statements provided to the Modoc County Sheriff's Department and given to the defense after the trial had concluded." The statements he referred to were founded on Munholand's accusation more than three months earlier. Alvarez continued, "The prosecutor went on to have Chief Barnes describe the eviction letter addressed to Ms. Rhoades and read Ms. Rhoades's purported notebook writing—"A bunch of bullshit!!!"—to the jury in an attempt to persuade the jury that Ms. Rhoades was angered and raged over the eviction." According to Alvarez's motion, none of this evidence would have been admitted had Chief Barnes not perjured himself. Without Chief Barnes's testimony the backpack would not have been introduced into evidence. The jury would not have considered this evidence during its deliberation on whether Cherie acted with premeditation and deliberation.

Before Judge Beason ruled on the motion for a new trial, Alvarez said that while Cherie had "already been found guilty, the only issue left is whether she gets death or life without parole. However, if my motion for a new trial is granted then there is the possibility of a plea bargain, at least on my part." Outside the courtroom Alvarez added that he did not believe "Barnes had any reason or intention to lie during his backpack testimony, but was obligated to file his motion because the integrity of the case may have been compromised."

As Cherie's sentencing date drew near, Funk prepared his rebuttal. On April 6, 2017, he ran a small display ad in the local newspaper. Following Cherie's sentencing he would hold a town hall meeting at Modoc High School in response to the claims of Dowdy, Munholand, and Poindexter. The date for the town hall gathering was April 12, two days after Judge Beason was to rule on Alvarez's motion for a retrial and before the anticipated sentencing. Refreshments would be served. Funk invited Poindexter and Dowdy to attend.

Funk set up his PowerPoint presentation at the high school's social hall. About thirty people attended. Poindexter and Dowdy did not. The district attorney refuted their and Munholand's claims that Barnes had perjured himself. Although the backpack was not entered as evidence until five days after the shootings, it was photographed in the conference room immediately following the shootings. Its location was documented in a detailed crime scene drawing by a specialized team of forensic investigators. Lead investigator Barnes testified that he saw the backpack the day after the shooting in the exact location documented by Department of Justice and that Dowdy collected it five days later. Cherie was caught on video carrying it into the conference room before the shooting. The defense attorneys did not interpret Barnes's testimony as conflicting. They did not cross examine him on Munholand and Dowdy's theory of perjury.

"Munholand, Dowdy, and Poindexter willfully misinterpreted and misunderstood Barnes's testimony," Funk said. He reminded the audience that Barnes had disciplined Dowdy after what he called a dust-up in the office of a previous district attorney. The city council upheld the chief's decision and Dowdy resigned. "Poindexter and

Dowdy were predisposed to their misinterpretation because of their anti-Funk and anti-Barnes animosity," Funk explained. "This led to an ignorant, ill-conceived effort in an attempt to overturn a death verdict in a mass murder in the service of their political agenda to embarrass Barnes and myself."

Funk later said, "Munholand failed to consider or comprehend the possibility of an ulterior agenda by Dowdy and Poindexter." At the root of the problem, he said, was her steadfast refusal to accept that he was in charge of the case, not her, not Dowdy, not Poindexter, not Hedi Bogda, the tribe's attorney, or Rurik Davis's daughters. "Munholand put the backpack in the closet after Department of Justice had documented the crime scene," Funk said. "After reviewing the video Barnes realized the backpack was brought in by Rhoades and needed to be collected, so he sent Dowdy back to get it." Barnes testified that he saw the backpack on the conference room floor. His testimony was backed up by the criminalists who photographed it there. What angered him, Funk said, was the sheriff's holding evidence in reserve for two and a half months "and no one said boo to me." If Poindexter and Dowdy were concerned about Barnes's testimony they were required to inform the district attorney instead of sending letters to Alvarez.

As Funk was preparing to expose Poindexter, a half-day National Crime Victims' Rights Week conference was held on April 6, 2017, at the SuAnne Big Crow Center in Pine Ridge, South Dakota. The subject: gun violence in Indian Country. The center is named for SuAnne, a star basketball player for Pine Ridge High School who died in a car accident in 1992 on her way to receiving the "Miss Basketball Award." The U.S. Attorney's Office, the Oglala Sioux Tribe, and the Bureau of Alcohol, Tobacco, Firearms and Explosives were conference sponsors. Munholand and Poindexter were invited to share their stories of survival and the effect the shooting had on their community. Munholand canceled a few days before the conference was to begin. There was no formal explanation for her cancelation. It was well known that the tribe wanted to avoid publicity that would perpetuate their being identified as the "Mass Murder Tribe." There was also speculation that Munholand may have started distancing herself from the county sheriff. Poindexter, who styled himself a "constitutional sheriff" and made numerous public appearances, went back to Pine Ridge for the half-day conference. Constitutional sheriffs pledge not to enforce federal laws they believe are unconstitutional, but they strongly support the Second Amendment. They believe they have plenary power to deny the enforceability of any warrant issued by any judge—state or federal. Joe Arpaio, the infamous Maricopa County sheriff pardoned by President Trump, is a constitutional sheriff.

On sentencing day, April 10, 2017, Judge Beason listened to both sides of the retrial motion. While Alvarez's associate Serita Rios was defending the motion for a retrial based on the Poindexter allegations of perjury, Beason interrupted her. "Can I caution you? I understand your argument, but I had intended to not delve into local politics. This episode is an unfortunate attempt, I believe perhaps on both sides, to use defense counsel and to use the court for purposes that are not germane to this proceeding and not the purview of this court." As an admonishment to the witnesses and spectators, the judge added, "People can come up with all sorts of conspiracy theories, intentional misconduct, without evidence to back those up . . . and it pains me when I see that happen." She noted that in the course of the two trials, statements were made by people she did not identify who were upset that "other individuals" were not arrested and charged in the case. She said there would not be sufficient evidence to prove beyond a reasonable doubt that anybody else was involved.

"There are other things where people complain," she continued. "And I understand it when it's a layperson of how the proceedings work, or why certain things weren't held to answer at the preliminary hearing. But those things are tangential, and they don't go to the heart of why we are here, why this community, why the lawyers, the court system has been called upon to evaluate this most sad situation."

Funk was next.

"You have a classic conflict of recollections," he told the judge. "I regret that I was not more careful in my questioning because I've opened the door for this tempest in a teapot, and it's entirely my fault."

He said Barnes made it clear that the day after the murders he was in the conference room and remembered Dowdy bringing the backpack to his attention. Funk asserted that the defense knew that the actual collection of the backpack was at a later date. "So they were aware of the incongruity, if there was one, and did not choose to cross examine Barnes about it." He admitted to "sloppy questioning," but evidence of Rhoades's guilt was in the video and audio tapes. Funk ended with another apology. "I'm sorry for the errors. I've created a firestorm unnecessarily because I wasn't careful."

Judge Beason did not acknowledge Funk's apologies. Instead she went directly to the question of whether there was any evidence that Barnes actually perjured himself. She said there was not. "There is no evidence of any perjury or suborned perjury or conspiracy or anything of the nature that the court observed, based on the testimony that was presented in court." Then she denied the defense motion for a new trial. The dispute over Barnes's alleged perjury was decided by Judge Beason. However, Alvarez said it could reach the California Supreme Court, which automatically reviews death penalty cases.

At the beginning of 2018 Poindexter said he was not going to seek election to a third term. Other than alluding to "some sleepless nights," he gave no reason for his decision. He did, however, announce his "full support" for Dowdy to replace him as the county's sheriff.

Russo went public after Alvarez moved for a new trial. In a written statement to a regional television station, he wrote:

"I believe this motion for a retrial lacks merit and is disingenuous in its motivation. I am confident District Attorney Funk will have this motion dismissed. I fully support him in this effort as well as how he conducted the trial. I prayed every day for justice in this case, and with the death penalty conviction, we got it. For Sheila and me this was a personal victory. It brought me a sense of closure. I felt that my wife could finally rest in peace and that I could begin to move forward with my life. I see this motion for retrial as another form of re-victimization of the victims and survivors of this heinous mass murder. I can only hope that one day we will finally get to see a system that refuses to disregard the rights of the victims over the rights of criminals and murderers."

36

CHERIE RETURNED TO THE Alturas courtroom on April 10, 2017, three years after the multiple murders. She wore the requisite bullet-proof vest over her black and gray–striped jail uniform. Her hands were manacled in front of her. Her wavy brown-to-gray hair fell past her waist. It was cut in a mullet and dyed purple on top. The survivors of the mass killings and their friends sat in the next-to-back row of the gallery reserved for them. They wore black or a variation on a black theme with Native design overtones—a statement, a symbol of their bonding.

Judge Beason dismissed Alvarez's argument that Chief Barnes had perjured himself. She denied his motion for a new trial. She denied an automatic motion to reduce the death penalty to life in prison without parole. "I find that the aggravating circumstances are so substantial in comparison with the mitigating circumstances that it warrants death instead of life without parole." Then she asked if anyone wanted to make surviving victim statements which would automatically be reviewed by the California Supreme Court. When she finished she was visibly struggling to contain her emotions.

One by one the survivors stood at a lectern and faced Cherie.

Holly Cox described the routine she and Rurik Davis shared the day he was killed. They had coffee together. Got the kids ready for school. Packed for a tribal business trip to Hawaii. And she told how difficult it was at the end of that day to break the news to her sons that their father figure was dead. "I'm glad she got the death penalty, and whatever happens, it still doesn't bring back those four beautiful people."

Brandi Penn said her children know they have seen people murdered, but they don't remember who they are anymore, and that's the pain. "And it's really sucky because of all the pain you go through, you kind of numb yourself. And with so much numbness you kind of, like, start to—like, memories are fading." Speaking directly at Cherie who was seated only a few feet away, she said: "I hope you start hating yourself. But suicide would be too easy for you. The death penalty is too easy for you. But you're Cherie, you don't care. But that would be my last wish to you, Cherie, I hope you start caring."

Hedi Bogda called herself a survivor and not a victim. In staggering personal detail she recounted the killings, their aftermath, and her nightmares. She told about the victims and what they meant to her. Rurik "was so happy and excited because the tribe was finally exercising their sovereign authority by holding their very first court hearing." She spoke poignantly about nineteen-year-old Angel Penn, "I recall Angel walking into the building that day, so excited to see me, to show me baby Nico." When she addressed Cherie she was indirect, referring to her in the third person. "She has shown no remorse, and no punishment other than death is fitting for her."

Rurik's former wife, Diane Henley, said her daughters and the other survivors were gathering strength together and together they would lead the tribe. "But not you, Cherie. Not your son. Not your grandchildren. Nobody. You disgust me. You always have. You've always been a bitch. You've always been mean, cruel, and disgusting. And you know that. You really do deserve to be where you're at. And I hope you live a long, long life there."

When Patricia Lenzi took the lectern she said the effects of the murders on the Cedarville Rancheria Northern Paiute Indians had been inadequately addressed in the course of the trial. For the next hour she gave the court and listeners a lesson in Native American sovereignty. She explained the responsibilities of the tribe's executive committee, its community council. She explained the basic differences between the "western system" of law and traditional tribal systems. She told of cultural traditions and the meaning of genera-

spoke with the confident voice of entitlement and scribed herself as the tribe's "grandmother," s historical cause. Her purpose was to show mbers of the Cedarville Rancheria were not

"The tribal court is designed generally in a western style, so in many ways it is similar to this criminal court," Lenzi said. "But in other ways it is different." Western systems want judges and juries who have no knowledge of the facts or the people in the case. Tribal courts ensure that people making the decisions are at the very least aware of the ways of the community. Sometimes they also know the people or the disputes involved in order to settle them, particularly in peacemaker and traditional talking circles types of courts.

Lenzi said it was necessary to ask for both permission and forgiveness from the tribe's leaders "in a traditional way." The oldest and therefore elder of the tribe did not actually live on the Rancheria. So the responsibility of being the elder of the tribe fell to Melissa Davis, twenty-eight, chair of the executive committee, a title Lenzi said was seen by the tribe as equivalent to president of the United States. Lenzi explained that she had asked for forgiveness of the absentee elder for being so bold as to speak for the tribe when she was not one of its members. That forgiveness was granted, she said. And because Melissa Davis was the elected leader of the tribe, Lenzi asked for both her forgiveness and permission to speak on behalf of the tribe. This seeking of forgiveness and permission was staged symbolically in front of Beason when Lenzi and Davis performed the traditional exchange of the "talking stick." The talking stick in its various forms is a symbol of free speech. For centuries Natives used it so that everyone was heard equally. Only the person holding the talking stick could speak and be heard without interruption.

"So, now, Melissa, I'm going to ask you for permission to speak on behalf of the tribe," Lenzi told Melissa Davis, who was standing before her.

"I give you permission to speak," Melissa answered.

"You have a traditional talking stick. In Native communities the person holding the stick is the only one that's allowed to talk. So I'm going to ask if you give me permission by giving me the talking stick."

"I give you permission."

"And do you forgive me for being so bold as to speak on behalf of your community and your tribe?"

"I forgive you."

Melissa handed it to Lenzi and they hugged. The talking stick w thin twigs with a few feathers and beads attached.

Lenzi ranged from defiance of Beason's admonitions to avoid hearsay to ignoring the purpose of victim's impact statements. After the melodramatic talking stick exchange she detailed how tribal courts must consider customs and traditions of the tribe in addition to its written laws. She reminded Beason that it was she, Patricia Lenzi, who presided over the telephonic hearing when Cherie opened fire. But when Lenzi tried to relate a scene where Funk made a derogatory remark about Natives to Melissa Davis, Beason quickly and firmly ordered Lenzi not to relate hearsay in a court of law. Lenzi argued, "Even though it may sound like I'm specifically targeting the district attorney at certain times, or saying some of what happened, you can't understand the trauma to the tribe, the effects, the delays in our court, unless you understand how they tied into this process in your court." Beason countered, telling her, "My nights are filled with circumstances of this case. And it's not the only death penalty case I have ever handled. I've handled several. So I ask that you be mindful of those things in your remarks." Momentarily undeterred, Lenzi made a second attempt at exposing the insulting scene she said allegedly took place in Funk's office with Melissa Davis.

"So when Melissa approached the district attorney outside the penalty phase to ask why we had not been given more time to speak, he said, 'Why don't you go to the hotel, get drunk, have a big party, and write a letter to the editor and tell him everything I did wrong.' That is harm that could not have happened to this tribe had this criminal not committed this offense. Those are the things that I need you to understand," Lenzi told Beason. That was when Beason stopped Lenzi again and ordered her not to continue.

"The court is going to require that you not delve into those types of hearsay statements that can only serve at this point not to add to the court's decision, not to allow the Supreme Court of the State of California to know the impact of the loss here of each of these individuals, which is indescribable, but certainly will only serve to inflame the local community, and there is no opportunity for Mr. Funk or anyone else to rebut those claims. So I am going to order that you eliminate those matters from your statement." Detouring Judge Beason's admonition, the tribe's criticisms of Funk found their way into the court record. In the county's formal probation report on Cherie, Hedi Bogda took direct aim at Funk as well as the U.S. Attorney's Office.

Bogda wrote: "I think about the fact that we will continue to be victimized. The U.S. Attorney's Office for the Northern District of California has refused to take the embezzlement case as the monetary value is not high enough for them. However, they haven't even fully investigated how much money was actually stolen. We also have the county attorney who has consistently treated us with rudeness. He did not prepare prior to the preliminary hearing and as a result, he lost three of the counts including my own. He did not prepare any of the witnesses prior to that hearing, and he failed to prepare any of us during the trial. He has made derogatory remarks to several of us before and during the trial and he also failed to look into other individuals who, most likely, had a hand in the planning of the murders."

The probation report also noted that Sheila Russo's parents "want the court to know they are morally opposed to the death penalty unless there is a possibility the defendant would be released, then they would agree to death. They never want the defendant to walk free for the rest of her life."

Lenzi switched her approach and talked about survivors' determination. How the nine adult active members were committed to continuing their heritage and customs. Brandi Penn temporarily took over as tribal chair. Non-Native Nikki Munholand, supported by Hedi Bogda, stepped in to fill the role of Sheila Russo. Lenzi went on to the suffering Natives have historically endured, not just the Cedarville Rancheria.

"But suffice it to say, American history, manifest destiny, westward expansion, the six eras of federal Indian policy described and identified by Vine Deloria Jr. and Clifford M. Lytle—the Discovery, Conquest, and Treaty-Making Era; Removal and Relocation Era; Allotment and Assimilation Era; Reorganization and Self-Government Era; Termination Era; and Self-Determination Era—took their toll on this little tribe just as they have on every tribe in this country. The survivors of this horrific crime may bear the scars of historical trauma that all Indian people bear, and also the scars of this crime," she predicted.

She said removing Cherie from office, evicting her from Rancheria housing, and subjecting her to loss of tribal privileges was equivalent to "shunning," a tribal penalty in the Paiute tradition for serious offenses. And a state court–imposed sentencing of life without parole or the death chamber was the same as "banishment," where the person is never allowed to be part of the tribal society again. As for the punishment Cherie deserved, Lenzi was impartial.

"For me personally, do whatever you want with this criminal you sentence today. I don't say her name, as that gives her identity, respect, and power that I will not allow her to ever have. She's nothing to me. Others here today very much do care what happens to her, though. They most definitely want you to impose the death penalty, as directed by the jury."

Judge Beason formally sentenced Cherie to be executed for the murders of her half-brother, niece, nephew, and tribal administrator and life without the possibility of parole for attempting to murder her nieces Melissa and Monica, plus a combined 150 years to life for the intentional use of a firearm to harm or kill. She was to be credited for the 1,146 days she spent in the Modoc County jail and transferred to the state penitentiary within ten days. As the judge read the sentence, Cherie held her face in her hands. She looked down and shook her head as if she were saying "this can't be."

Philip Russo addressed Cherie directly. "Cherie Rhoades, you will be an embarrassment to your family for generations. You will be forgotten, and you will die alone." He told the judge he had been waiting to make direct eye contact with Rhoades and it finally happened when he stepped up to the podium. "I saw empty, black, blank eyes," he said. "It was like looking at evil."

37

LLOYD THOUGHT IT CURIOUS that Judge Lenzi brought a talking stick into the courtroom. Was she trying to establish precedent? Can Native tradition be used in the courts?

"The talking stick could be a feather, could be a rock, a pencil, it could be anything," Lloyd said. "It didn't have to be decorated as an Indian thing or anything. It's just a tool to say, 'I have the floor. You have to respect me. While I hold this, if you have something to say I will give the stick to you.'" He knew the talking stick was important to them, but Lloyd never heard of a talking stick being passed in that manner. Talking sticks, he said, are "pan-Indian" now. Lloyd used pan-Indian to describe something that is meant to identify an Indian; in this case, an Indian with no specific identity. Lloyd uses the talking stick with kids because he can't keep them from talking over each other. His Chickasaw tribe didn't use it in tribal courts and never in a regular court. It was an assumption based on experience, but he was certain a Modoc County courtroom was the only place the talking stick scene could take place. Certainly not in Sacramento or another large city.

"I'm sure it wouldn't have happened. It wouldn't have been tolerated. Lenzi saw an opportunity. They're an independent nation and they hold rank. They're equal to everyone else. She wanted to show they had culture and spirituality and were Native. The whole scenario."

For Lloyd it went back to the question of sovereignty, and he told the story of a young Native girl whose face had been burned.

"In the past, welfare workers came into Indian homes and took kids out because they were sleeping on the floor. Well, Indian kids have been sleeping on the floor forever. They still got a roof over their heads and they're being fed," Lloyd said. A welfare worker wanted to take the girl out of her home because she wouldn't wear a mask on her face. And the mother didn't want it. The girl had a serious burn and the welfare people wanted to keep it bandaged. This was when Lloyd was in school, and his teacher had to intervene. The case went to court, and the judge was ready to take the girl from her home. The teacher explained why the girl wouldn't wear the mask. What no one realized was that the girl didn't want to wear the mask because it was 114 degrees in her trailer. It was too hot to wear the mask. The trailer was in the middle of the desert, and they didn't take any of that in consideration. So Lloyd's teacher, an Indian expert, told the court to buy the girl's family an air conditioner. A swamp cooler. And they did, and then the little girl wore the mask. "Native American traditional living," Lloyd said, "in this instance in the desert without air conditioning, is part of our sovereignty. Sovereignty gives Native Americans the right to live in their traditional ways, but often the court system doesn't take cultural issues into consideration. The simple remedy, to make the home cooler with AC, took care of the problem. Like the talking stick, it's the same thing. The courts have to be shown that we have our truths and our way of doing things. Bringing the talking stick into the court, that was just more leverage to show that we're here and we have rules and laws and spirituality,"

Judge Lenzi was showing that. What's the solution? Would a central form of government be a solution? Could Natives possibly ever achieve a central government? "I don't think so," said Lloyd. "We haven't in hundreds and hundreds of years. We couldn't even come together to save ourselves. People think sovereignty is more than it is, too. Natives are still under state and federal government control. We still have to abide by the laws." Using the talking stick at Cherie's sentencing gave the impression that these were culturally connected people. But in Lloyd's experience they were not. Lloyd said giving the impression that Glenn Calonico was a potential medicine man was the farthest thing from the truth. Lloyd knew him. He took Glenn to trainings and spent a lot of time with him. To Lloyd, Glenn had the desire to be a leader. If he could have maintained his sobriety, he had potential. At the time he certainly was not a medicine man. Yes, Lloyd conceded, Glenn was interested in the cultural aspects of the Northern Paiutes, but he didn't attend Lloyd's sweat lodges,

Lloyd wondered if there is any hope the tribe will accept and learn the traditions, adapt them? He didn't know. He thought that would be difficult. They have to have elders who are cultural. When Cherie and Rurik's mother Virginia was the leader, she was against anything cultural. So the tribe would have to start somewhere. He didn't know how they would get to that place. They were never culturally active. He knew Rurik's daughters were not brought up as Native. They came to the Rancheria as political leverage to unseat Cherie. "They'd never been to the Rancheria. I knew that all the time I was there. I knew them for what, fifteen years, and they never were up here. In the time of my employment with the tribe and later, as Rurik's friend, I never knew them to visit the Rancheria. Instead, Rurik went down to the Sacrament area a lot. Or he met them in Reno, took them to the car shows and that kind of thing. They were not involved in any way."

The question, as Lloyd saw it, was: what are they doing now? It's been three years. Has anything changed? Are they any more Native than they were then? He's no longer at the Rancheria, so he admits he doesn't know. But he hasn't heard that they are trying to bring back any culture. They don't know what their culture is. He said some elders from Pit River and Pyramid Lake Paiute came to the services for Rurik and Angel and offered their eldership. It wasn't accepted. A ceremony was performed, but it wasn't done in a traditional manner. No one asked Lloyd.

"They assumed I would do it, but no one came with the traditional offer of tobacco. No one thanked me, even afterwards. I wasn't expecting anything, but the family usually gives a traditional gift. And there wasn't anything. They have no tradition. To learn their heritage, to try and learn their culture there has to be a council of elders. Pyramid Lake Paiute Reservation has a council of elders. Fort Bidwell Reservation could be recourse, but Bidwell is splintered and confused about cultural things. Trying to get culture back and move ahead financially? That's very muddy."

The services for Rurik and Angel were an opportunity to do the Wiping of the Tears or other ceremonies meant to help people with grief. Lloyd didn't know if they did any of them, other than the outside influence from that inter-tribal wellness group from Oregon. But that wellness session didn't have a real cultural meaning to the tribe's Paiute culture.

"They did a Choctaw dance and other Native customs, but it really wasn't Northern Paiute. And it wasn't really well attended by the tribal members. So is that going to change? I doubt it. They lost their cultural connection when Rurik died. He was proud of his Indianness," Lloyd said. Can members of the Cedarville Rancheria tribe, without a resident elder to pass on the traditions, learn their culture, their language, their spirituality? "Being a Native in the spiritual way is every day, it's your life. It's not like going to church and that's the day we're spiritual. It's a part of your life. It's layers of who you are. And they don't have the layers. Some layers are good and some layers are bad. People come into Indian Country thinking that Indians are all spiritual and all cultural and all that. That's another layer. There are layers of pain, of Indianness. When you talk to another Indian person, we know, like, we don't have to say the words. We know what those are. Then some non-Native comes in, tries to be an Indian, uses words like many moons and things that we never even use, I have to laugh. Things that you see on TV. As long as the grass shall grow. All this stuff."

It's as if they're wearing somebody else's skin, walking around in somebody else's shoes, or robe. They don't know what that means. They might talk about generational trauma, but they don't have a clue what that is. "Generational trauma is being molested by your uncles and your brother and your parents and your aunties. And you're told to keep quiet. That's just one horrible aspect of it. Handling family problems within the family and not letting them out. Keeping a lot of secrets. That's all generational trauma," he said.

"So for a person to come in, even a tribal person who hasn't had a Native upbringing—Rurik's daughters, for example—it would be like pounding a square peg into a round hole. It's about education, getting the opportunity at an education. But if you're promised a big load of money all the time, you don't go to school. Why would you go to school and become involved? So, without Rurik Davis now, they've lost it."

Lloyd said his purpose in being at the Cedarville Rancheria was to learn how to take care of tribal affairs and to work with kids. He went to the training sessions to learn how to work within the tribe's constitution, how to police the Rancheria from drugs, and how to do a home inspection. He went to Washington DC and Florida to represent the tribal interest. The tribal council members rarely attended, or even when they did, they hung out in the pool at the hotel. The tribal members said it was for him to bring that information back.

"It wasn't on me to bring that back. It was for them to learn. So they'd get used to something. They think it's never going to change. That this life they have, this money was going to continue to come."

He thought they could find some Indianness by living on a reservation. "Right now, there is a lot of grief. But how healthy are they and how healthy were they before all this? How mentally healthy were they? The people I knew were not healthy. How many people were living under Virginia's roof? She couldn't take care of so many kids with so many problems. There were drugs and alcohol. It was constant stress, constant craziness all the time. So could Virginia feel some degree of that? Yes. And what was she fighting for? I used to watch them fight over nothing. You know, just, absolutely nothing. Could be a bag of beans. There was so much anger between them all. Some anger came from money, wanting more money. And then power. The oppressed become the oppressors. If you've been oppressed, you're seeking some way to find power. And it's not always the healthiest power that you find. Cherie found her power through anger and aggression."

Lloyd predicted that blood quantum related to per-capita income will eventually play into the tribe's future. "Cedarville Rancheria is probably meeting bare minimum blood quantum. This could cause problems with the disenrollment issue. The more who can enroll, the lesser amount of money the others get. The pot is divided by the total number of eligible tribe members. They want the money. Tribes are becoming their own worst enemies in some respects."

"The county didn't control Cherie. They looked the other way. I did child abuse reports, of beatings, and nothing ever happened," he said. "I've seen some horrible stuff that Cherie did. I called the sheriff out on her lots of times for things she did. And they just wouldn't deal with it, because she was such a force, so angry and loud and obnoxious." People just looked the other way. When things like that happen, others started believing that they're empowered, he explained. Cherie got away with so much that others thought they could do what they wanted without consequences. He said meth was being used on the Rancheria. Mental illness peaked. It didn't happen one night. This was a buildup. "These are the layers, he said. Layer after layer after layer." He is convinced the system empowered her to become who she was because the system didn't know the Indian world. County social services knew nothing about Indian child welfare. He had to explain to them that every Indian child was covered by the Indian Child Welfare Act.

"The baby Angel was holding when she was killed, he might be the future," he said. "You never know. They say you can't count 'em out. You never know when that seed is going to show up. I mean the person who shows that spirit in them. But right now, at least for me, there's closure. With that death sentence, I was able to stop. I haven't thought about it. Sometimes I tried to think about it, but, you know, I'm done. We've got closure. But our culture doesn't stand still. We evolve. And that's another thing. They want to keep the Indians in the past. Well, we're in the future. We are in the future now."

38

ON APRIL 20, 2017, Modoc County sheriff's deputies took Cherie Rhoades to the Central California Women's Facility in Chowchilla. Twenty other women are awaiting execution at the state's largest women's prison—some have been there as long as thirty years. She was not allowed to take her penis drawings with her. On departure all she said was, "Bye."

39

WHAT IF HEDI BOGDA had convinced Rurik Davis and Glenn Calonico to give Cherie more time to prepare her case? What if they had followed Judge Lenzi's advice and put the hearing off until the next day? Was it a misuse of sovereignty that led to the murders? Or a misunderstanding? What if Cherie had listened to Lenzi when the judge told her the hearing was a first, to be followed by a second hearing? What if the tribe had not been in a rush to judge Cherie guilty of embezzlement? Cherie saw a simple answer to these questions: "This all happened because of the stupid court thing." She believed the victims brought their deaths and wounds on themselves because she was right. She was wrongly evicted and the court was being lied to. Judge Lenzi rationalized the murders differently. She said Cherie was an experienced tribal leader who ignored customs and traditions.

"She actually established some of the customs and traditions of this tribe, which in turn became laws I was bound to apply in her eviction hearing because their laws say that," Judge Lenzi observed. "That is why I asked her what other options she had. If anyone knew of other ways to handle evictions beyond the tribe's written laws and policies, it was her. She had presided over these eviction hearings in the past. She was the one who helped establish the laws of the tribe vis-à-vis custom and tradition. She either deliberately ignored custom and tradition of the tribe that would give her an opportunity to stay in the housing, just so that she could commit her crime in this selfish way, or she knew the customs and traditions that she helped create would work against her desires. Therefore she planned to carry out her crime and evil while disrespecting the laws she created.

"So instead of cornering her with that question about other options, it actually was an opportunity for her that opened doors and windows. She could say how to handle the eviction. She knew this better than anyone, including me. To call it railroading her or bullying her is completely wrong. It was the opposite. She alone knew if there was another way under Cedarville Rancheria Northern Paiute customs and traditions to legally address her eviction. Instead she chose violence and evil as her path."

District Attorney Funk found a deeper reasoning in the murders, asking the persistent question: what does it mean to be a Native American tribe in modern America?

"In the course of the trial I learned that 'eviction' is a severe sanction to a Native American. To sanction Rhoades by evicting her from the tribe, in the face of virtually no evidence of her embezzlement, set the stage for the carnage that followed. In no way did it justify what Rhoades did, but I can't help wondering but for her eviction, what some may argue was a hasty and ill-supported decision, would she have slaughtered her family and tribe? If the process she received from the tribe was not the process she was due, I can't help wondering if she would have killed had she been treated differently? It's a lesson that shooting victims often learn too late. There are some people with whom one has to be very careful. Cherie Rhoades was such a person. You have to have a deep-seated character flaw to slaughter your own family and tribal government for any reason. But we have to ask what could or should we have done differently?

"Honestly, from where I stood throughout this case the concept of the Cedarville Rancheria as a 'tribe' with a cultural identity of its own had little credence. Apart from Rurik Davis, I did not see that any of the current members were interested or immersed in their culture or their identity as Native Americans. They were plagued by many social ills. Their legacy was bequeathed to them in large measure by a reservation system which strikes me as horribly destructive of Native American culture.

"The tribe's claim to be regarded as fully Native Americans seemed to me somewhat disingenuous. But again, is it all the tribe's fault? To what extent is tribal dysfunction and the dysfunction present in contemporary Native American culture something that state and federal policy, especially gambling policy, incentivizes? My impression of the Cedarville Rancheria was that they're simply a loose collection of people who have just enough genetic composition to meet the legal threshold to claim Native American status—to receive benefits.

"But, for most of them, especially the younger generation, there is little or nothing underlying their claims to be 'Native.' I think Rurik Davis was interested in and committed to the traditions of his Native fathers. In addition to very much looking Native American, Rurik, from what I learned, seemed genuinely interested in recalling and perpetuating Northern Paiute culture. But my impression of many of the rest of the tribal members, especially the younger ones, is that their claim to revere and value their heritage is not deeply held. They receive their gambling subventions, then use those benefits to function entirely as whites in a white culture. And often dysfunctionally and with barely a tip of the hat to their own heritage.

"Yeah, it was a seminal case, but because it was out in the middle of nowhere; no one appreciated that."

EPILOGUE

ONE YEAR AFTER THE murders the tribe's executive committee exercised its sovereign rights by performing its first adoption. The child was Angel Penn's baby Nico. Melissa Davis took him as her own.

Cherie Rhoades is the only woman mass murderer tried and sentenced to death in the U.S., but it's unlikely she will be executed any time in the near future. The death penalty in California became moot in 2019 when newly elected Governor Gavin Newsom signed an executive order placing a moratorium on further death row executions. Trial attorney Antonio Alvarez said he doubted Cherie is getting any treatment for her mental illness from the California Department of Corrections and Rehabilitation. As far as he knew she hasn't sought out treatment, adding that personality disorders are "unlikely" to be "something the CDCR will address."

Kandi Maxwell and Lloyd Powell moved to a small community in the Sierra Foothills to be closer to their children and grandchildren. Lloyd continues to conduct sweat lodges and helps with special cultural events for the Native youth who attend RISE trips out of town. He also volunteers at an equestrian therapeutic center as a mentor and assistant therapist for at-risk teens. Kandi's health has declined, making active participation in the Native community difficult. She continues to sing with her drum group, Thoz Womenz, when she is able. She also works with RISE director Dr. April Lea Go Forth on writing projects and behind-the-scenes planning for recordings, youth activities, and special events.

Jordan Funk ran for reelection in the June 2018 primary. He lost to Samuel Kyllo, the county's contract public defender. Kyllo was a member of Richard A. Ciummo and Associates, the Fresno law firm that employs Cherie's attorney, Antonio Alvarez. The firm was the single largest contributor to Kyllo's campaign. Another large contributor to Kyllo's campaign to upset Funk was the wife of Sheriff Mike Poindexter. Soon after the election Funk moved his law practice to another county.

Philip Russo's campaign to have his wife Sheila remembered for her altruistic compassion, not only for the Cedarville Rancheria but for all people of Indian Country, reached its height during the trial. Hedi Bogda, the tribe's attorney and Sheila's best friend, praised Sheila for her dedication and devotion to the Native American cause. Russo moved to Redding.

In a rare courtroom appearance Monique Davis testified that she had a fear of trusting strangers and family—without saying anything further. She did not file a victim's statement for the county probation report, and she did not appear before the court when Rhoades was sentenced. Instead, Tribal Judge Patricia Lenzi spoke for her at the sentencing. Lenzi said Monique and her father "were working to mend the emotional distance between them from the past" when he was killed. Monique lives in the greater Sacramento area.

Hedi Bogda continued as tribal attorney. She did the legal work required to complete Rhoades's eviction after the murders, explaining in detail the reason for the delay and giving a description of the killings.

Brandi Morning Dove Penn was arrested on a charge of hit and run in October 2014, eight months after the killings. She was booked into a sobering cell a few feet from Cherie, who was awaiting trial. They were not in sight of each other. Brandi was sentenced to forty-eight hours on a DUI and has other related convictions. Following the murders she was the temporary chair of the tribe's executive committee. Later she reportedly married and moved away but returned to the Rancheria with her two children.

Spencer Bobrow pleaded no contest in April 2016 to a misdemeanor charge of "corporal injury to spouse, cohabitant, fiancé, girlfriend or child's parent." He was sentenced to three years' probation and thirty days in the county jail—at the same time Cherie Rhoades was being held there. He was also ordered to pay a fine of $1,180 and required to complete a one-year aggression response control program.

Richard Lash, like Monique, did not make a statement at Cherie's sentencing or for the probation report. He was a member of the local militia when the murders occurred. A recruitment poster on the Cedarville post office bulletin board identified Lash as the militia's squad leader and membership contact. In 2018 he was elected to a one-year term as chair of the tribe.

Jenica McGarva is no longer associated with the tribe and prefers anonymity because she does not want her children "Googling my name and having something like that come up."

Jack Stockton Jr. was working for a cable TV installation company at the time of his mother's trial.

Patricia Lenzi was re-appointed tribal judge.

Tina Penn was vice chair of the tribe at the time of the murders, but she was not at the fatal eviction hearing. She was the mother of Angel Penn, Glenn Calonico, and Brandi Penn. Rurik Davis was her brother, Cherie her half-sister. She died on April 20, 2016, of alcoholic hepatitis. She was fifty-four. Her death certificate listed her occupation as caregiver.

Nikki Munholand became the tribe's administrator, its social services department, and the lead tribal court clerk.

Erin Stockton was hired in 2016 as an instructional assistant in the Modoc County Education Office's Early Intervention Program.

Holly Cox kept financial books for the tribe at the time of Rhoades's sentencing. She worked in the same offices where her boyfriend Rurik Davis and the others were killed.

Duanna Knighton, a force in key tribal decisions, left her position as administrator prior to the murders. At the time of the trial and sentencing she was in litigation with the tribe over insurance premium payments and her retirement fund.

While its population fluctuates when members move away and then move back, it is estimated that perhaps eight adults and five or six children are currently living at the Cedarville Rancheria. Most are blood related. The dominant family is Cherie Rhoades's branch— the Lashes.

ACKNOWLEDGMENTS

A HINDRANCE TO ACCESSING the inside workings of nearly all tribes—not just the Cedarville Rancheria—is that because of their sovereign status they live, work, and act legally or illegally largely in the absence of a watchdog press.

A legal issue that surfaces in open court can become a public document. The disenrollment epidemic was widely covered by state and national press because of victims' public complaints. But typically the internal activities of tribes cannot be examined by the public. An exception, of course, was the mass murder trial of Cherie Rhoades, which was held in an open California Superior Court.

I'd like to acknowledge the Native American Journalists Association, which is challenging this impasse. As the NAJA reports, "Tribal nations have the sovereignty to decide how they want to protect freedoms of the press and information. More and more do but the problem is that too many still do not." However, NAJA has found some progress is being made in the coverage of Indian Country issues. Examples are the Osage Nation's Independent Press Act of 2008 and the Cherokee Nation of Oklahoma's Free Press Protection and Journalist Shield Act of 2012. Additionally, Washington state courts have recognized a right to certain information under state public records laws, and some access to federal documents involving tribes has been obtained through the federal Freedom of Information Act. By contrast, the California Public Information Act does not apply to Indian Country.

The press does not have the First Amendment to fall back on in the absence of due process under tribal constitutional laws. This is compounded by government agencies that are too inept to comply with the California Public Records Act or knowingly stonewall investigative efforts to uncover what limited public records exist revealing the inner workings of tribes. As a consequence tribes are faceless, living in a world largely removed from public view by both self-imposed and socially imposed restrictions. If the social and political workings fueled by a bitter family feud at the Cedarville Rancheria had been open to public view—by even the most routinely responsible media coverage—there may have been an outside chance that the tribe would not have lost the promise of its ancestral core when Rurik Davis was killed.

The story of the Cedarville Rancheria killings could not be fully told without also telling the story of the community-at-large and its cultural and socio-economic history—especially as it related to Indian Country. The two cultures, one Native, one white, without choice, are inextricably entwined. Obviously Kandi Maxwell and Lloyd Powell, who gave every minute I asked of them, are the best examples a writer could have when saying, "I couldn't have written this book without them." And my thanks to Dr. April Lea Go Forth for her sage advice.

But there are many others who helped in varying ways, people who remained in the background but were essential in my research and writing. In my formative days as a rookie newspaper reporter I caringly called them the "Courthouse Gang." That elite membership has changed from one county to another during my passage through time, but their spirit has not. Thank you, Ronda Gysin, Shannon Pedotti, Teresa Eames, and Michele Dancer in Modoc County. And down in Placer County my thanks go to Layne Anderson at MOA–California Court Reporters. Lori Behle put a fine polish on the notes and bibliography. And no researcher can do without historical archives. Thank you Sheryln L. Hayes-Zorn, curator of manuscripts at the Nevada Historical Society in Reno. For advice and insights on sovereignty I am also indebted to Tony Cohen and James Diamond. Thanks, too, to the California-based First Amendment Coalition for giving me astute advice on how to wade through the government morass. I would not have acquired critical information without the FAC's help and the use of both the California Public Records Act and Freedom of Information Act.

For illuminating email correspondence spanning 2014–19 I thank Antonio Alvarez, Marlys Big-Eagle, Jane Braxton-Little, Edward Bronson, Melinda Dollarhide, Jack Duran Jr. (Duran Law Office), Grant Duwe (Baylor Institute for Studies of Religion), Kevin Fagan (*San Francisco Chronicle*), Fair Punishment Project, Rick Fakhre (Tulelake High School), Jordan Funk, John Geldreich (Modoc High School), Doug George-Kanentiio (Hiawatha Institute for Indigenous Knowledge), Greg Glazner, Cheewa James, Zaid Jilani (*Intercept*), Lee Juillerat, Brendan Lindsay (California State University, Sacramento), Sal Martinez (Manchester Band of Pomo Indians), Terry Miller (Surprise Valley Unified School District), Michael (Michelle) Moreno (Inter Tribal Council of California), National Indian Gaming Commission, Chester Robertson (chief administrative officer, Modoc County), Steve Russell (Indiana University, Bloomington), James A. Sandos (University of Redlands), Deborah Smith (National Center for State Courts), Lorissa Soriano, Michelle M. Sotero (University of Nevada, Las Vegas), Darryl A. Stallworth, Darryl Babe Wilson, and Lynda Zambrano.

If in my memory search I have left someone out, I apologize. The beers are on me.

On a personal side, no writer can make it through the lengthy ordeal of research and putting words down without the moral support and confidentiality of family and friends. My daughter, Melissa, gave a fresh eye to the manuscript and pointed to some of the obvious flaws her dad missed. John W. (Jack) Frost's periodic calls gave me the strength to go five sets if I had to. Mike Marron, Esq. guided me through many a legal document maze. Eric Brazil, a colleague from my early newspaper days, quietly monitored me like the great *USA Today* Los Angeles bureau chief he was. Mark Charlton took me on an eye-opening theological tour. On the pragmatic side a writer has to have a machine with the gears always well oiled, and Larry Watson of CSI Computers in Klamath Falls, Oregon, was patiently there for me. And I am grateful to Dr. Bennett Pafford for his thoughtful support.

Always in my memory as I wrote this work was Gabriel Garcia Marquez's *News of a Kidnapping* and John Dos Passos's *USA Trilogy*. I also read Julien Cornell's fascinating *The Trial of Ezra Pound: A Documented Account of the Treason Case by the Defendant's Lawyer*. I am indebted to other readings as well. In researching the Modoc War story I came across *Torture Team* by Philippe Sands. This is a riveting book that took up much of my evening reading, but in finishing it I came away with a thorough understanding of this country's rationale for torture that far exceeds the legal decisions of 1873. Two other exceptional books that showed great style and depth are *The Unquiet Grave* by Steve Hendricks and *Killers of the Flower Moon* by David Grann. These examples may seem unrelated to this book, but all my reading, research, and writing are cumulative.

And I want to add former U.S. Poet Laureate Juan Felipe Herrera, who once asked during a pizza break for poets at the Squaw Valley Writers' Conference, "What would wild sister do?" "Wild sister," of course, is my wife Barbara, winning poet, my first line reader, and always tolerant of my time away.

APPENDIX

I HAD AN ERRATIC correspondence with Cherie Rhoades while she was in the county jail waiting for her trial to start. Our correspondence covered roughly a two-year span. I specifically told her the purpose of my questions and that I was preparing to write a book about her for the University of Nebraska Press. I asked her about Native sovereignty and its effect on the Cedarville Rancheria. Did she feel she had exhausted all her options in fighting her eviction? Would she permit me to see her pre-trial mitigation findings? I offered to send her a money order to cover her mailing costs. I told her I was making visiting arrangements with her attorney Antonio Alvarez. In my last letter I asked if she believed she was being disenrolled from the tribe instead of evicted. Using a pencil and in clear, legible handwriting that was loosely cursive, she wrote back in rambling sentences with numerous spelling errors. Her replies were not always to the point of my questions. She was willing to be interviewed but unwilling to discuss tribal law or events when she was chair. She did say that in her opinion there was a need for more access through federal courts than there is now, but she did not explain why. She shielded her son Jack and used him to threaten me. She often went from being defensive to being offensive. There was always a tone of frustration. She wrote that a former cell mate sent her a thank you card for saving her life when she was choking on a sandwich. As time went by, her letters dwindled in length. In her first letter she was cooperative and wrote over a thousand words. After that each letter was shorter than the last. By her last letter, at just over two hundred words, her mood was terse and final. She did not reply to my final question, but I had her response during the jail interview.

July 30, 2015

In my first letter I thanked her for remembering me in court the day before and regretted that we'd been interrupted by the bailiff. In telling her I was researching a book about her case and Native sovereignty, I reminded her that when we talked in court she inferred that the Cedarville Rancheria was corrupt. "Within the broad subject of Native sovereignty laws can you share with me what you saw as flaws or faults of the tribal system?" I asked. Was there a feeling of helplessness and did she feel there was an adequate avenue within the tribal system to have her voice heard?

August 3, 2015

Cherie led off her reply telling me she could not discuss her case. She then said Duanna Knighton did a great job as the tribe's administrator. She went on in detail explaining tribal sovereignty as it relates to federal government controls. Her conclusion was that sovereignty has its limitations and ends where federal control begins. Tribes have their own constitutions "with the help of the Bureau of Indian Affairs." She ended saying she hates to write because she gets sidetracked. In a postscript she apologized for not writing more because she had to wait until she had money to buy paper.

August 7, 2015

I addressed my letter to Cherie as "c/o Modoc County Sheriff's Dept." and said I was particularly interested in matters of sovereignty and its effect on the Cedarville Rancheria. I did not hear from her until December.

November 10, 2015

In this note I told Cherie that although I had not heard from her, she had given me time to continue researching Native sovereignty and its application to the Cedarville Rancheria when she was chair of the executive committee. I specifically asked if she had been denied "due process of the law" and how did that figure into the tribe's constitution?

December 17, 2015

In her first sentence she said I didn't have to write to her c/o the sheriff's department. By her fourth sentence she told me I wasn't worth spending stamp money on. In her fifth sentence she said she wouldn't talk about her time as chair of the tribe's executive committee. In her seventh sentence she blasted the tribe's management of Rabbit Traxx, calling them stupid and saying that things go to hell in a handbasket when stupid people are in charge. Karma is a bitch, she said.

She repeated her textbook take on tribal constitutions, adding that the sheriff's department kept the stamps I sent her and that she didn't like to write. She wished me "Merry Christmas, Happy Honaka Ect. Or bah humbug if your a witness."

December 23, 2015

I told Cherie I appreciated her comments on the faults of the tribal system and I wanted to follow up on that subject. I told her I was making arrangements with the sheriff's department to visit her after the New Year. And I asked that she give her attorney Antonio Alvarez permission to let me see the mitigation findings to be used at trial. She didn't answer right away, so I followed with another letter in February 2016.

February 23, 2016

Hello Cherie,

I had hoped to hear from you regarding my letter of Dec. 23, 2015, but no luck. I can appreciate your reluctance to hand write a letter, as you have expressed, but if it is any relief for you my handwriting is totally unreadable while yours is perfect by comparison. So, until I can arrange to meet with you personally it would be helpful if you could give Antonio Alvarez your permission to share the mitigation findings with me. In the meantime, I hope you are agreeable to answering the following questions:

What's happening at Rabbit Traxx? I get the impression all is not going smoothly.

Can you share with me your opinion of how the Cedarville Rancheria was run when you were chair and how its management changed after you were voted out?

Do you feel you exhausted all your options to be heard when your eviction was upheld by the executive committee?

March 4, 2016

"The initial questions I have are in my letters, if you still have them."
I wrote and offered to send a money order to pay for telephone calls.
I reminded her that I had not heard from her. Was she serious when
she said she didn't like to write?

March 7, 2016

After my letters in December, February, and my most recent, I finally
heard from Cherie. She was more personal. She'd had her first "roommate." The roommate was being pushed around in the dorm section
of the jail, and although she had said she didn't like murderers she
requested to be placed in Cherie's cell. Cherie said the roommate
lived to see the courtroom and two more roommates had also made
it out of her cell in one piece. One of the roommates was choking
on a sandwich when Cherie stepped in. "I did save her life when she
was choaking on her sandwich," Cherie wrote, "but hay I didn't need
another charge, right."

She explained the routine for our jail interview and said if there
were any problems to bring her letter with us.

March 11, 2016

I thanked Cherie for making the effort to reply to my letters and asked
for specifics I didn't have at the time: where she was born and raised,
schooling, and when she came to the Rancheria.

March 21, 2016

I thanked Cherie for the jail interview and her willingness to talk
with Barbara and me.

In this letter I asked Cherie one question: "In a word or more how
would you describe the members of the Cedarville Rancheria's ability to govern themselves?"

March 23, 2016

Cherie replied that she hated it when I didn't write my name on the
envelope. She said I was treating her like a dirty little secret. She
didn't trust me and I was not honest in my intentions. She accused
me of writing "shit" in our newspaper about Rabbit Traxx and said

that her son Jack hated me and had been rubbed wrong by my stupidity. In her postscript she said I should not show my dumb ass on his doorstep. She signed off with have a nice day. Cherie never did answer my question about the tribe's ability to govern itself. This was the last letter I received from her.

September 3, 2016

Hello Cherie,

I am hoping you will take a moment to answer this question: Did you believe you were being disenrolled at the Feb. 20, 2014 hearing instead of evicted?

I did not hear from her again.

NOTES

This book is a journalist's recording of events as they unfolded. I then reorganized and sequentially structured the material for improved flow of the story. I relied heavily on firsthand, for-the-record accounts, such as interviews and supporting documents of public record. The murder scene and trial coverage, including witness statements, were drawn directly from official audio, video, trial transcripts, and Cherie's probation report. Email correspondence and telephone and personal interviews with Modoc County District Attorney Jordan Funk, Defense Attorney Antonio Alvarez, and Modoc County Sheriff Mike Poindexter occurred over the entire length of the Cherie Rhoades case, with the mutual agreement that information obtained would not be used until after the trials. Many of the principals allowed me to record our lengthy interviews and quote them. Frequently I went back over the transcripts with their help to clarify any ambiguous information or unclear text intended for use as direct quotes. Where I have attributed exact quotations to the principals those quotes came from the person quoted or from public files, such as probation reports, personal documents, or contemporaneous newspaper accounts. Email correspondents are listed in the acknowledgments. Various sources were used for familiarization of subject matter only and have not been cited in either notes or bibliography. They include the National Indian Law Library, Tribal Law and Policy Institute, National Park Service, *Native Max* magazine, Nativenewsonline.net, Centers for Disease Control and Prevention (CDC), historycommons.org, recoveryranch .com, and Inter-Tribal Council of California. This is an original story never before told in depth or in the broad context of Modoc County's history, which explains the general absence of archival materials as sources. References to historical events, as they apply, can be found in the bibliography. For more detail on the gathering of information for this work, see my author's note opening the book.

1

The information for this chapter comes from public records, primary sources, court documents, trial transcripts, and audio-video surveillance evidence.

2   **"Let me know how it goes"**: Jack Stockton's testimony during first trial.

4   **Richard Lash who was sitting:** Scene from surveillance evidence.

4   **as chair of the executive committee:** *Knighton v. Cedarville Rancheria of Northern Paiute Indians*, 234 F. Supp. 3d 1042 (E.D. Cal 2017).

11   **"Who brings children?":** Modoc County Probation Report.

13   **the chairs and tables:** Scene from surveillance evidence.

13   **"I would never think she would start":** Brad Knickerbocker, "Alturas Tribal Shooting: Was Embezzlement, Eviction Behind Family Revenge?" *Christian Science Monitor*, February 23, 2014; Associated Press, "Woman, 47, Who Opened Fire."

13   **"The people of Modoc County are stunned":** Evan Schreiber, "Small Community Devastated by Mass Shooting," KRCA–TV, February 21, 2014.

14   **"also killed was":** Press coverage of the murders uniformly referred to Sheila Russo as "also killed." An example is the widely distributed AP report "the other person killed was identified as Sheila Russo, 47, who was not related to the suspect." February 21, 2014.

14   **He invited a regional television crew:** Ian McDonald, "Husband Recounts Chilling Lead-Up to Alturas Shooting," Fox 40 TV, March 19, 2014, https://fox40.com/news/california-connection/husband-recounts-chilling-lead-up-to-alturas-shooting/.

14   **he posted an opinion piece:** Russo, "Please Stop Turning Killers into Celebrities." Huffington Post, May 14, 2014, https://www.huffpost.com/entry/stop-turning-killers-into_b_5320362.

14   **"It is our responsibility":** Read Russo, "Holding the Media Accountable, One Phone Call at a Time." Huffington Post, July 25, 2014, https://www.huffpost.com/entry/holding-the-media-account-sensationalism_b_5618854.

2

Information for this chapter comes primarily from Bureau of Indian Affairs files via the Freedom of Information Act and for-the-record interviews with firsthand sources.

15   **sent his first dispatch:** BIA weekly report, February 21, 2014.

15   **and look for outside help:** The BIA search for a CISM team is documented throughout the initial exchange of emails between officials.

15   **"We are in the process of getting":** Joshua Simmons to Sid Caesar, email, February 21, 2014.

16   **"A critical stress management team":** Jay Hinshaw to DOI Watch Office, email, February 21, 2014.

18   **In the meantime the BIA continued:** Jay Hinshaw to Sue Bush, email, February 21, 2014.

18   **Its purpose is to provide healthcare:** Strong Family Health Center is a nonprofit receiving federal funds for services such as eye and dental care, medications, diabetes, and substance abuse. It does not provide in-house crisis counseling. See https://strongfamilyhealthcenter.com.

19   **Deaton, too, might be a victim:** There are victims in a mass shooting other than those killed. They are the wounded survivors, intended victims, eyewitnesses, family, and citizens who happen on the scene. The most frequently unrecog-

nized are the first responders: police, fire fighters, paramedics and emergency medical technicians. Through the tribe's outside attorney, Deaton declined to answer the following questions: 1. Please describe who the resources were you worked with when you came forward as the tribe's contact person. *". . . she indicated that she is working with county and other partners and believes she has all resources currently or en route at this time."* (See Jay Hinshaw's emails of February 24, 2014, at 4:58 p.m. and 5:00 p.m.) 2. In your "needs assessment" what did you determine those needs were? *"She's doing a needs assessment and will let us know on Monday if there are any unmet needs."* (See Jay Hinshaw's emails of February 24, 2014, at 4:58 p.m. and 5:00 p.m.) 3. What counseling did Strong Family Health provide survivors in place of a "critical incident stress management" (CISM) team? And when? 4. Did the three-day wellness session in June 2014 fulfill the need for crisis counseling, or was that a separate effort by Strong Family to assist survivors and community?

19   **Tina Penn, the surviving vice chair:** Over a two- to three-day period BIA internal emails note that Tina Penn was missing. However, no indication was ever given that she was located.

20   **"I am shocked":** William Wiley to Sue Bush, email, February 22, 2014.

20   **Its main goal:** See U.S. Department of the Interior, Office of Justice Services, www.bia.gov.

21   **"I agree we need to coordinate":** Darren Cruzan, email to Jay Hinshaw, March 13, 2014.

21   **an after action report was completed:** From BIA, Pacific Region, March 17, 2014.

22   **Beretta PX4 Storm semi-automatic:** The Beretta is intended for personal defense and law enforcement, according to its website. And "Besides being a custom-looking touch, the Commander-style hammer is lighter; hammer-fall during firing is therefore crisper and will not disrupt your aim." See Beretta.com.

22   **It was the second deadliest:** Kutner, "What Led Jaylen Fryberg to Commit the Deadliest."

22   **and formed their own CISM team:** See Native Nation Events, Second Tribal Security Symposium, "Why You Need an Active Shooter Plan," Sycuan Casino Resort, El Cajon CA, October 28–29, 2019, www.nativenationevents.org.

22   **"Mom, how can you guarantee":** Interview with Lynda Zambrano, October 15, 2019. In answer to her son's question, Zambrano said she is working with a panel of tribal representatives proposing that an emergency management training curriculum be included at college level. No such curriculum currently exists in higher education, she said.

22   **In late 2019:** BIA response to author's query, October 17, 2019.

3

Information for this chapter comes primarily from news accounts, personal observations, for-the-record interviews with firsthand sources, and the Bureau of Indian Affairs files via the Freedom of Information Act.

24 **The petition asked the Bureau:** "Rancheria's Plan for Truck Stop Meets Opposition in Cedarville," *Modoc Independent News*, June 2005.

25 **The store keeper was the first to sign:** The petition, dated May 5, 2005, is on file with the Bureau of Indian Affairs office in Redding, California.

25 **Yes, the tribe conceded:** "Rancheria's Plan for Truck Stop," *Modoc Independent News*.

25 **"I believe that a truck stop in this town":** Letter from Sandra Parriott, Page's Market, to BIA, May 10, 2005.

4

The information in this chapter comes entirely from interviews with firsthand sources and email exchanges with the principals.

29 **The BIA does not set blood quantum:** U.S. Department of Interior, Indian Affairs, www.bia.gov.

29 **"statistical genocide":** Caitlyn M. May, "Who's In and Who's Out: Tribal Courts and Boards Feud over Membership," *Statesman Journal* (Salem OR), September 19, 2016.

29 **the Karuk of California:** American Indian Enterprise & Business Council, www.aiebc.org.

30 **Most Modoc tribal members:** Email interview with Cheewa James, March 9, 2019.

5

The information for this chapter comes primarily from public records, primary sources, court documents, and interviews with firsthand sources.

32 **These five tribes continue:** American Indian Records in the National Archives, Commission to the Five Civilized Tribes (The Dawes Commission), 1893–1914, Dawes Rolls, https://www.archives.gov/research/native-americans/dawes/tutorial/intro.html.

33 **"They don't look like Indians to me":** Graham et al., "An Oral History of Trump's Bigotry."

6

The information for this chapter comes primarily from public records.

34 **The twenty-acre tract:** From the U.S. Government Printing Office, www.gpo.gov.

35 **Of the nearly six hundred:** From www.USA.gov.

7

The information for this chapter comes primarily from trial testimony, the probation report, and a for-the-record interview with Cherie Rhoades.

37 **"reality-based pathological component":** Dr. Alex Yufik's testimony under cross-examination by District Attorney Jordan Funk.

37 **"When we were in meetings":** From jail interview with Cherie Rhoades.

37 **she pushed her chair back:** From Cherie Rhoades's trial testimony.

38 **"This all happened because":** From Modoc County Probation Report.

38 **"Rurik was a piece of shit":** From jail interview with Cherie Rhoades.

8

The information for this chapter comes primarily from public records, primary sources, court documents, and interviews with firsthand sources.

39 **a disenrollment epidemic was raging:** James Dao, "In California, Indian Tribes with Casino Money Cast off Members," *New York Times*, December 12, 2011, https://www.nytimes.com/2011/12/13/us/california-indian-tribes-eject-thousands-of-members.html.

39 **at least two dozen California tribes removed:** Dao, "In California, Indian Tribes with Casino Money."

40 **The first, *Santa Clara Pueblo v. Martinez*:** See U.S. Supreme Court, *Santa Clara Pueblo v. Martinez* (1978), No. 76–682.

40 **Cabazon and Morongo bands:** There are many sources covering *California v. Cabazon Band of Mission Indians*, including U.S. Supreme Court case files 480 USA.202 (1987) and Washington and Lee University School of Law online files.

41 **The majority of the eighty-nine tribes:** From the California Gambling Control Commission, www.cgcc.ca.gov.

42 **Only in the 1990s did banishment:** Wilkins and Wilkins, *Dismembered*, 52.

43 **The Cedarville Rancheria's enrollment:** From the Cedarville Rancheria's enrollment ordinance and from Cedarville Rancheria's constitution and by-laws, Article IX–Bill of Rights, Section i: "the protections guaranteed by Title II of the Civil Rights Act of 1968 (82 Stat. 77), against action of a tribe in exercising its powers of self-government, shall apply to the Cedarville Rancheria its officers and all persons within its jurisdiction." See also Amy Stretten, "Something Is Threatening Native Americans and It's Called Tribal Disenrollment." Splinter (blog), March 4, 2014, https://splinternews.com/something-is-threatening-native-americans-and-its-calle-1793840961.

9

The information in this chapter comes entirely from for-the-record interviews and email exchanges with Kandi Maxwell.

10

The information in this chapter comes entirely from for-the-record interviews and email exchanges with Kandi Maxwell.

11

The information in this chapter comes entirely from for-the-record interviews and email exchanges with the principals.

49   **"A Call for Justice over a Mass Shooting"**: See Jennie Stockle, "A Call for Justice over a Mass Shooting in Indian Country." *Rewire.News*, July 21, 2014. https://rewire.news/article/2014/07/21/call-justice-mass-shooting-indian-country/.

12

The information in this chapter comes entirely from for-the-record interviews with Lloyd Powell.

13

The information in this chapter comes entirely from for-the-record interviews with Lloyd Powell.

14

The information for this chapter comes primarily from public records, primary sources, court documents, and interviews with firsthand sources.

56   **January 9, 2014:** McDonald, "Husband Recounts Chilling Lead-up to Alturas Shooting."

56   **to take matters into their own hands:** McDonald, "Husband Recounts Chilling Lead-up to Alturas Shooting."

56   **first to discover the bookkeeping discrepancies:** Case Title; Cedarville Rancheria. Office of Inspector General, U.S. Department of the Interior.

56   **"Munholand believed":** Case Title; Cedarville Rancheria. Office of Inspector General, U.S. Department of the Interior.

57   **The audit also revealed:** Case Title; Cedarville Rancheria. Office of Inspector General, U.S. Department of the Interior.

15

The information in this chapter comes entirely from for-the-record interviews with Lloyd Powell.

16

The information for this chapter comes primarily from public records, primary sources, court documents, and interviews with firsthand sources.

61   **Modoc County led California:** California Opioid Overdose Surveillance Dashboard, https://www.cdph.ca.gov/opioiddashboard; www.newsbug.info, May 27, 2019; Anne Ternus-Bellamy, "County Targeting Opioid Abuse with Medication-Assisted Treatment," *Davis (CA) Enterprise*, October 12, 2018, www.davisenterprise.com

62   **"I guess our little community":** Evan Schreiber, "Small Community Devastated by Mass Shooting," KCRA-TV, February 21, 2014.

62   **Mayor Dederick and the City of Alturas:** Author's note: The U.S. Department of the Interior, Office of the Assistant Secretary–Indian Affairs, issued a news release on February 28, 2014—a week after the murders. No evi-

dence was found that Governor Brown sent a condolence letter. There was no response to repeated attempts to reach Alturas officials as of May 30, 2016. Modoc County Administrator Chester Robertson confirmed, according to memory, that the board of supervisors did not send a letter of condolence.

17

The information for this chapter comes primarily from public records, personal observations, and for-the-record interviews with firsthand sources.

64   **with net assets of about $1.5 million:** IRS Form 900 "Return of Organization Exempt from Income Tax, 2014."

18

The information in this chapter comes entirely from for-the-record interviews and email exchanges with Lloyd Powell.

19

The information for this chapter comes primarily from public records, personal observations, and for-the-record interviews with firsthand sources.

72   **The 1969 occupation of Alcatraz:** March, "On the 40th Day of Indian Occupation."

73   **"It's about generational trauma":** From author interview with Charles Tailfeathers.

20

The information in this chapter comes entirely from for-the-record interviews, email exchanges, with the principals, and public records.

76   **Two years after Philip Russo's initial:** "Remove the Brady Campaign's 'Zero Minutes of Fame' Video from Circulation," Change.org petition, www.change .org/p/the-board-of-the-brady-campaign-to-prevent-gun-violence-remove-the -brady-campaign-s-zero-minutes-of-fame-video-from-circulation/c/441603224. Note: www.change.org appears to be an online app that facilitates the originating of petitions, in this case the Brady Campaign to prevent gun violence. As of November 22, 2016, the website noted that Russo "hasn't started any petitions yet."

76   **"My wife was murdered":** See www.change.org/p/the-board-of-the-brady -campaign-to-prevent-gun-violence-remove-the-brady-campaign-s-zero -minutes-of-fame-video-from-circulation/c/441603224.

77   **Why is it that a criminal gets publicity:** Melissa Davis, letter to the editor, *Modoc County Record*, August 13, 2015.

77   **"That's why you will never hear":** Richard Gonzales, "New Zealand PM Ardern Urges Her Nation to Make Gunman Nameless," NPR, March 18, 2019.

The information in this chapter comes entirely from for-the-record interviews and email exchanges with Kandi Maxwell.

The information in this chapter comes primarily from for-the-record interviews and email exchanges with Kandi Maxwell.

The information for this chapter comes primarily from for-the-record interviews with Dr. April Go Forth and public records.

87 **A new report said:** Wood, *Boarding Schools to Suspension Boards.* The study, based on the self-reporting of school districts statewide, was compiled by the Sacramento Native American Higher Education Collaborative (SNAHEC) and the Community College Equity Assessment Lab (CCEAL), a national research laboratory under the Interwork Institute at San Diego State University.

88 **"One noticeable pattern":** Wood, *Boarding Schools to Suspension Boards.*

88 **During the 2018 fall football:** Pat Wood, "Braves Tradition," letter to the editor, *Modoc County Record*, October 25, 2018.

The information in this chapter comes primarily from for-the-record interviews, email exchanges with the principals quoted, and public records.

89 **The county, in acting as the airport's:** Email correspondence with Chester Robertson, Modoc County administrative officer, October 4, 2019.

89 **a small band of Modoc Indians:** McNally, *The Modoc War*, 310.

89 **influenced President George W. Bush:** Memo from John Yoo, deputy assistant attorney general, to Jay S. Bybee, assistant attorney general, January 9, 2002, in Byrd, *The Transit of Empire*; "Yoo Memo Says U.S. Not Bound by International Laws in War on Terror," January 9, 2002, www.historycommons.org.

90 **That plan was dropped:** *Tule Lake Committee v. City of Tulelake and Modoc Tribe of Oklahoma*, declaration of Barbara Takei.

91 **More than three hundred:** Email correspondence with Barbara Takei, October 2, 2019; *Tulelake Committee v. City of Tule Lake et al.*, verified complaint for temporary restraining order.

91 **"All this seems to be forgotten":** Barbara Takei speaking on behalf of the Tule Lake Committee before the Tulelake City Council.

92 **"In memory of this Nation's dark":** See Tule Lake Committee Facebook page.

92 **Red Cedar Services that defrauded:** Taylor et al., "Stretching the Envelope of Tribal Sovereign Immunity?"

93 **Modoc County came in with a verbal offer:** Email correspondence from Chester Robertson, Modoc County Administrative Officer, to author, October 4, 2019.

93 **call the prison site "just dirt":** *Tule Lake Committee v. City of Tulelake and Modoc Tribe of Oklahoma.*

94 **"Japanese Americans had it much better":** Lee Juillerat, "Tule Lake Committee Seeks Injunction to Stop Airport Sale," *Herald and News* (Klamath Falls OR), August 22, 2018; *Tulelake Committee v. City of Tule Lake et al.,* verified complaint for temporary restraining order.

94 **"We (Tule Lake internees)":** February 18, 2015, www.discovernikkei.org.

95 **"One wonders that a small":** *Tulelake Committee v. City of Tule Lake et al.,* verified complaint for temporary restraining order.

97 **The War Memos:** Memo from John Yoo, deputy assistant attorney general, to Jay S. Bybee, assistant attorney general, January 9, 2002, in Byrd, *The Transit of Empire*; "Yoo Memo Says US Not Bound by International Laws in War on Terror," January 9, 2002, www.historycommons.org.

25

The information for this chapter comes primarily from the author's view.

26

The information for this chapter comes primarily from interviews with firsthand sources.

105 **After the preliminary hearing:** Email correspondence from Jordan Funk to author, January 8, 2018.

106 **"Bogda was haughty":** Email correspondence from Jordan Funk to author, January 8, 2018.

27

The information for this chapter comes primarily from public records, interviews with principals, and personal observations.

110 **"No rational person":** Maura Dolan and Victoria Kim, "California Death Penalty Unconstitutional, Judge Says," *Los Angeles Times,* July 16, 2014, https://www.latimes.com/local/lanow/la-me-ln-california-death-penalty-unconstitutional-judge-says-20140716-story.html.

111 **"I am appealing the court's decision":** David Siders, "Kamala Harris Will Appeal Death Penalty Ruling," *Sacramento Bee,* August 21, 2014. There are several sources documenting Harris's position on the death penalty. See Weil, "Kamala Harris Takes Her Shot."

111 **Jerry Brown could have conceded:** Mugambi Jouet, "Why Does Kamala Harris Defend the Death Penalty?" *San Francisco Chronicle,* September 2, 2015.

111 **"make a courageous":** Philip Pullella, "Pope Calls for Worldwide Abolition of Death Penalty." Reuters, February 21, 2016.

The information for this chapter comes primarily from public records, primary sources, court documents, and deep background interviews with firsthand sources.

114 **had qualified over two hundred times:** Bronson correspondence to Antonio Alvarez, December 30, 2014.

114 **"It is important to observe":** Bronson correspondence to Antonio Alvarez, December 30, 2014.

115 **"Racial blood lines":** Phil Willon, "Suspect Was Known for Her Temper," *Los Angeles Times*, February 23, 2014.

The information for this chapter comes primarily from personal observations, public records, correspondence with principals, and an interview with Cherie Rhoades.

118 **Cherie took several prescribed:** Modoc County Probation Report.

The information for this chapter comes primarily from guilt phase trial transcripts and for-the-record interviews with firsthand sources.

123 **Placer's poverty level:** U.S. Census Bureau, July 1, 2018.

124 **more than any other county:** From report by the Death Penalty Information Center, a Washington DC-based nonprofit group.

135 **refer to Cherie's IQ as average:** Data on average IQ scores in the United States varies by sources, but a commonly accepted range is 90 to 110. It was later learned her IQ was at the low end of average.

138 **Poor recognition of comorbid:** See Goodwin and Jamison, *Manic-Depressive Illness*.

139 **there was no evidence:** Modoc County Probation Report.

149 **The expression of remorse and its role:** References to remorse in this chapter are from the following sources: Bandes, "Remorse, Demeanor, and the Consequences of Misinterpretation"; Greenwald, "What Explains the Power of Dzhokhar Tsarnaev's Middle Finger?" Intercept, April 23, 2015, https://theintercept.com/2015/04/23/power-dzhokhar-tsarnaevs-middle-finger/; Zhong, "So You're Sorry?"

156 **"you've crossed the Rubicon":** There are numerous accounts of this event in history, including Redonet, "How Julius Caesar Started a Big War."

The information for this chapter comes primarily from post-trial for-the-record interviews and email exchanges with District Attorney Jordan Funk.

The information in this chapter comes primarily from penalty trial transcripts, for-the-record interviews, and email exchanges with the principals.

165　**letter written by Philip Russo:** Philip Russo, letter to Editor, "Justice Is Served," *Modoc County Record*, January 12, 2017.

33

The information for this chapter comes entirely from post-trial for-the-record interviews and email exchanges with District Attorney Jordan Funk.

34

Information for this chapter comes entirely from post-trial for-the-record interviews and email exchanges with District Attorney Jordan Funk.

35

Information for this chapter comes primarily from public records, primary sources, and for-the-record interviews.

169　**Nikki Munholand stopped to talk:** Correspondence by William Dowdy to Antonio Alvarez, February 24, 2017.

169　**It's not clear who initiated:** *People of the State of California, Plaintiff, vs. Cherie Louise Rhoades, Defendant*, Case No. F14–073, Defendant Cherie Rhoades' Notice of Motion and Motion for New Trial, March 16, 2017.

169　**She told Dowdy:** *People of the State of California, Plaintiff, vs. Cherie Louise Rhoades, Defendant*.

170　**"Make no mistake about it":** Comstock. "False Testimony Investigation Could Lead to Retrial in Cherie Rhoades Case." Fox 40 TV, March 24, 2017, https://fox40.com/news/local-news/false-testimony-investigation-could-lead-to-retrial-in-cherie-rhoades-case/.

170　**Two weeks before Cherie was:** Correspondence by Mike Poindexter to Antonio Alvarez, February 22, 2017.

170　**Poindexter built an argument:** Correspondence by Poindexter to Alvarez, February 22, 2017.

171　**The sheriff's answer was:** Comstock, "False Testimony Investigation."

172　**Outside the courtroom Alvarez:** Comstock, "False Testimony Investigation."

173　**a "constitutional sheriff":** See member list at www.consitutionclub.ning.com.

175　**"victims over the rights of criminals":** Comstock, "False Testimony Investigation."

36

The information for this chapter comes primarily from the sentencing transcript, probation report, and personal observations.

37

The information in this chapter comes primarily from for-the-record interviews with Lloyd Powell.

38

The information for this chapter comes primarily from sources within the Modoc County jail.

39

The information for this chapter comes primarily from the probation report and for-the-record interviews with District Attorney Jordan Funk.

Epilogue

The information for this chapter comes from primary sources, public records, trial transcripts, for-the-record interviews, and deep background interviews with first-hand sources.

193 **by performing its first adoption:** Melissa Davis, correspondence to Elizabeth Appel, Office of Regulatory Affairs and Collaborative Action, Indian Affairs, Department of Interior, May 19, 2015.

193 **Governor Gavin Newsom signed:** Willon, "Gov Gavin Newsom to Block California Death Row Executions" *Los Angeles Times*, March 12, 2019; Kelli Saam, "Death Sentences Plummet across California. Riverside County, Which Led the U.S. in 2017, Has Had Zero This Year," KRCA-TV, ABC News, March 13, 2019.

194 **arrested on a charge of hit:** Modoc County Superior Court records.

194 **pleaded no contest in April 2016:** *Modoc County Record*, "Court Activity," April 21, 2016.

195 **Her death certificate listed:** Certificate of Death, Modoc County, California, April 20, 2016.

195 **Erin Stockton was hired:** See www.modoccoe.k12.ca.us, County Office of Education.

Appendix

201 **I had an erratic correspondence:** The use of "erratic" is the author's expression of frustration at Cherie's avoidance in answering questions directly. The letters have been edited for length and clarity. Grammar and misspellings have been retained.

BIBLIOGRAPHY

Associated Press. "Woman, 47, Who Opened Fire at Northern California Tribal Meeting Killed Three Relatives and Was 'Being Investigate for Embezzling $50k.'" February 21, 2014.

Bandes, Susan A. "Remorse and Criminal Justice." *Emotion Review* 8, no. 1 (October 2015), DOI: 10.1177/1754073915601222.

———. "Remorse, Demeanor, and the Consequences of Misinterpretation: The Limits of Law as a Window into the Soul." *Journal of Law, Religion and State* 3 (2014): 170–99.

Boon, Kristen E., Aziz Huq, and Douglas C. Lovelace Jr., eds. *Terror-Based Interrogation.* Vol. 109 of *Terrorism: Commentary on Security Documents.* New York: Oxford University Press, 2010.

Brown-Rice, Kathleen. "Examining the Theory of Historical Trauma among Native Americans." *Professional Counselor* 3, no. 3 (2013): 117–130, www.tpcjournal.nbcc.org.

Byrd, Jodi A. *The Transit of Empire: Indigenous Critiques of Colonialism.* Minneapolis: University of Minnesota Press, 2011.

California Department of Education. "Common Core State Standards." www.cde.ca.gov.

California Gambling Control Commission. Notification of Anticipated Indian Gaming Revenue Sharing Trust Fund (RSTF) Shortfalls for FY 2016–17 (memo), May 13, 2016. http://www.cgcc.ca.gov/documents/rstfi/2016/Notification_of_Anticipated_Indian_Gaming_Revenue_Sharing_Trust_Fund_Shortfalls_for_FY_2016-17.pdf.

———. Revenue Sharing Trust Fund Report (memo), June 30, 2016 and October 19, 2017. www.cgcc.ca.gov.

California Proposition 66, Death Penalty. www.Ballotpedia.org.

California Secretary of State, California General Election Results, 2016. www.vote.sos.gov.

Chomsky, Aviva. "Making Native Americans Strangers in Their Own World." Tom Dispatch (blog) November 29, 2018, https://www.tomdispatch.com/blog/176501

/tomgram%3A_aviva_chomsky%2C_making_native_americans_strangers_in
_their_own_land.

Collman, Ashley. "Eastern Band of Cherokee Indians Chief Voices Support for Elizabeth Warren After She Sparked Controversy for Taking a DNA Test to Provide Her Native American Ancestry." *Business Insider*, October 16, 2018, https://www.businessinsider.com/richard-sneed-cherokee-chief-voices-support-for-elizabeth-warren-2018-10.

Cothran, Boyd. *Remembering the Modoc War: Redemptive Violence and the Making of American Innocence*. Chapel Hill: University of North Carolina Press, 2014.

Cuevas, Rick. "Report: BIA Director Amy Dutschke's Conflict of Interest Wilton Rancheria Does Not Qualify for Restored Lands Exemption and Thus, No Casino in Elk Grove," Original Pechanga's Tribal Disenrollment Blog. January 9, 2017, https://www.originalpechanga.com/2017/01/reportbia-director-amy-dutschkes.html.

Denny, C. H., D. Holtzman, R. T. Goins, and J. B. Croft. "Disparities in Chronic Disease Risk Factors and Health Status Between American Indian/Alaska Native and White Elders: Findings from a Telephone Survey, 2001 and 2002."*American Journal of Public Health* 95, no. 5 (May 2005) 825–27, https://dx.doi.org/10.2105%2FAJPH.2004.043489.

"Five Lynched by a California Mob—The Lookout Lynching." Strange Fruit and Spanish Moss (blog), May 31, 2015, https://strangefruitandspanishmoss.blogspot.com/search?q=Five+Lynched+by+a+California+Mob%E2%80%94The+Lookout+Lynching.

Galanda, Gabriel S., and Ryan D. Dreveskracht. "Curing the Tribal Disenrollment Epidemic: In Search of a Remedy." *Arizona Law Review* 57, no. 2 (2015), https://arizonalawreview.org/pdf/57-2/57arizlrev383.pdf.

Goldberg-Ambrose, Carole, and Timothy Seward. *Planting Tail Feathers: Tribal Survival and Public Law 280*. Los Angeles: American Indian Studies Center, UCLA, 1997.

Goodwin, Frederick K., and Kay Redfield Jamison. *Manic-Depressive Illness: Bipolar Disorders and Recurrent Depression*, vol. 1, 2nd ed. New York: Oxford University Press, 2007.

Gore, Donna R., "Where's the Heart in Journalism for the Plight of Victims of Violent Crime?" Lady Justice Blog, July 22, 2014, https://donnagore.com/2014/07/22/wheres-the-heart-in-journalism-for-the-plight-of-victims-of-violent-crime/.

Graham, David A., Adrienne Green, Cullen Murphy, and Parker Richards. "An Oral History of Trump's Bigotry." *Atlantic*, June 2019.

Grann, David. *Killers of the Flower Moon: The Osage Murders and the Birth of the FBI*. New York: Simon and Schuster, 2017.

Hansen, Kenneth, and Tracy A. Skopek. *The New Politics of Indian Gaming: The Rise of Reservation Interest Groups*. Reno: University of Nevada Press, 2015.

Hendricks, Steve. *The Unquiet Grave: The FBI and the Struggle for the Souls of Indian Country*, New York: Thunder's Mount Press, 2007.

Hinckley, Stuart W. "Capital Punishment." In *The Encyclopedia of Mormonism*, Harold B. Lee Library, Brigham Young University, 1992, https://eom.byu.edu/index.php/Capital_Punishment.

Ikeda, Andrea. "Cowboys, Indians, and Aliens: White Supremacy in the Klamath Basin, 1826–1946." Senior thesis, University of California, Berkeley, 2015.

Indian Country Today Media Network.com. "Tribal Leaders Must Talk About Disenrollment." June 10, 2015.

Internal Revenue Service. Form 990 for 2014, www.guidestar.org.

Johnson, Troy R. *We Hold the Rock: The Indian Occupation of Alcatraz, 1969 to 1971*. San Francisco: Golden Gate National Parks Conservancy, 1997.

Juillerat, Lee. "Tulelake Council Approves Airport Land Sale." *Herald and News* (Klamath Falls, Oregon), August 2, 2018.

Kimberlin, Sara, and Amy Rose. "Making Ends Meet: How Much Does It Cost to Support a Family in California?" California Budget and Policy Center, December 2017, https://calbudgetcenter.org/resources/making-ends-meet-much-cost-support-family-california/.

Krogstad, Jens Manuel. "One-in-Four Native Americans and Alaska Natives Are Living in Poverty." FactTank, Pew Research Center, June 13, 2014, https://www.pewresearch.org/fact-tank/2014/06/13/1-in-4-native-americans-and-alaska-natives-are-living-in-poverty/.

Kutner, Max. "What Led Jaylen Fryberg to Commit the Deadliest High School Shooting in a Decade?" *Newsweek*, September 16, 2015.

Lindsay, Brendan. *Murder State: California's Native American Genocide, 1846–1873*. Lincoln: University of Nebraska Press, 2012.

March, Ray A. "On the 40th Day of Indian Occupation of Alcatraz Island." *San Francisco Business*, February 1970

McKay, Jim. "Opioid Crisis Affects First Responders and the Whole Community." *Emergency Management*, October 11, 2019, https://www.govtech.com/em/safety/Opioid-Crisis-Affects-First-Responders-and-the-Whole-Community-.html.

McNally, Robert Aquinas. *The Modoc War: The Story of Genocide at the Dawn of America's Gilded Age*. Lincoln: University of Nebraska Press, 2017.

Modoc County Record. "Rhoades Attorney Files Motion for a New Trial, Claiming Perjury," March 23, 2017.

———. "Funk Blasts Sheriff's Interference in Trial." April 20, 2017.

———. "Proposed Truck Stop/Mini Mart Creates Some Angst in S.V." May 26, 2005.

Modoc Independent News. "Rancheria's Plan for Truck Stop Meets Opposition in Cedarville." June 2005.

Mullen, Frank X., Jr. "Shoshone Mike: New Theories Emerge 100 Years After 'Last Massacre.'" *Reno Gazette-Journal*, February 19, 2011, https://www.rgj.com/story/travel/destinations/explore-nevada/2015/06/02/shoshone-mike-new-theories-emerge-100-years-after-last-massacre/28331071/.

Murray, Keith A. *The Modocs and Their War*. Norman: University of Oklahoma Press, 1959.

National Research Council of the National Academies. *Assessment of the Bureau of Reclamation's Security Program*. Washington DC: National Academies Press, 2008, www.nap.edu.

Neyfakh, Leon. "Sorry, Not Sorry." Slate, November 4, 2015, www.slate.com/news-and-politics/2015/11/remorse-judges-and-juries-think-they-can-tell-when-a-defendant-is-sorry-they-cant.html.

Obama, Barack. "On My Upcoming Trip to Indian Country." Indian Country Today, June 5, 2014. https://indiancountrytoday.com/archive/on-my-upcoming-trip-to-indian-country-1In7Gf0xPEaQgAZaMyuLqg

O'Brien, Sharon. *American Indian Tribal Governments*. Norman: University of Oklahoma Press, 1989.

People of the State of California v. Bonilla (2007). Case No. SO45184, 41 Cal. 4th 313.

Pevar, Stephen L. *The Rights of Indians and Tribes*. Carbondale: Southern Illinois University Press, 1992.

Philbin, Patrick F. "Legality of the Use of Military Commissions to Try Terrorists, Memorandum Opinion for the Counsel to the President," November 6, 2001, https://fas.org/irp/agency/doj/olc/commissions.pdf.

RafuShimpo. "API Legislative Caucus Opposes Tulelake Airport Fence," October 16, 2017, http://www.rafu.com/2017/10/api-legislative-caucus-opposes-tulelake-airport-fence/.

———. "Tule Lake Committee Files Lawsuit to Stop Transfer of Airport to Modoc Tribe," August 25, 2018, https://www.rafu.com/2018/08/tule-lake-committee-files-lawsuit-to-stop-transfer-of-airport-to-modoc-tribe/.

Redonet, Fernando Lillo. "How Julius Caesar Started a Big War by Crossing a Small Stream." *National Geographic History*, March–April 2017, https://www.nationalgeographic.com/history/magazine/2017/03-04/julius-caesar-crossing-rubicon-rome/.

Russo, Philip. "National Crime Victims' Rights Week 2014." Huffington Post, April 14, 2014, https://www.huffpost.com/entry/national-crime-victims-ri_b_5126775.

———. "Mixed Emotions Over the Evidence." Huffington Post, July 8, 2014, https://www.huffpost.com/entry/mixed-emotions-over-the-shelia-russo_b_5559381.

Sands, Philippe. *Torture Team—Rumsfeld's Memo and the Betrayal of American Values*. New York: Palgrave Macmillan, 2008.

Schwarz, Jon. "The Assassination of Orlando Letelier and the Politics of Silence." Intercept, September 21, 2016, https://theintercept.com/2016/09/21/the-assassination-of-orlando-letelier-and-the-politics-of-silence/.

Shapiro, Nina. "Native Lawyer Takes on Tribes That Kick Members Out." *Seattle Times*, December 19, 2015.

Sotero, Michelle M. "A Conceptual Model of Historical Trauma: Implications for Public Health Practice and Research." *Journal of Health Disparities Research and Practice* 1, no. 1 (Fall 2006): 93–108.

Stutz, Howard. "Report: Indian Gaming Revenue Hits Record $28.3 Billion in 2013." *Las Vegas Review Journal*, March 30, 2015, https://www.reviewjournal.com

/business/casinos-gaming/report-indian-gaming-revenue-hits-record-28-3
-billion-in-2013/.

Sullivan, Patrick. "Tribal Gaming Revenue Sharing in California." *National Law Review*, March 20, 2013, https://www.natlawreview.com/article/tribal-gaming -revenue-sharing-california-0.

Swift, Mary. "Banishing Habeas Jurisdiction: Why Federal Courts Lack Jurisdiction to Hear Tribal Banishment Actions." *Washington Law Review* 86, no. 4 (December 2011): 941–80.

Taylor, Kyra, Leslie Bailey, and Victoria W. Ni. "Stretching the Envelope of Tribal Sovereign Immunity?" Public Justice Foundation, November 2017, https://www .publicjustice.net/wp-content/uploads/2018/01/SVCF-Report-FINAL-Dec-4.pdf.

Trouillot, Michel-Rolph. *Silencing the Past: Power and the Production of History.* Boston: Beacon Press, 1995.

U.S. Bureau of Indian Affairs. Weekly Report, Northern California Agency, February 21, 2014.

U.S. Department of Homeland Security. *Security Guidelines for General Aviation Airports.* Washington DC: Transportation Security Administration, 2004.

Vockrodt, Steve. "Modoc Tribe Settles with Feds over Payday Probe." *Kansas City Star*, June 29, 2018.

Weil, Elizabeth. "Kamala Harris Takes Her Shot." *Atlantic*, May 2019.

Wilkins, David E., and Shelly Hulse Wilkins. *Dismembered: Native Disenrollment and the Battle for Human Rights.* Seattle: University of Washington Press, 2017.

Wood, Luke. *Boarding Schools to Suspension Boards: Suspensions and Expulsions of Native American Students in California Public Schools.* Sacramento Native American Higher Education Collaborative (SNAHEC) and Community College Equity Assessment Lab (CCEAL), September 2019.

Zhong, Rocksheng, Madelon Baranoski, Neal Feigenson, Larry Davidson, Alec Buchanan, and Howard V. Zonana. "So You're Sorry? The Role of Remorse in Criminal Law," *Journal of the American Academy of Psychiatry and the Law Online* 42, no. 1 (March 2014): 39–48.